MW01281818

The Majority Press

THE PAN-AFRICAN CONNECTION:
From Slavery to Garvey and Beyond

TONY MARTIN established himself as the leading scholar of the Garvey Movement with his *Race First: The Ideological and Organizational Struggles of Marcus Garvey and the Universal Negro Improvement Association* (1976). He followed this up with *The Pan-African Connection* (1983) and *Literary Garveyism: Garvey, Black Arts and the Harlem Renaissance* (1983). He also edited *The Poetical Works of Marcus Garvey* (1983) and co-authored *Rare Afro-Americana: A Reconstruction of the Adger Library* (1981).

Martin is professor and chairman of the Black Studies Department at Wellesley College, Massachusetts. He did his M.A. and Ph.D. in history at Michigan State University and the B.Sc. in economics at the University of Hull, England. In 1965 he qualified as a barrister-at-law at Gray's Inn, London. He has taught at the University of Michigan-Flint, the Cipriani Labor College (Trinidad) and St. Mary's College (Trinidad). He has been visiting professor at the University of Minnesota and Brandeis University.

Marcus Garvey Remembered

Books from The Majority Press, Inc.

THE NEW MARCUS GARVEY LIBRARY

Literary Garveyism: Garvey, Black Arts and the Harlem Renaissance. Tony Martin. $19.95 (cloth), $9.95 (paper).

The Poetical Works of Marcus Garvey. Tony Martin, Ed. $17.95 (cloth), $9.95 (paper).

Marcus Garvey, Hero: A First Biography. Tony Martin. $9.95 (paper).

The Pan-African Connection. Tony Martin. $10.95 (paper).

Message to the People: The Course of African Philosophy. Marcus Garvey. Ed. by Tony Martin. $22.95 (cloth), $9.95 (paper).

Race First: The Ideological and Organizational Struggles of Marcus Garvey and the Universal Negro Improvement Association. Tony Martin. $12.95 (paper).

The Philosophy and Opinions of Marcus Garvey. Amy Jacques Garvey, Ed. $14.95 (paper).

Amy Ashwood Garvey: Pan-Africanist, Feminist and Wife No. 1. Tony Martin. Forthcoming.

African Fundamentalism: A Literary and Cultural Anthology of Garvey's Harlem Renaissance. Tony Martin, Ed. $14.95 (paper).

THE BLACK WORLD

Brazil: Mixture or Massacre? Essays in the Genocide of a Black People. Abdias do Nascimento. $12.95 (paper).

Studies in the African Diaspora: A Memorial to James R. Hooker (1929-1976). John P. Henderson and Harry A. Reed, Eds. $39.95 (cloth).

In Nobody's Backyard: The Grenada Revolution in its Own Words. Vol. II, Facing the World. Tony Martin, Ed. $22.95 (cloth).

Guinea's Other Suns: The African Dynamic in Trinidad Culture. Maureen Warner-Lewis. $9.95 (paper).

Carlos Cooks: And Black Nationalism from Garvey to Malcolm. Robert, Nyota and Grandassa Harris, Eds. $9.95 (paper).

From Kingston to Kenya: The Making of a Pan-Africanist Lawyer. Dudley Thompson, with Margaret Cezair Thompson. $10.95 (paper).

The Jewish Onslaught: Despatches from the Wellesley Battlefront. Tony Martin. $9.95 (paper).

Marcus Garvey/Makis Gave. Florie-N Chevry-Saintil. $9.95 (paper). [In Haitian Creole].

Eyes to My Soul: The Rise or Decline of a Black FBI Agent. Tyrone Powers. $14.95.

The Progress of the African Race Since Emancipation and Prospects for the Future. Tony Martin. $5.00.

Reflections on Our Pastor: Dr. Martin Luther King, Jr. at Dexter Avenue Baptist Church, 1954-1960. Wally G. Vaughn, Ed. $12.95.

Best Poems of Trinidad. A.M.Clarke, Comp. $10.95.

Order from The Majority Press, Inc., P.O. Box 538, Dover, MA 02030, U.S.A.
Mass. residents add 5% sales tax.

The Pan-African Connection

From Slavery to Garvey and Beyond

by TONY MARTIN

The New Marcus Garvey Library, No. 6

THE MAJORITY PRESS
Dover, Massachusetts

Copyright © 1983 by Tony Martin
Wellesley, Mass.

Library of Congress Cataloging in Publication Data

Martin, Tony, 1942–
  The Pan African connection.
  (The New Marcus Garvey library; no. 6)
  Includes index.
  1. Garvey, Marcus, 1887–1940. 2. Pan-Africanism—
History. I. Title. II. Series: Martin, Tony, 1942–.
E185.97.G3M368   1983   305.8′96′024   82-19521
ISBN 0-912469-10-2
ISBN 0-912469-11-0 (pbk)

First published in 1983.

First Majority Press edition, 1984.

Second printing December 1985

10 9 8 7 6 5

The Majority Press
P.O. Box 538
Dover, Massachusetts 02030
Printed in the United States of America

Table of Contents

Preface

Pan-Africanism may be defined as the attempts by African peoples to link up their struggles for their mutual benefit. The pioneers of the movement thought largely of global linkages, but the dream of continental unity, of a United States of Africa, also buttressed their endeavors. In time the spirit of Pan-Africanism came also to infuse regional groupings within the African continent. The term itself was first popularized by Henry Sylvester Williams, the Trinidad lawyer who founded a Pan-African Association in England in 1897. The permanency of the term was assured when Williams lent it to his Pan-African Conference, held in London in 1900. If Williams popularized an expression, however, he certainly did not found a movement. For the Pan-African movement had experienced its first stirrings, even without benefit of a name, many years before 1897.

Pan-Africanism became inevitable with the inception of the transatlantic slave trade. Europe, by scattering Africa to the winds, inevitably if unwittingly set in motion the process which would bring scattered Africa together again, at a higher level. It was inevitable that the forcibly uprooted Africans would yearn to rediscover their homeland. It was inevitable that the journey to rediscovery would be a journey against the colonialism that had uprooted Africa in the first place. It was inevitable that a final reunification of scattered Africa could come only at the expense of colonial Europe. Thus was set in motion, by the transatlantic slave trade, a process whose course, even now, has not yet fully run.

New World Africans in time lost the sharp edge of their specific African nationalities. Thousands of miles and several generations away from the African homeland, it mattered less than before whether one was Yoruba, Hausa or Mandingo. As the years rolled by, fewer and fewer New World Africans knew exactly from whence in the African homeland they had sprung. They were already an amalgam of African ethnicities. But of one thing they could be certain—they were African. Often the slaveowner left the mark of his dominance indelibly stamped on the forehead of the New World African. But even this unfortunate circumstance could never totally obliterate the remembrance of Africa.

And always, remembrance walked hand in hand with desire. Often the desire to return to Africa manifested itself on an individual level. But by the eighteenth century organized moves were already afoot. From England, from Nova Scotia, from Rhode Island, came tidings of emigration and repatriation schemes. Such organized efforts became a permanent feature of New World African life, which lasted until our own time in the twentieth century.

Meanwhile the simple desire to return went through further refinements. New World Africans felt an obligation to assist in the development of Africa. The politically astute of the nineteenth century foresaw the gathering imperialism that would ere long engulf the continent. They tried to sound a warning.

In Africa itself the advent of colonialism and imperialism similarly quickened the pace of Pan-African consciousness. Ancient rivalries, though they did not disappear, could now partially be subsumed into a greater common struggle against the European colonizer. In the process, Africans at home reached out to Africans abroad and, in a more general way, to all struggling peoples in the great quest for freedom and dignity. One African, Chief Alfred Sam of the Gold Coast (Ghana), even journeyed to North America and led one of the largest emigrationist movements there, prior to the advent of Marcus Garvey.

In the New World, Pan-Africanism has generally been associated with Black nationalism. In North America especially, those who favored a proud, self-reliant and separate race have always striven energetically to cement the African link. W. E. B. DuBois, in his four Pan-African Congresses (1919 to 1927) has represented the most important liberal integrationist strain within the Pan-African movement. Marxists of varying description, such as George Padmore and C. L. R. James, have brought further ideological diversity to the Pan-African ideal.

In its Black nationalist aspect Pan-Africanism has been an important component of the dominant ideology of the Black masses of North America. The largest mass movements of Afro-America have been nationalist and have included a strong African consciousness. The Liberia Exodus Association of Martin R. Delany and others in the years after 1877; the Akim Trading Company of Chief Alfred Sam up to 1914; the Universal Negro Improvement Association of Marcus Garvey in its post World War I heyday; the Nation of Islam of Elijah Muhammad at its peak in the 1960s; these have been Afro-America's largest and most powerful mass movements. They have all revolved around the principles of race first, self-reliance, nationhood and Pan-Africanism. In the

Caribbean, too, Africa has been prominent in the largest mass movements, from slave revolts to Black Power.

If Black nationalism / Pan-Africanism has been the dominant ideology of the New World African masses, it has also been a heavily persecuted ideology. The powers that be have sought to destroy nationalist movements with a fervor not usually experienced, even by less conservative integrationist organizations.

The present volume represents a convenient collection in a single place of articles on the subject, published or delivered as lectures by the author. They appeared originally, between 1970 and 1981, in a variety of forums—in academic journals, in a newspaper, in pamphlet form. The spread of countries in which these articles first appeared is itself reflective of something Pan-African. They include the United States, Trinidad, Kenya, Jamaica and England.

To the author's own essays in this volume are appended four very rare documents illustrative of facets of Pan-African history. Three of these have never been published before.

One or two of the essays bear the influence of the time and place in which they were written. But no attempt has been made to rewrite for this compilation. Apart from a single essay, where a couple of paragraphs have been deleted, the articles remain as first published. Some minor repetition is inevitable under these circumstances. That is not necessarily a bad thing.

Together these essays and documents touch upon many of the main currents of the Pan-African experience. There is material here on the international exchange of ideas among African communities; on emigrationist movements; on African cultural survivals in the New World; on the Afro-centric view of African history; on the role of Black missionary activity in Africa; on Pan-African organizations, and more. About half of the essays and documents deal with Marcus Garvey and the Universal Negro Improvement Association. Garvey was the most complete of Pan-Africanists, reaching organizationally into the lives of African peoples around the globe. He has no equal in this regard. The materials herein collected show his impact on the United States, Jamaica, Trinidad, the Caribbean generally and Southern Africa.

The complete publishing history of the contents of this volume is as follows.

   ● "The Caribbean and Africa—Historical Perspectives" was delivered as a public lecture at the Trinidad Public Library, Port-of-Spain, on July 29th, 1980. The event was under the auspices of the Caribbean Research Unit and the library's adult education program. The lecture was subsequently published in pamphlet form (Port-of-Spain: Caribbean Research Unit, 1981). ● "Some Reflections on Evangelical Pan-Africanism, or, Black Missionaries, White Missionaries and the Struggle for African Souls, 1890–1930," appeared in *Ufahamu*, I, 3, Winter 1971, published by the African Activist Association at the African Studies Center, University of California, Los Angeles. ● "Revolutionary Upheaval in Trinidad, 1919: Gleanings from British and American Sources," was published in the Association for the Study of Afro-American Life and History's *Journal of Negro History*, LVIII, 3, July 1973. ● "Marcus Garvey and the West Indies" was written for the monthly *Caribbean Contact* (April 1978). ● "Marcus Garvey and Trinidad, 1912–1947," was first presented, in preliminary form, at the International Seminar on Marcus Garvey at the University of the West Indies-Mona in 1973. This seminar was organized by the African Studies Association of the West Indies. In its present form it was delivered at the annual meeting of the Association of Caribbean Historians in Trinidad in 1980. ● "Garvey and the Beginnings of Mass-based Party Politics in Jamaica" was read at the annual meeting of the Conference of Black Political Scientists in Chicago in 1976. ● "Attempts to Bring Garvey Back to the United States" appeared in the *Negro History Bulletin*, XXXVIII, 1, December 1974–January 1975. ● "Carter G. Woodson and Marcus Garvey" appeared in the same journal, XL, 6, November–December 1977. ● "Marcus Garvey and Southern Africa" was prepared as a background paper at the request of the United Nations Special Committee Against Apartheid. The occasion was the committee's 1979 conference in Jamaica, honoring six West Indians, Garvey included, who had contributed significantly to the struggle against apartheid. The version of the paper circulated at that conference was expurgated by the committee's chief civil servant, for reasons of personal ideological preference. The full version is reproduced here. ● "George Padmore as a Prototype of the Black Historian in the Age of Militancy" was published in Kenya by the *Pan-African Journal* (IV, 2, Spring 1971), one of the periodicals of the now defunct East African Literature Bureau. ● "C. L. R. James and the Race/Class Question" saw the light of day in *Race* (now *Race and Class*), XIV, 2, October 1972, a journal of the Institute of Race Relations, London. ● "Rescuing Fanon from the Critics" appeared in the *African Studies Review*, organ of the African Studies Association of the United States (XIII, 3, December 1970).

● The first document, "Benito Sylvain of Haiti on the Pan-African Conference of 1900," was contained in a book published by Sylvain in Paris in 1901. It remains mostly unknown. The present author's translation from the French appeared in *Pan-African Journal*, VIII, 2, Summer 1975. ● Sam Manning's "The Yorubas of Carapichaima, Trinidad, Pre-1910" is a document in the possession of Mr. Lionel Yard of Brooklyn, New York, to whom grateful acknowledgement is made. ● Amy Ashwood Garvey's "The Birth of the Universal Negro Improvement Association" is extracted from her unpublished biography of Marcus Garvey, contained in the Amy Ashwood Garvey Papers in London. Grateful acknowledgement is made to Joey and Lera Morris for permission to use this. ● The collection ends with "My Advent, Work, Persecution, Indictment, Conviction, Appeal, Imprisonment and Liberation in the United States of America—the Land of My Friends and My Enemies." This is the text of an important autobiographical speech delivered by Marcus Garvey in 1927, shortly after his deportation to Jamaica from the United States. It is as appropriate a note as any on which to end a Pan-African collection.

September, 1982   Tony Martin
                                                            Wellesley, Massachusetts

Acknowledgments
    The author would like to thank the following for permission to reprint articles.
Regents of the University of California *(Ufahamu)*.
Association for the Study of Afro-American Life and History *(Journal of Negro History* and *Negro History Bulletin)*.
Institute of Race Relations *(Race)*.

PART I

Essays

1

The Caribbean and Africa—Historical Perspectives*

Over fifty years ago, in the 1920s, the famous Afro-American poet, Countee Cullen, pondered his position as an African in the West. Here he was, three hundred years removed from his African homeland, and yet the remembrance of that continent pulsated in his being. As he wrote, he could yet feel the throb of the drums in his brain. Africa for him was a very personal, a very close thing after three hundred years, and he wrote a poem about it, a poem which he called "Heritage". If he had written it in 1980, he might have called it "Roots", but he called it "Heritage," the same thing. Here is how Countee Cullen began that poem—

> What is Africa to me:
> Copper sun or scarlet sea,
> Jungle star or jungle track,
> Strong bronzed men, or regal black
> Women from whose loins I sprang
> When the birds of Eden sang?
> One three centuries removed
> From the scenes his fathers loved,
> Spicy grove, cinnamon tree,
> What is Africa to me?

This question, "What is Africa to me?" is a question which has dominated the history of African peoples in the Western world ever since we were forcibly uprooted from our ancestral homeland and herein lies what seems to me to be a central paradox in the history of our people in the Caribbean. For on the one hand, the remembrance of Africa has dominated our being, our very existence. We have never forgotten

*Originally delivered as a lecture in 1980

3

Africa and yet, at the same time, the powers that be have never felt comfortable with this remembrance. Throughout our history there has been a conflict—at times a muted conflict, at times an out and out violent conflict—between those who would remember Africa and those who would suppress that memory.

At times governments have paid lip-service to that memory, at times they have suppressed it violently and over the next hour or so I would like to trace the development of that sentiment in the West Indies over the last few hundred years.

Naturally during slavery times many of the Africans in this part of the world were actually born on the African continent. So it is not surprising to find that during slavery there were all kinds of manifestations of African consciousness in the Caribbean. We all know about the maroon slaves who escaped; and whenever they escaped they did their best to re-create the Africa that they had known. They created African communities. I am talking about people like the Djukas of Suriname, the so-called Bush Negroes. I am talking about people like the Maroons of Jamaica. I am talking about people like the so-called Black Caribs of St. Vincent in the 17th and 18th centuries. They recreated the African environment through language, through religion, through architecture, through social organization, and in any other way that they could. But this is not surprising, for many of them were born in Africa.

As time went on and increasing numbers of Africans were born here in the West, that desire to reunite with Africa in any form or fashion, either physically or spiritually, continued to manifest itself. And there were many other ways in which Africans during the era of slavery manifested that desire. For example, researchers in Afro-America have shown that the slave songs and many of the old spirituals contained in their lyrics that desire to go back to Africa. Sometimes the words were couched in religious terms because the slaves had been fed with the Bible. But in essence very often these slave songs showed a desire to return. Their lyrics often equated Africa with heaven. Similar references to Africa have been found in 19th century African-Caribbean songs.

Often we are told that the slaves even went so far as to commit suicide in the hope and expectation that having departed this life, their spirits would reunite with their ancestors in the African homeland. And throughout the era of slavery we find that slaves, and especially revolutionary slaves, always had the idea of Africa not very far from their activities. No sooner had Toussaint L'Ouverture vanquished his European adversaries and imposed his will on revolutionary Haiti than he turned his thoughts to Africa. He made elaborate plans for leading an expedition to West Africa to liberate the homeland from the slave traders.

Again, we have the case of the Jamaican Maroons who were exiled by the British to Nova Scotia in Canada in the late 18th century—we find them asking to be sent to Africa once they got to Nova Scotia. The result was that in 1800 some 500 Jamaican Maroons were shipped from Nova Scotia to Sierra Leone at their own request. Again—and this next example highlights the point I am making that revolutionary slaves especially, nurtured the remembrance of Africa—in 1839, there took place in Cuba a most remarkable slave insurrection, the Amistad mutiny. Amistad was the name of a ship which was being used to transport slaves from one port in Cuba to another. During the trip these African slaves revolted under the leadership of Cinqué. They killed all the white men on the ship except one, the pilot. They told the pilot that the reason they spared his life was because they wanted him to guide them back to Africa. The pilot set out in the direction of Africa, towards the east. But he played a trick on the slaves. He would sail towards the east at night, when the Africans could verify their direction from the stars; but once the day came, he would tack towards the north, so that the Amistad eventually ended up in Long Island, New York. There was a long celebrated trial, after which the slaves were eventually freed and they did in fact get back to Africa. This just highlights the point I am making, that revolutionary slaves often did what was necessary to get back to Africa.

DAAGA

Here in Trinidad, we have a very interesting and by now I guess a very well known example of a similar phenomenon. I am talking about the case of the Daaga mutiny in St. Joseph in 1837. Daaga was a "liberated African" as they used to call them. This was just before the end of so-called apprenticeship in the British colonies. At that point the British navy was intercepting slave ships—Portuguese, Cuban and other slave ships—and "liberating" their cargoes. Some of these newly freed slaves were sent to the West Indies where many were more or less forced to join the West India Regiment.

Now this Daaga apparently was a person of royal background in

Africa. He belonged to the Pawpaw nation from Dahomey and he was tricked into slavery as many Africans had been tricked into slavery before. He actually came to the shore to sell slaves to the Portuguese and the Portuguese enticed him on board their ship and before he knew what was happening, he was a slave too.

On the way over to the West Indies, Daaga sought to make his peace with his fellow captives by promising to lead them to freedom later on. And so, in St. Joseph in 1837, after they had been impressed into the West India Regiment, Daaga led a mutiny. This mutiny is described by E. L. Joseph, a Scotsman who was living in Trinidad at that time and I do not know if he can be fully believed or not.

According to Joseph, Daaga and his band of mutineers walked eastwards in the direction of Arima, in the hope that somehow they might reach Africa. This is a phenomenon which has been described by other people too. In fact, Joseph himself says that white convicts in Australia, tried to walk to China. I do not know why they wanted to walk to China.

Now Daaga was a very remarkable person both physically and in terms of leadership capacity. And I want to read you a description of Daaga by this white man in Trinidad in 1837. This account is one of my favorite examples of the racism which white writers on Black affairs have frequently exhibited but which they exhibited more openly in the 19th century. Listen to this Scotsman describing Daaga, a revolutionary African who led a mutiny in the hopes of reuniting with his motherland.

> Daaga was just the man whom a savage, warlike, and depredatory tribe would select for their chieftain, as the African negroes choose their leaders with reference to their personal prowess. Daaga stood 6 feet 6 inches without shoes. Although scarcely muscular in proportion, yet his frame indicated in a singular degree the union of irresistible strength and activity. His head was large; his features had all the peculiar traits which distinguish the negro in a remarkable degree; his jaw was long, eyes large and protruded, high cheek-bones, and flat nosed:his teeth were large and regular. He had a singular cast in his eyes, not quite amounting to that obliquity of the visual organs denominated a squint, but sufficient to give his features a peculiarly forbidding appearance;—his forehead however, although small in proportion to his enormous head, was remarkably compact and well formed. The whole head was disproportioned, having the greater part of the brain behind the ears;

How Joseph figured this out, I have always wondered. He continued, but the greatest peculiarity of this singular being was his voice. In the course of my life I have never heard such sounds uttered by human organs as those formed by Daaga. In ordinary conversation he appeared to me to endeavour to soften his voice—it was a deep tenor; but when a little excited by any passion (and this savage was the child of passion) his voice sounded like the low growl of a lion, but when much excited, it could be compared to nothing so aptly as the notes of a gigantic brazen trumpet.

That is Mr. Joseph, a native of Scotland, describing Daaga. And I read this especially to give you an illustration of the kind of racist writing on Black people which was very, very common in the 19th century. Black people somehow seemed to be a peculiar species and they were described with a type of awe and derision with which one might describe an animal. Not even Joseph's prejudice, however, could totally obscure the strength and power that Daaga obviously exuded. Also, Joseph did leave us one interesting fact. He says that Daaga was very upset at having been tricked into slavery, and "This transaction caused in the breast of the savage a deep hatred against all white men—a hatred so intense that he frequently . . . declared he would eat the first white man he killed. . . ." So Daaga exemplifies that trend of revolutionary Africans in the era of slavery to reunite with the African homeland. Daaga unfortunately was captured and executed at St. Joseph on Auguest 16, 1837.

After the end of slavery, this African desire continued to well in the beings of Africans in the Caribbean. You found all kinds of people either going back to Africa physically (many are still doing so today—more than is generally realized), or trying to lobby on behalf of Africa in a variety of different ways. Some of them, despite slavery, despite suffering, had managed to gain a certain amount of technological knowledge here in the West. And once slavery was ended, the thoughts of thousands of ex-slaves turned to the question of how could they go back home to Africa to impart some of the knowledge which they had gained—some of the technical knowledge which they had gained in the West. And you find this trend running through the whole of the 19th century.

Some Caribbean Christian missionaries were among those who returned to Africa after slavery. Now missionaries often have a very bad reputation in Africa, and for very good reason. It is very interesting to note, however, that these Black missionaries were often motivated by different kinds of concerns than white missionaries. The white missionaries were usually agents of colonialism and imperialism. The Black missionaries, however, often found themselves drawn into conflict with the white missionaries. The white missionaries for their part tried their best to prevent Afro-Caribbean and Afro-American missionaries from going to Africa because they knew that if Black missionaries would spread out throughout Africa, then the work of the white missionaries, the racism of the white missionaries, would have been made much more difficult.

One of the earliest groups of West Indian missionaries who went over there was a group from Codrington College in Barbados. They formed an organization known as the West Indian Church Association and, beginning in the 1850s, they went to a place called Rio Pongo in what is now Guinea, the country now ruled by Sékou Touré.

One of the outstanding persons who joined this missionary trek was a man by the name of Edward Wilmot Blyden. He started off trying to be a missionary but he did not remain a missionary very long. Blyden left his home in St. Thomas in the Virgin Islands in 1850 and went to the United States. There he tried to enroll in a theological seminary, but the racism in the U.S.A. was so great at that time that he was refused on account of his colour. Blyden therefore left right away in 1850 and went to Liberia. He later became one of the most outstanding African intellectuals in the whole world. He had a very great influence on two or three generations of African intellectuals and one of the most important persons who Blyden influenced was Marcus Garvey.

In Trinidad after slavery, you had the same phenomenon taking place. There was a group of Mandingoes here in Port-of-Spain who were trying very hard to get back to Africa at about the same time as Daaga was leading his mutiny. One of them succeeded, a man by the name of Mohammedu Sisei. From the name you can guess he was a Muslim and I might mention that there were Muslim slaves here in Trinidad and elsewhere in the Americas during slavery times. Some of them were literate in Arabic. In Cuba, too, you had the same thing happening. In Cuba around the turn of the century there were several thousand Africans from the Congo. And I might mention that in Cuba slavery only ended in 1886. So around the turn of the century these people would have been right out of slavery and they also tried very hard to get back to the Congo—what is now Zaire today. A few succeeded.

During this period, a lot of West Indians also were already beginning to emigrate to North America. West Indian emigration to North

America is not a new business. It was happening in the 19th century. And then as now a large number of the Afro-Americans who distinguished themselves in this quest for Africa were in fact people born in the Caribbean. One such was John B. Russwurm, a Jamaican and a man who co-founded the very first Afro-American newspaper. Here was a Jamaican, co-founding the very first Afro-American newspaper in 1827, a paper known as *Freedom's Journal*. Russwurm emigrated to Liberia in 1829. In Liberia, he published the first English language newspaper in West Africa—the *Liberian Herald*. He later became governor of an area in West Africa known as Maryland, an area which today is part of Liberia.

In 1859 another Jamaican, Robert Campbell, joined the Afro-American, Martin R. Delany, in a two-man expedition known as the Niger Valley Exploration Mission which went to the Niger Valley in what is today Nigeria. Their idea was to settle there and encourage Western Africans to come back home to impart whatever skills they had gained. Robert Campbell himself was a teacher and a chemist. This mission failed, partly due to opposition by the British who were then establishing themselves in Nigeria, and partly because of the onset of the United States Civil War. But Robert Campbell himself settled in Lagos, Nigeria and became a well-known and distinguished member of the community.

In 1865 a shipload of 346 Barbadians emigrated to Liberia under the auspices of a North American group, the American Colonization Society. These Barbadians prospered in Liberia. One of them, Arthur Barclay, was president of Liberia from 1904 to 1912. His son Edwin Barclay, was secretary of state and acting president of Liberia in the 1920s. So these were people going back to Africa to live and to make a contribution to their ancestral homeland.

But as the 19th century wore on, you had another group of people emerging in the Caribbean and also, of course, in Afro-America. (But tonight I am mostly concerned with the Caribbean). These were members of the first generation to self-consciously describe themselves as Pan-Africanists. The previous group that I mentioned were people who were primarily interested in going back to live, to teach, to help, to contribute. In the case of the pioneer Pan-Africanists, however, even though some of them did go back to live, this was not their primary aim. Their primary aim was to develop a worldwide community of African peoples. These people whom I am going to deal with in a minute were imbued with the idea that Africans, no matter where they lived, were basically one people. Whether they were living on the continent of Africa, in Afro-America, or in Brazil or Europe or the Caribbean, they were basically the same people. They had a similar history, a similar experience, and, in essence, a similar culture.

Another reason for these early Pan-Africanists beginning to organize in the 19th century was because they were acutely aware of the fact that Africa was about to be gobbled up by Europe. Because these Africans in the West had grown up in the belly of the monster, to use a common expression, because they had grown up in direct contact with Western society, they could see the signs of impending doom for Africa.

Africans on the continent at this time were unfortunately, a very very nice, humane people. Africans in the 19th century were people who would open their houses to the European explorers, tend them when they were sick, give them food, resuscitate them, carry their bodies for hundreds of miles to the nearest white settlement when they were dead. You had people like the Scotsman David Livingstone in the 19th century walking from one end of Africa to the next. For over thirty years, from the 1840s to the 1870s, he walked up and down the people's continent. Nobody killed him, nobody told him to go back. They said we used to be cannibals, but nobody ate him. Here was a lone white man walking through vast areas, in most of which the inhabitants had never seen a white man before. But this was the kind of place, unfortunately, that Africa was. I say unfortunately because African hospitality was Africa's downfall. If they had been less hospitable to the white man, they might have escaped colonialism.

However, the Africans who grew up in the West, they knew the white man and they saw the explorers going to Africa. They saw the European consulates being opened up and they knew what was going to come next. And it is one of the ironies of our history as African people that these Africans in the Caribbean and Afro-America saw what was going to happen, they tried their best to prevent it, but they did not really have the resources. Nevertheless, one has to acknowledge their effort.

And so these early Pan-Africanists began to agitate. They began to tell Black people that they needed to unite on an international basis to save Africa. Of course, as we know, Africa was not saved. At least not immediately. Because between 1870 and the first World War of 1914–1918, practically the whole of Africa was conquered by Europe. For even though Europeans had enslaved Africans for over 400 years from the 1440s up until the late 19th century, still after 400 years most of Africa remained free and independent. The European slave traders never got much further than certain coastal enclaves. But beginning around 1870 that was to change.

The subjugation of Africa is a very recent phenomenon. It only happened about 100 years ago. So these West Indians and these Afro-Americans, they knew. They knew that as soon as David Livingstone started walking from one end of Africa to the next and drawing maps, and finding out where rivers went and where diamonds were, and where the gold was, they knew what was going to happen next. They knew that that was the beginning of the end for Africa and they tried their best. Many of the people who distinguished themselves in this struggle to save Africa from the European scramble were West Indians. They were men like Benito Sylvain, a Haitian who lived in France for many years. In the 1890s Benito Sylvain journeyed to Ethiopia, one of the furthest parts of Africa from the Western World; and the reason why Sylvain journeyed there was because of an event which took place in Ethiopia in 1896. In 1896 at the Battle of Aduwa, Ethiopia, under the Emperor Menelik II, became the only African country to militarily defeat the European colonialists in the midst of their scramble for Africa. Menelik inflicted one of the most humiliating defeats that Europeans ever received in Africa and was able to save Ethiopia at least for the time being, from what happened to the rest of Africa. The Emperor Menelik actually made Sylvain a sort of representative of Ethiopia, a sort of diplomat. In Paris, Sylvain also organized the Black community. In 1898 he founded the Black Youth Association of Paris. In 1900 he was one of the people who participated in the first ever Pan-African Conference. Which brings us to Henry Sylvester Williams, another outstanding pioneer in that early history of Caribbean Pan-Africanists.

HENRY SYLVESTER WILLIAMS

Henry Sylvester Williams was a son of our soil, born in Arouca. Like so many of these Pan-Africanists, he was very widely travelled. West Indians then, like West Indians now, are some of the most travelled of peoples. You find us everywhere. Henry Sylvester Williams travelled in North America. After studying in Canada, he went to England where he studied law. In 1897 he founded something known as the Pan-African Association and the main purpose of this association was to lobby. Williams was living in London at the heart of the British empire and so he was in a very strategic position to lobby on behalf of Africa. He was very concerned about the scramble for Africa in general, but he was especially concerned about the South African issue. Even as far back as that, South Africa was already the focal point of some of the worst atrocities in European-controlled Africa.

In 1900 Henry Sylvester Williams convened the first ever Pan-African Conference. He is the man who really put the word Pan-Africanism in the dictionaries. There were Pan-Africanists before him but they had not used the expression Pan-Africanism. Williams was the man who really, you could almost say, coined that term, Pan-Africanism. At this conference in 1900, some 30 odd delegates got together from the Caribbean, from Afro-America, from Canada, from Europe and from Africa itself. They discussed together how they could try to unite the African world into one solid body which would be strong, which would fight on behalf of Africa, and which would rescue Africa from that European scramble which by 1900 was already in full swing.

Henry Sylvester Williams toured the West Indies after that conference. He came to Trinidad, went to Jamaica. He founded many branches of his Pan-African Association. In 1903 he emigrated to South Africa of all places. Here was a man who was so committed to the work that he was doing, that he actually emigrated to South Africa. He was very active in South Africa for a couple of years, until he left. He died in Trinidad in 1911. He was still a young man when he died, only forty-two years old.

There were many other Trinidadians involved in this struggle at this time. I will mention just one more. There was a man by the name of F.E.M. Hercules, born in 1888, who while a student at Queen's Royal College founded a Young Men's Coloured Association. In 1907 he was a founder of the Port-of-Spain Coloured Association. Hercules went to England during the First World War and became a leader of the Black community there; and there was a Black community there. There were seamen and students and there were travellers. In fact all over Britain, in 1919, there were very bloody race riots and quite a few Black people were actually repatriated to the West Indies.

During these riots there appeared in the *London Times* a letter from a retired British colonial administrator who had worked in Grenada and Africa. This old colonialist suggested the deportation of Britain's Black population and blamed the riots on Black men who were having affairs with white women. The average Englishman, this functionary wrote, was revolted by the idea of sexual contact between white women and Black men. Hercules wrote a reply to the *London Times* in which he pointed out that when the European exploiters left Africa and the West Indies that would be enough time for English people to talk about Black people leaving England. He pointed out that in the West Indies and Africa the slavemasters and their descendants had always forced their attentions on Black women. Hercules recalled from his West Indian experience cases where girls as young as twelve had fallen victim to the white man's lust. He reminded the aging colonialist that in South Africa there were millions of so-called coloreds. (And let me say here that this is one of the strange paradoxes about racial relations. In the most racist societies, you normally find the largest numbers of half-caste children—in the southern United States, in South Africa today). And where did they come from? They are the children of the white South Africans. So Hercules pointed out these paradoxes and contradictions. He was also secretary of the London-based Society of Peoples of African Origin (SPAO). The SPAO's mostly West African and West Indian leadership included Audrey Jeffers of Trinidad, who in 1921 founded her well-known Coterie of Social Workers. Hercules, like Sylvester Williams before him, and like Marcus Garvey in 1937, made a lecture tour of the West Indies in 1919. In Jamaica the British authorities accused him of causing strikes and unrest. He came through Trinidad and spoke to packed audiences at the Princes Building in Port-of-Spain and at other venues in other towns. Many people joined his Society of Peoples of African Origin. From Trinidad he went to Guyana. A few weeks later he returned to Trinidad, but was not allowed to land. His wife and children were here, but the British authorities could not care less. Trinidad at the time was in the grip of strikes and unrest. Anti-colonialist and anti-white feeling were running high, and the authorities were alarmed at the enthusiastic local response to Hercules' call for race pride, freedom and self-reliance.

Other groups of West Indians who experienced Africa in the 19th century and up into the early 20th century were soldiers and civil servants. Some of these unfortunately played a somewhat negative role. One of the unfortunate realities of colonialism all over the world is the fact that the colonialists can dispense rewards. They usually have the power to divide and rule and so everywhere that the European colonialist went, he was able to use one section of the conquered people against another. Africa was not unique in this respect. And so you had the formation of the West India Regiments in the late l8th century. These were regiments of Black soldiers and they were used to fight British imperialist wars everywhere. They fought in the endless inter-European wars in the Caribbean. They were used to put down slave rebellions here in the West Indies. They took part in the ill-fated British expedition to New Orleans in 1814/15 and the more successful British assault on Mobile, Alabama in 1815. They were used to help put down the Jamaica Rebellion in 1865. They were used all over Africa. They participated in the conquest of large pieces of West Africa for Britain. A lot of the British soldiers in the Ashanti wars were actually men from the West India Regiments. C.D.B. King, president of Liberia in the 1920s, was the son of a Jamaican ex-soldier. During the First World War the West India Regiments served in Sierra Leone, the Cameroons and in East Africa.

The overwhelming majority of the regiment's members in the earlier decades of the 19th century were African born. These included over l2,000 "liberated" slaves by 1840. The fear of another Daaga rebellion, though, caused the British to ease up a little on this kind of recruitment after 1837. By the end of the century African born soldiers were in the minority. There were some Afro-American recruits too, at the beginning. These regiments remained in service right up to after the First World War. The officers of course were white, as always in this period.

Some at least of the West India Regiment veterans lived long enough to realize they had been used by the British. When the Garvey movement came into being some of the members were West India Regiment ex-soldiers who, because of what Garvey was saying, were able to turn their knowledge of Africa to a more positive purpose. A lot of West Indian civil servants also worked in Africa. Many went to help build and operate railways, especially in Nigeria. Others went as teachers and policemen. These people were still being sent over up until well into the 20th century. Some of them are still alive. I have spoken with one or two of them.

During the mid-19th century, the remembrance of Africa was also fed by the presence here in the Caribbean of Africans who were coming in as indentured servants. As in the case of the soldiers, many of these had previously been liberated from slave ships by the British navy. Between 1841 and 1867 13,969 of these free African workers entered British Guiana, 10,003 went to Jamaica, 8,385 came to Trinidad and a further 3,763 went to other British colonies, for a grand total of 36,120. They came mainly from St. Helena, Sierra Leone and

Liberia. Thousands more went to Cayenne, Martinique, Guadeloupe and the Dutch colonies.

In addition, demobilized West India Regiment soldiers, many of course African born, were settled in the Caribbean, especially in Trinidad, throughout the 19th century. Others settled in West Africa, especially Sierra Leone, thus fostering the ongoing African-Caribbean cross fertilization.

There was yet another group of free Africans who settled in the West Indies, this time even before the end of slavery. These were Afro-American veterans of the War of 1812 between Britain and the United States. Throughout Afro-American history, whenever the South in particular, and the United States in general, has been under external attack, large numbers of Afro-Americans have sided with whoever the enemy happened to be. In this case they sided with the British against their American slavemasters. In return they extracted from the British a promise of freedom. The British kept their promise and resettled these troops in Trinidad's famous "Company Villages" at the war's end.

Some of these Afro-American veterans were doubtless African born and in Trinidad they referred to themselves as Africans, even if persons outside their community often called them Americans or "Merikins". Up to this day (1980), older inhabitants of these villages still refer to their parents, grandparents and great-grandparents as "the Africans." The Spiritual Baptist faith is among the legacies of this Afro-American community in Trinidad.

The Europeans had a practice of exiling troublesome African leaders to the West Indies and this, too, helped to foster interest. For example, when I was a little boy growing up, my mother had an expression that went something like this, "Who do you think you are, King Jaja?" And I always thought that King Jaja was a fictional character from some story book. It's funny but I never thought of asking who King Jaja was. I am not even sure she herself knew who he was. But imagine my surprise when I went to graduate school in the United States, studying African history, and discovered that not only had there been a King Jaja, but that he had in fact been exiled to the West Indies in the late 19th century. The fact that the memory of him continued in our folklore means that he must have had some impact on the population here. And in fact he did. King Jaja of Opobo (in modern day Nigeria) was a merchant who gave the British so much competition in their trade that they got rid of him. And so in 1888 they put him on a ship and sent him off to the West Indies. He eventually stayed in St. Vincent. He stopped in other islands, too, along the way. King Jaja later became ill and in 1891 they put him on a ship back to Africa. He died on the ship on his way back. He never saw his native land again. But West Indians demonstrated and agitated on behalf of King Jaja. And so his name lived on in our folklore. One of his wives is said to have settled in Trinidad after his death.

The French did the same thing to King Behanzin of Dahomey, the country that Daaga had sailed from many years before. Behanzin waged a bitter armed struggle against the French colonialist aggressors (and their Senegalese troops), but was eventually defeated. In 1894 the French exiled him to a fort in Martinique, installed a puppet ruler in his place and broke his country up into a colony and protectorate. Behanzin was kept in Martinique until 1905 and then transferred to the Algerian town of Blida, where he died in 1906.

Half a centruy later, in that same Algerian town, an African son of Martinique, Frantz Fanon, would join the Algerian revolution and help bestow on France its greatest defeat in Africa. And King Behanzin's nephew, Prince Kojo Tovalou Houénou, in the 1920s became an avid supporter of the Jamaican Marcus Garvey, the scourge of the European colonialists in Africa. Houénou is even said to have led a Garvey inspired uprising against the French in Dahomey in 1923. The God of Africa, too, moves in mysterious ways, his wonders to perform.

AFRICAN COMMUNITIES

All of these varied African immigrants—the soldiers, the indentured servants, the liberated Africans plain and simple, the exiles, and of course, the slaves—helped keep alive the memory of Africa. And perhaps this may be part of the reason, though not the whole reason, why way up into the 20th century you found many African communities here. And when I say African communities now I do not simply mean people of African descent, but communities of Africans who self-consciously regarded themselves as African communities; who tried to preserve, in whatever ways they could, the traditions of their particular ethnic group. The Congo people I mentioned in Cuba were one example.

In Trinidad you had Mandingo communities, you had Yoruba communities, Hausa communities, Congo communities; a Rada community in Belmont was still alive and well in the 1950s. It was communities like these, creatively applying their African cultural heritage to a new environment, that gave us calypso and steelband.

I came upon a manuscript the other day, written by Sam Manning, a famous old time calypsonian, who apparently grew up in or near a Yoruba community in Carapichaima. He was describing the Yorubas of Carapichaima around the turn of this century. He described them as a very proud group of people, a people who were very thrifty and industrious. Many of them were cocoa farmers, according to Manning's account. These Yorubas of Carapichaima looked down to some extent on the Congoes of nearby Alexander Village, among other things because they (the Congoes) were prone to racial intermixture with the whites. The Yorubas on the other hand, were very proud of their race.

So this brings us to the early 20th century. We have seen that by this time West Indians had long been manifesting their interest in Africa in all kinds of ways. Some were going back to Africa physically, some were agitating on behalf of Africa, some were trying to prevent the European scramble for the continent, some were going as civil servants and soldiers, some were living in African communities in the West Indies.

MARCUS GARVEY

Then in the early 20th century, there appeared Marcus Mosiah Garvey, who in a way gathered up most of these trends that I have been describing. And Marcus Garvey in a most amazing fashion was able to gather up all this in his career and was able to have an unprecedented impact on the whole African world and indeed the whole world in general—an impact which I do not really think has ever been equalled.

Marcus Garvey founded and led the largest Pan-African movement in history. People like Henry Sylvester Williams, Edward Wilmot Blyden, F.E.M. Hercules and the others had written books and articles, lectured widely, held conferences and generally agitated on Africa's behalf. Where they had tried to form organizations, these had not lasted very long. Garvey combined the best qualities of all these men. He had the vision. He had the organizing ability. He had the staying power. But he probably could not have done what he did had it not been for the history of similar struggles that were waged before his time. In a way he stood on the shoulders of those who had gone before him—the Blydens, the Sylvester Williamses, because nobody ever arises in a vacuum. We all build on the work of previous generations.

Garvey, a descendant of Jamaica's Maroons, was born on August 17, 1887, exactly fifty years and a day after the execution of Daaga in Trinidad. Like so many other major Pan-Africanists, he was widely travelled. Many of the major Pan-African figures over the years have come from the West Indies. And the fact that we have travelled so widely may have something to do with our ability to see the struggle of African peoples in a global perspective. Garvey travelled throughout Central America. He travelled in South America. He went to Europe and travelled through seven countries. He went to the United States. He travelled through thirty-eight states in a year. He travelled in Canada. He was always on the move. He knew the Black world personally and well.

Garvey had a tremendous impact on African nationalist struggles. A large number of the major nationalist figures in Africa in the 1920s, '30s, '40s, 50s even '60s and '70s, even today, were influenced directly or indirectly by Marcus Garvey. People like Harry Thuku in Kenya in the 1920s—the person who was the head of the organization that Jomo Kenyatta joined as a young man. Thuku corresponded with Garvey. People like Kwame Nkrumah of Ghana. Nkrumah wrote in his auto-biography that of all the books he read, the one which had the greatest impact on him was Garvey's *Philosophy and Opinions*. Nkrumah also went to Garveyite and West Indian nationalist meetings as a student in New York.

Nnamdi Azikiwe, who was the first governor general of independent Nigeria, also wrote in his autobiography of the impact that Garvey had on him. As a young man in 1920, Azikiwe wrote, he saw his first copy of Garvey's newspaper, the *Negro World*, and that changed his life. It had a mighty effect on him. And when he wrote his autobiography half a century later, he was still celebrating that event—the day he read a copy of Garvey's newspaper.

In South Africa, the same place that Henry Sylvester Williams had earlier emigrated to, the African nationalist movement was thoroughly organized by Garvey. There were two major African organizations in South Africa in the 1920's and both of them had Garveyites in their leadership. One was the African National Congress, which is still today an important part of the struggle for freedom and justice in South Africa. The other one was the Industrial and Commercial Workers Union (ICU). Not only were some of the leaders of that union Garveyites, but some were actually West Indians. There was a West Indian community in South Africa in the 1920's and some of them were leading the struggle there.

In the Garvey Movement, therefore, we have another example of that continuing effort by West Indians to contribute directly to African struggles in Africa. It illustrates also the effort on the part of Pan-Africanists to develop African peoples worldwide into a single, strong community. It demonstrates further the role that Africa has played in broadly based social movements in the West Indies. For the Garvey Movement, apart from everything else, was a movement against colonialism and imperialism and for racial justice and social change. Unfortunately, it also demonstrates the fact that African movements in the Caribbean have often been suppressed and harassed.

Many Garveyites were deported from various places, including Trinidad. Garvey himself was almost prevented from landing in Trinidad in 1937. Captain A.A. Cipriani had to write a letter to the Colonial Office in London, asking them to allow Garvey to land. Many Garveyites were jailed for reading his paper, the *Negro World*. The newspaper was banned here in Trinidad from 1919. Under the Seditious Publications Ordinance of 1920, you could be put in jail for reading it. Nevertheless Garvey was a great success in so far as he stirred the people to greater consciousness of self and provided a nursery for young politicians and trade unionists. As late as the 1950s, many of the politicians in power in the West Indies were people who had either grown up in the Garvey Movement or whose parents were Garveyites. And even today, there are still one or two around.

Now the Garvey Movement began to decline by the 1930s. It did not die, but it began to decline. But Garvey had planted the seed of African consciousness so strongly, that even though his own movement, the Universal Negro Improvement Association (UNIA), began to decline, that seed continued to flower in all kinds of other areas. And so from the time of Garvey you found African consciousness continuing to flower in the West Indies in all kinds of ways.

RASTAFARIAN MOVEMENT

One of the ways in which it flowered early in the 1930s was in the Rastafarian Movement in Jamaica. Many of the people who began that movement were people who had been members of Garvey's UNIA. What tended to happen not only in the Caribbean but in Afro-America too, was that as the UNIA declined, new organizations tended to come into being. And even though these new organizations went off in slightly different areas, they all had a common origin in Garvey. They all considered Garvey as a prophet and a forerunner and they all preached basically what Garvey was preaching—race pride, self-reliance, African redemption and the question of reuniting in some form or fashion either spiritually or physically with the African homeland.

The Rastafarians were one of the major manifestations in the Caribbean of that development of new groups growing out of Garvey's organization. The movement started right around the UNIA in Kingston. Many of the early Rastafarian leaders used to hang around with the Garveyites at Liberty Hall (as UNIA meeting places were called all over the world). In fact, some of the Rastafarians at one point in the early 1930s actually had an office in the Kingston Liberty Hall.

We all know that the question of Ethiopia is central to Rastafarianism. And one does not have to look far in the Garvey Movement to see where these early Rastafarians may have developed that interest in Ethiopia. I am not saying that the Garvey Movement was the sole or exclusive source of their knowledge of, and interest in Ethiopia. But nevertheless, the question of Ethiopia was so widespread, so pervasive in the UNIA that those early Rastafarians who came out of the Garvey Movement could not help but have imbibed a lot of knowledge of Ethiopia from their association with Garvey and Garveyism. For example, as early as 1922 Ras Tafari, who at that time was prince regent (he became emperor in 1930), sent a message to the UNIA in New York inviting Africans in the West to come back home to Ethiopia and help build the country.

Garvey himself often used the word Ethiopia. Now the word Ethiopia in ancient times used to mean not only the country which we call Ethiopia today, but Africa in general. During Garvey's youth, this use of the word was still popular. In Trinidad, for example, you had an Ethiopian Association formed in Princes Town in 1910. The ancient Greeks were the ones who actually coined the word. It literally means, "land of the people with burnt faces," burnt faces being the Greek method of describing black skin. Ethiopia played a very important role in ancient Greek mythology. The Ethiopians were seen as a sort of especially blessed people, so much so that the Greek deities used to journey to Ethiopia every year to sojourn with the Gods of Ethiopia.

In the Bible also, there are all kinds of references to Ethiopia. Marcus Garvey was especially fond of the prediction contained in the 68th Psalm and the 31st verse, that "Princes shall come out of Egypt, and Ethiopia shall soon stretch forth her hands unto God." He used it to signify that Africa would soon be free. Anybody in the Garvey Movement must have been aware of that quotation.

The national anthem of the UNIA was known as the Universal Ethiopian Anthem. It illustrated very well Garvey's frequent use of Ethiopia and Africa as one and the same. The opening verse and chorus went like this—

I

Ethiopia, thou land of our fathers,
Thou land where the gods loved to be,
As storm cloud at night suddenly gathers
Our armies come rushing to thee.
We must in the fight be victorious
When swords are thrust outward to gleam;
For us will the vict'ry be glorious
When led by the red, black and green.

CHORUS

Advance, advance to victory,
Let Africa be free;
Advance to meet the foe
With the might
Of the red, the black and the green.

That's how the Garveyite anthem began. So an early Rastafarian coming out of the Garvey Movement would have been familiar with all this. In fact, just around the time that the Rastafarian Movement was being founded in Jamaica, quite a few Garveyites were actually emigrating to Ethiopia. Beginning in 1930, quite a few of them went over, led by Barbados born Rabbi Arnold J. Ford. Ford had lived in Afro-America for many years and had been musical director of the UNIA.

These Garveyites went to Ethiopia and played useful roles. None of them became super-famous or anything but they all quietly made their little contributions in whatever way they could. Some of them started schools. In fact, the first secondary school in Ethiopia for women was started by one of these Garveyites. Arnold Ford himself was a master musician. He taught music to some of the emperor's family. So these people were going there at the same time as the Rastafarians were getting started.

Now one of the events which it is normally said gave great impetus to the formation of the Rastafarian Movement was the coronation of Haile Selassie I, as King of Kings, Lord of Lords, and Conquering Lion of the Tribe of Judah in November 1930. At that time Garvey was back in Jamaica, having been deported from North America. His Jamaican newspaper, the *Blackman,* along with other newspapers both Black and white carried the coronation of Haile Selassie in big bold type on the front page. The *Blackman* also carried huge portraits on the front page of both Garvey and Haile Selassie. And Garvey pointed out around that time, that Haile Selassie would welcome back, and had in fact already extended an invitation to, Africans from the West, to come and help build Ethiopia. And as I said, some were actually on their way to Ethiopia at that very time. So all of this may help to explain the connection between the early Rastafarian Movement and Marcus Garvey.

Another event in the 1930s which again demonstrated that continuing link with Africa also involved Ethiopia. This time, it was what is known in the history books as the Italo-Ethiopian War.

In 1935 the Italian fascist dictator, Benito Mussolini, invaded Ethiopia. No event since the beginning of the Garvey Movement had such a tremendous impact on the African peoples in the West. All over Afro-America and the Caribbean, and in Europe too, African communities mobilized to help in whatever way they could to send medicine, to raise money, to lobby and to publicize the Ethiopian cause. In Trinidad here, dockworkers refused to handle Italian ships. There were large public meetings attended by thousands here in Trinidad. Thousands of people here and throughout the West Indies petitioned the government to be allowed to go and fight for Ethiopia. Although the British government refused all such requests, thousands of young men, here in the West Indies, expressed that desire by signing petitions to go and fight for Ethiopia. Such was the feeling on behalf of Ethiopia among Afro-West Indians in the 1930s.

Marcus Garvey left Jamaica this same year (1935) to live in England. There he continued publishing his *Black Man* magazine, a successor of the *Blackman* newspaper. Garvey was very supportive of the Ethiopian struggle against Mussolini. Issue after issue of the *Black Man* contained articles bitterly hostile to Mussolini in particular and the Italians in general. Garvey was a poet among other things and I am going to read an extract from one of his poems written against Mussolini. This poem is entitled "The Smell of Mussolini." Garvey said Mussolini smelled stink from Addis Ababa down to sinful Rome. Let me just read a portion of this poem published in 1936—

> Let all Italians live and die in shame,
> For what their Mad Dog did to our dear home:
> Their Mussolini's bloody, savage name
> Smells stink from Addis back to sinful Rome.
> No cause that links Italian liberty
> Shall have appeal to us, in peace or war;
> No one will ask us in our sobriety
> To help the Italian, near or far:
> In clash of arms, on Europe's fields of blood,
> No help must Negroes give to Roman cause,
> For it must be for ever understood
> That Italians keep no sacred laws.
> We shall march past the ancient Vatican,
> To sack the gates of Italian Rome,
> And make them feel the hand of vengeful man
> Who first was driven from his natural home:
> With English, German, French, or other hordes,
> We'll march to crush the Italian dog,
> And at the points of gleaming, shining swords,
> We'll lay quite low the violent, Roman hog.

Garvey was evidently very upset. However, despite his upset with Mussolini, and despite his support for the Ethiopian cause, Garvey had some mild criticism for Haile Selassie which got him in trouble with some of his followers. For Garvey could not help but remember the Emperor Menelik, who in 1896 had defeated these very same Italians. Something obviously had gone wrong between 1896 and 1935. Menelik had routed those Italians in 1896. At that time the Ethiopians had been able to procure modern weapons.

In the 1935 conflict, however, the Italians had a virtual monopoly of modern weapons. Not only did they have a monopoly of modern weapons, but they used modern technology in its most ruthless fashion. They used poison gas, something which had been outlawed by all kinds of international conventions. They dropped poison gas on the Ethiopians. The Ethiopians had no aeroplanes to counter the Italian air force. A Trinidadian, funny enough, Hubert Fauntleroy Julian, the famous "Black Eagle," tried to form an Ethiopian air force, but he did not have the resources at the time.

And so Garvey criticized Haile Selassie for allowing Ethiopia to fall into this weakened condition. He argued that Haile Selassie should have modernized Ethiopia. And when, as the war progressed, Haile Selassie left Ethiopia and went into exile in Europe, Garvey argued that Selassie should have stayed to rally his forces. Now Garvey was not against Selassie per se, he was not against Ethiopia, but he did voice these mild criticisms. And of course coming at a time when Ethiopia was under siege, many people misunderstood what he was saying and attacked him on this score. He was strongly attacked by a lot of people.

NEGRITUDE

At about the same time that the Rastafarians were getting started in Jamaica, the African literary world was swept by a movement known as "Negritude". West Indians were involved in this as usual. Among the leading exponents of the new development were Léopold Sédar Senghor, now president of Senegal, Aimé Césaire of Martinique and Léon Damas of Cayenne. Negritude was basically a response to European cultural imperialism. Its poets and other writers tried to show that everything white was not pretty, that everything black was not ugly; that whites were not inherently superior in intelligence, and Africans were not naturally stupid. Praiseworthy as were the goals of the Negritude writers, some of them went overboard and fell into all kinds of contradictions. In their efforts to extol the humanity of Africans some Negritude poets suggested, like the European racists, that Africans had never invented anything and that Europeans had some sort of monopoly over scientific intelligence. Some of the Negritude poets who later went into politics seemed quite content to play a neocolonial role, despite their poems about beautiful naked Black women and tom-tom drums.

The 1930s were also a time when the nationalist struggles in Africa and the Caribbean were beginning to gather momentum. At this stage you find West Indians once again distinguishing themselves in the African phase of this struggle. For example, in England there were many small bodies which played an important role in the history of that struggle. One of these was the International African Friends of Abyssinia (Ethiopia), founded by C.L.R. James in response to the Italian aggression against Ethiopia. And when you look at the membership of that organization, you find people like Jomo Kenyatta, who later became the head of Kenya. You find people like I.T.A. Wallace-Johnson, a well-known Sierra Leone nationalist. You find people like George Padmore of Trinidad, who later played a distinguished role in Nkrumah's Ghana. You find people like Amy Ashwood Garvey, the first wife of Marcus Garvey. So here you find West Indians very involved with Africans, planning this phase of that protracted struggle that would lead eventually in the 1950s and '60s to independence.

In that same decade George Padmore organized the International African Service Bureau in London. This was superseded later by his Pan-African Association. There, too, you found the same kinds of names. In 1945, in Manchester, England, there took place the Fifth Pan-African Congress—one of the most important gatherings to take place in that struggle for independence in Africa and the West Indies. This congress was organized by George Padmore of Trinidad and Kwame Nkrumah of Ghana.

Padmore, by the way, was born in 1902 in Arouca, which happened also to have been the home town of Henry Sylvester Williams. (His childhood friend, C. L. R. James, was born in 1901 in nearby Tunapuna). Padmore emigrated to the U. S. A. in 1924 and immediately became active in the Afro-American struggle. He joined the Communist Party in due course and was sent to Moscow. Here and at other posts in Europe he played an important Pan-African role as head of the Negro Bureau of the Red International of Labor Unions (Profintern). He eventually broke with the communists in 1934 when Soviet foreign policy ran counter to his Pan-African sensibilities. In 1935 he moved to London.

Padmore and Nkrumah's Fifth Pan-African Congress in 1945 was important because after that congress, the delegates decided that the time had come for them to return home and intensify the struggle. Prior to that, many of them had been based in Europe. Nkrumah returned home about one year after the congress. By 1957, he was leader of independent Ghana, the first of the British African and Caribbean colonies to gain its independence. Jomo Kenyatta also went back home after that congress, to lead the struggle in Kenya. So in this period, too, you find West Indians playing an integral part. And in fact when Ghana became independent in 1957, George Padmore became Nkrumah's advisor on African affairs. So here you had a Trinidadian advising one of Africa's most outstanding leaders on African affairs.

There could be no more intimate contact between the Caribbean struggle and the African struggle. Here you had the very first African country to gain its independence from Britain and who did you have as an advisor to the Prime Minister on African affairs? A Trinidadian, George Padmore. And there were many other West Indians and Afro-Americans in Ghana at that time. Padmore is just the most outstanding. He was by no means a unique phenomenon.

Nkrumah also paid homage to the role West Indians had played in his struggle by naming Ghana's new steamship company the Black Star Line, after Marcus Garvey's earlier shipping company. He named a square in Accra (that is, the capital city), the Black Star Square. He had an Order of the Black Star, which he conferred on the Emperor Haile Selassie, a few years afterwards. So that link between the West Indies and Africa was very, very intimate right at the beginning of that new era of post-colonial African independence.

Around that same time you had Algeria in North Africa moving towards independence. When one thinks of the link between Africans and West Indians one normally thinks of West Africa especially, perhaps East, Central and South Africa to a lesser extent. But very few people think of North Africa. Of course the European often caused us to forget the North existed with his talk of Africa, south of the Sahara. Africa, of course, is one indivisible continent. And even in far away Algeria, you found a West Indian playing a leading role in the struggle for independence in the 1950s and '60s and this was Frantz Fanon of Martinique.

FRANTZ FANON

Fanon had been a psychiatrist practising quietly in Algeria when fate caused the Algerian struggle to begin. He found himself clandestinely helping wounded guerillas until he could take it no more. He packed up his practice and joined up full time with the guerilla underground. Fanon eventually edited *El Moudjahid ("The Freedom Fighter")*, the official revolutionary journal of the Algerian government in exile. He also served as an ambassador to various African countries. He was one of the leaders of the Algerian revolution.

In the West Indies meanwhile many of us were moving quietly, not as fast, not as violently, to our formal independence, which came in due course. Local people replaced the European colonialists. But still the African consciousness would not go away, all contrary efforts of the ruling classes notwithstanding. And the history of the West Indies from the 1950s has been one of continuing mass identification with Africa—an identification which the post-colonial powers have been just as uneasy with as were their European predecessors. Sometimes they have tried to pretend it does not exist—the kind of pretense that could allow an island of over 90 per cent Africans to proclaim its motto to the world as "Out of many, one people." The United States, France, Holland, the Soviet Union, England and South Africa under white oppression are all more multiracial than most West Indian islands; but cock will probably get teeth before you will here the likes of England and France boasting about "Out of many, one people". Sometimes, of course, governments have tried to violently suppress this kind of activity. More typically they have tried other means. There is the well-known case a few years ago of the Sixth Pan-African Congress in Tanzania, where the governments in the Caribbean prevented non-governmental pro-African organizations from going to Africa to participate in that kind of activity.

Sometimes governments have tried to partially accommodate this African consciousness. For example, in Jamaica in 1961, the government actually helped finance a "Mission to Africa," where representatives of the Rastafarians, Garveyites and other pro-African groups toured Ethiopia, Liberia, Nigeria, Sierra Leone and Ghana to see how receptive African leaders were to the question of repatriation.

Jamaica, I might add,is possibly the country in the Caribbean which has the strongest mass interest in Africa. There, unlike in some other Caribbean countries, it is not always possible for governments to ignore that interest. It is just too widespread. And so in Jamaica you find in 1964 that Marcus Garvey was made a national hero. He became their very first national hero. Which puts Jamaica in a sense ahead of many of the other islands in giving that kind of honor to a Pan-Africanist. Indeed, even now, with 1980 elections in the air, there is taking place in Jamaica an unprecedented spectacle of all the major political parties locked in intense struggle over which one is the real recipient of Garvey's legacy. Opportunistic as some of the actors in this drama might be, the fact is still of great importance that the populace of one Caribbean island has compelled the socialist Peoples National Party, the conservative Jamaican Labour Party and the communist Workers Party of Jamaica to all vie bitterly with one another for the mantle of heir to Garvey the Pan-Africanist.

CENTRAL ROLE

So what does all this mean for the Caribbean? How can we conclude? It is obvious that Africa has played a central role in the history of African peoples in the Caribbean. Slavery was not able to destroy that role. Post-slavery colonialism was not successful in destroying that role. Independence has not gotten rid of that role. It is obvious that this interest in Africa, this deep desire for Africa, will continue, even if, as too often over the last 500 years, it has to be asserted in the face of official indifference, intolerance or worse.

It should be equally obvious that the celebration of Africanness in the Caribbean has historically provided the impetus for movements attempting broad social change. This is not surprising, for Africans have usually been liberally represented among the wretched of the Caribbean earth. Perhaps this is why the powers that be have over the years so often viewed Africa-related movements with suspicion and/or hostility. For the Djukas of Suriname celebrated their Africanness by defeating the Dutch troops, punishing their former slavemasters and forcing all and sundry to respect their freedom. The Maroons of British Jamaica did likewise, though they did lapse into the occasional contradiction. The Maroons of Saint-Domingue helped prepare the way for the Haitian Revolution. Daaga of Trinidad and Cinqué and the Amistad revolutionaries of Cuba engaged in serious struggle in pursuit of their African desires. Henry Sylvester Williams fought against apartheid in South Africa and for freedom and justice for African peoples everywhere. F.E.M. Hercules in 1919, like Stokely Carmichael in 1967, was banned from his own native land for telling the people like it was. Marcus Garvey's African program was wide enough to include a relentless struggle against racism, colonialism and imperialism and for self-government and a federation of the West Indies. George Padmore and Frantz Fanon had profound effects on African nationalist struggles. The Black Power activists of the 1960s and '70s sought ways to democratize political and social systems and reached out in solidarity to other oppressed groups in Caribbean society.

None of this is to suggest that all of these individuals and organizations were always correct all of the time. That would not be humanly possible. This is merely to say that the remembrance of Africa and movements for broad social change have more often than not gone hand in hand in the Caribbean experience.

Those who attempt to suppress this historical reality will forever be spinning top in mud, because you cannot ask a human being to suppress his roots. The African consciousness which has refused to disappear from our history is a manifestation of a very deep human urge. And as long as there are Africans in the Caribbean, they will continue to ask the question that Countee Cullen asked so long ago—

> What is Africa to me:
> Copper sun or scarlet sea,
> Jungle star or jungle track,
> Strong bronzed men, or regal black
> Women from whose loins I sprang
> When the birds of Eden sang?
> One three centuries removed
> From the scenes his fathers loved,
> Spicy grove, cinnamon tree,
> What is Africa to me?

2

Some Reflections on Evangelical Pan-Africanism
or
Black Missionaries, White Missionaries and the Struggle for African Souls, 1890–1930*

Christian proselytization by Europeans in Africa has, for the last five hundred years, been closely associated with European colonization and subjugation of that continent. The Portuguese pioneers set a pattern as they traded and raided their way around the African coastline from the fifteenth century onwards, which was not often fundamentally deviated from in the centuries that followed. The outstanding example of early Portuguese missionary activity centered around the almost legendary figure of the Mani Congo, whose son, appropriately renamed Dom Henrique, was elevated in the early sixteenth century to the status of bishop in the Church of Rome, a status which was not approached by any other African worthy for several hundred years afterwards. With the intensification of the slave trade, the Portuguese did not neglect the souls of their captives, though methods of mass production had perforce to be resorted to. This meant, in concrete terms, that slaves were baptized in lots and immediately afterwards

*Originally published in 1971

branded with hot irons on the Angolan coast, to signify that they had been received into the Church and that the King's duty had likewise been paid upon them.[1]

With the tendency dating from the late eighteenth century, among Afro-Americans and Black West Indians, to give organizational expression to their disenchantment with white churches whose Christianity balked at the prospect of racial brotherhood, the desire on the part of New World Africans to evangelize the mother continent grew. This desire was given an additional fillip by such events as the abolition of slavery in the West Indies, and paralleled a steady emigration of Africans from places as far apart as Brazil and Nova Scotia. Emigration began in earnest in the late eighteenth century and continued throughout the nineteenth and into the twentieth centuries.

The first Afro-American missionary to venture into foreign parts is supposed to have been one George Lisle, an ex-slave from Georgia who introduced the North American brand of Black religious nationalism into Jamaica in 1783. Lisle was a Baptist, and Baptists, both Black and white, were thereafter to be blamed by the colonial authorities for most manifestations of insubordination among the slaves.

With the abolition of slavery in the British West Indies in 1834 and the end of the short period of re-enslavement which followed (euphemistically referred to as "apprenticeship"), widespread manifestations appeared, often spontaneously, of a desire on the part of newly freed ex-slaves to make some tangible contribution to their brothers in Africa. European missionaries were often impressed and took steps to convert their desires into reality. Sometimes, however, the missionaries' home bodies discreetly evaded or discouraged such attempts.

Nevertheless, many West Indian missionaries made their way throughout the nineteenth century to such places as Fernando Po, the Gold Coast, the Congo, and several other locations along the West Coast of Africa, usually as subordinates of white missionaries.[2] (Thereby hangs a tale which will be briefly alluded to later in this paper). In 1846 one of these West Indians, a Joseph Merrick, made the first translation of the Bible into the language of the Isubu people living in the vicinity of the Cameroons River.[3] As late as the 1920s a school principalled and senior-staffed by four Jamaicans was described as the best of its kind in Africa by British Colonial Office functionary, Sir Hugh Clifford, and an educational commission staffed by Colonial Office and American "experts" on "Native Education." The latter was provided by the Phelps Stokes Fund.⁴ Such fulsome praise from such quarters means that these particular Jamaicans must have been of conservative bent.

More important for the purposes of this paper were the parallel attempts of Afro-American missionaries. From this source, too, there had been a steady if modest trickle of evangelical emissaries throughout the nineteenth century, particularly to Liberia, where ministers accompanied the first shipload of Afro-American settlers. Outside of Liberia, which was a special case due to its Afro-American population,⁵ the tendency, until late in the century, was for the occasional Black missionary to be sent together with white superiors by white church bodies.

By the last decade of the nineteenth century, however, a new situation seemed to be developing. Black Americans seemed poised to break into the African mission field in larger numbers than before—large enough numbers, indeed, to raise the question of a threat to the traditional hegemony which white missionaries enjoyed up till then over African souls. A large influx of Afro-Americans, cassocks or clerical collars notwithstanding, would also pose the problem of insulating the "Natives" from the "subversive" theories of Black Nationalism and race pride which flourished in Afro-American churches. And Africans had already given warning of a potential receptivity to these ideas, for nationalist "Ethiopian" churches had already appeared in Southern Africa, dating from the 1870s.

Why this threat to the colonial status quo should have been posed at this particular time was largely the result of the Civil War and the abolition of slavery which had taken place three decades earlier in the United States. The intervening thirty years had witnessed an improvement in the educational opportunities available to Black people which, even though still inferior, were nevertheless unprecedented. At about this time, too, new independent Black churches appeared to underscore the position of churches as one of the few autonomous areas within the Afro-American community, a factor which must have stood out starkly against the steady deterioration in the Black community's political position witnessed in the decades after Reconstruction.

The interest was also fanned by some white missionaries who, flooding the continent in the wake of the European scramble for Africa, often regarded the Afro-American missionary as a means to vindicate the institution of slavery. Out of evil cometh good, and from the evil of slavery God in His wisdom had produced, or so the argument went, the means of rescuing benighted Africa from eternal perdition. Many Black churchmen mouthed similar sentiments, and although some of them may have unwittingly or otherwise adopted the patronising language of their white counterparts, there was nevertheless a very genuine and fairly widespread sense of obligation to Africa, still often referred to as the fatherland, though the now more fashionable term of motherland also enjoyed currency.

The flavor of these sentiments can be garnered from a sampling of the statements of leading Afro-American churchmen of the period. Bishop Henry M. Turner of the AME church, for example, a leading nationalist of the period who was subsequently invited to (but could not attend) the first Pan-African Conference in London in 1900, in 1895 expressed such sentiments, in a heavy flood of melodramatic rhetoric:

> . . . I believe that the Negro was brought to this country in the providence of God to a heaven-permitted if not a divine-sanctioned manual laboring school, that he might have direct contact with the mightiest race that ever trod the face of the globe.[6]

Turner was the direct ideological forbear of Marcus Garvey and, like Garvey, in whom his thought found its highest expression, he used this hyperbolical introduction to lead up to the conclusion that "There is no manhood future in the United States for the Negro".[7]

And AME Bishop William H. Heard expressed a familiar sentiment when he landed not long afterwards in Freetown, Sierra Leone, together with Bishop Turner:

> As we reached this African town of forty thousand inhabitants and less than one fourth of them civilised, we felt good, for here we met our people. Up to this time we had been with the other race, which was not very customary to us.[8]

The Reverend Charles S. Morris of the Negro Baptists, who is thought to have accompanied the Nyasaland anti-colonialist hero, John Chilembwe back to Africa in 1900,[9] said in that same year:

> So, when I see the negroes of our Southern States; people who came here naked savages . . . and who, today, are four millions in number, redeemed, regenerated, disinthralled, I believe that God is going to put it into the hearts of these black boys and girls . . . [to] vindicate American slavery as far as it can be vindicated.[10]

The feeling of moral obligation was not the only argument advanced by Afro-American missionaries and those white churchmen who shared their views or considered it expedient to pay lip-service to the idea. Some voiced the opinion that Black Americans were more immune to African fevers. Whatever may have been the biological merits or otherwise of this argument, it did have at least a superficial historical validity, since there were well-known cases which seemed to prove the point.

Liberia in 1821 had fallen under the virtual governorship of a Black emigrant churchman, the Reverend Daniel Coker of the AME Church, after the white administrators had succumbed. The same had happened in the 1850s in the Rio Pongos mission where the West Indian J.H.A. Duport assumed control under similar circumstances. It had happened elsewhere.

Another argument advanced may have significantly influenced white missionary attitudes of hostility towards their Afro-American counterparts. The Reverend Charles S. Morris put it this way at the Ecumenical Missionary Conference in 1900:

> Within twelve miles of Lovedale I saw an American negro, who, last year, baptised some three hundred people in that country. And as I sat in his house the native men and women came and squatted on the floor and perched on the trunks and chairs, and there was such a freedom and a lack of formality as would be impossible in the house of any other missionary than a black man. Night came on . . . this missionary's little daughter slept in the middle and those two heathen girls on either side. That would be impossible to any other missionary than a black man.[11]

This type of situation led inevitably to charges of "sheep stealing" when Africans deserted white churches in favor of their Afro-American brothers. And it does not take much imagination to conclude that Afro-American missionaries would join with Africans in protesting the intrusions of racial discrimination into white churches. Morris himself continued the passage quoted above with a spirited defense of Ethiopianism and a catalogue of ills communicated to him by African Christians—being refused communion when white visitors were in the church; being served meals in the white missionaries' kitchens, and the like.[12]

Equally enthusiastic, and indeed oftentimes more so than Afro-Americans over this evangelical Pan-Africanism, were many white missionaries. Their actions sometimes belied their words, but of lip-service to the cause there was never a deficit. Which is not to say that it was all lip-service. There were obviously white missionaries who were genuine. Some of these made tangible earnests of their genuineness. But as so often happens, these "liberals" were not the ones whose counsels were sought by the wielders of power. On occasion, if they were radical enough, they might even be mentioned unfavorably in colonial despatches or excluded or deported from territories.

The most illustrious personage in this category during the period under consideration was undoubtedly Joseph Booth who, in his lengthy career in South and Central Africa, achieved the whole gamut of radical distinctions save only that of martyrdom à la John Brown. That supreme proof of radicalism was reserved for this first African convert, John Chilembwe, for whose Afro-American education, connections, assistance and ideological affinity Booth could justly take credit. Chilembwe "went down", to use the picturesque euphemism of his biographers,[13] together with a few dozen of his supporters in 1915, to give Africa yet another example of the truism that the voracious appetite of freedom will be assuaged only by the tragic immolation of Africa's noblest sons and daughters.

Though Chilembwe had drawn away from Booth after coming into contact with Afro-Americans, Booth seems never to have given up his vision of a large-scale Afro-American effort in Africa, and advocated the settlement of New World Africans in the motherland.[14]

The similarity of the sentiments expressed by white missionaries and others to those of Afro-American churchmen can be seen from the following quotation delivered by a white minister at the Congress on Africa held in Atlanta, Georgia in 1895: "The industrial, intellectual, moral and spiritual progress of the colored people in America is a prophecy . . . of what the native African is capable of becoming."[15] This sentence came to round off an explanation of the work of the white-run Stewart Missionary Foundation which propagandized Black people, including school children in the South, concerning the desirability of serving in Africa.

Even the Governor of Georgia got into the act during this conference and piously declared:

> A mysterious Providence has been over us. Slavery cannot be justified. But may not God have intended that you, who are the descendants of those whom slavery brought to this country, should pray and work for the redemption of your fatherland?[16]

History fails to enlighten us on whether these remarks were delivered tongue in cheek.

For many white missionaries and governmental officials, both in Britain and the United States, this desire for evangelical Pan-Africanism was only one aspect of a larger concern. For in the last decade of the nineteenth and early twentieth centuries British government officials and missionaries were still in the initial stages of formulating educational and administrative policies for the effective rule over their "new-caught, sullen peoples," as the poet Rudyard Kipling had characterized the newly-conquered subjects of the empire on which the sun never set.

The inhabitants of these countries had recently undergone painful and brutalizing experiences which did not unduly endear them to the white man. They were largely illiterate and innocent of Western ways. In a word, they were not unlike their brothers in the United States at the time of the emancipation of the slaves in the 1860s. And in the latter place, a tremendous job had been done in neutralizing the hate which was to be expected from persons who had recently emerged from the most horrible episode in human history.

Maybe it was like General Smuts, the South African "liberal" statesman averred a few decades later, during a speech in the United States, namely that next to the jackass, no animal approached the Negro in his boundless capacity for patience.[17] But for the European observer it seemed that there might be other lessons to be learned. Not the least important of these was the providing of a "suitable" type of education. And since "native education" was the specialty of missionaries, God and Caesar not unnaturally put their heads together on this problem. This cooperation was not, of course, a new phenomenon. Whatever the controversy over the existence of an identity of interests between missionaries and conquerors in Africa, the fact can hardly be denied that, whether by accident or design, the two more often than not found their paths converging, or deliberately or unwittingly facilitated each other's activities. Very often it was the missionaries, sometimes doubling as explorers, who preceded the armies and settlers. The cases of people like Livingstone and Moffat in Central Africa and the countless mission stations that preceded effective conquest in West Africa would be examples. Sometimes, though, it was the warrior who cleared the path for the missionary. Cecil Rhodes, for example, was so anxious to have his occupation of Mashonaland in 1890 followed up by missionary activity that he offered a grant of land to the American Board, a missionary society, by way of inducement.[18]

Meanwhile, what of the Africans? The advantages of Black missionaries from the African point of view have already been hinted at. And the general response of Africans to the idea of Black assistance may be fairly described as enthusiastic. African nationalists of this period were not loath to admit the educational and technological short-comings of their people. They had no illusions about coming to grips with the twentieth century. But there was a widespread feeling that if the required help could come from their own kind, it would be less likely to be accompanied by the violence and pain which had marked the descent of European imperialism onto the continent in the late nineteenth century.

As the AME Bishop to South Africa during the first few years of this century movingly expressed it when answering the charge of "sheep stealing" from the flocks of white pastors, " . . . they felt to be coming to their own, and for more reasons than is necessary for me to here name."[19]

Indeed the African reaction was a de facto approval of the argument which had moved New World Africans for so long, namely the special responsibility of those who had come into contact with Western tech-nology and material progress to impart this knowledge to their own. And the white man was seen, in this context, as a barrier to this return of the long-lost New World Africans. In 1929, for example, Jeremiah Gondwe, a Nyasaland nationalist preacher, explained to "discon-tented" Africans sentiments which are often echoed today:

> Some of them (whites) have returned to our elder brothers (Afro-Americans) and told them that we are monkeys and have tails. Our elder brothers have made aeroplanes and have come to see if the white people are telling the truth.[20]

Such racial affinity had its more bizarre moments, as when a Black missionary is supposed to have had his life spared in the Congo be-cause his would-be executioners purportedly believed that he was the reincarnation of a legendary chief.[21]

As a concomitant of all this, education in Black colleges in the Ameri-can South became a desirable goal for African students and such graduates of Southern colleges provided the leadership for many of the nationalist "Ethiopian" churches that spread throughout South and Central Africa in this period.

Established Afro-American organizations like the AME Church and the National Baptist Convention (which sponsored Chilembwe) were in the forefront of evangelical Pan-African activity in Southern and

Central Africa. But African enthusiasm also embraced in a very large measure the omnipresent philosophy of Marcus Garvey, Provisional President of Africa and most successful Pan-Africanist of all time. A Harlem banner had proclaimed, during Garvey's incarceration in the United States, that "Garvey is in Jail, but Garveyism is Abroad." In the 1920s, Garvey and his emissaries and publications were resolutely denied entry into British-occupied Africa, but his influence and ideas were nevertheless abroad.

Though much of Garvey's influence was secular, the religious aspects of his Univeral Negro Improvement Association (as exemplified in the African Orthodox Church) were not lost on "Ethiopian" adherents. One such South African organization, the Afro-Athlican Constructive Church, paid homage to Garvey in its credo: "We believe in one God, Maker of all things, Father of Ethiopia . . . who did Athlyi, Marcus Garvey and colleagues come to save? The down-trodden children of Ethiopia that they might rise to be a great power among the nations."[22]

Evangelical Pan-Africanism had therefore found favor with New World Black people, Africans, and an apparently large number of white missionaries. There was one fundamental consideration, however, which materially affected the situation. Africa might be Black and New World Africans might be Black, but the governors of Africa were white, a circumstance which had elicited Marcus Garvey's rhetorical lament—where is the Blackman's country? Where is his government?

And in the councils of white governments sat white missionaries, who, for all the lip-serivce which some of them may have paid to the desirability of Black missionaries, had very definite ideas concerning the type of Black persons who must be admitted to Africa. The machinations of these governments could keep Marcus Garvey out of even the nominally independent Black republic of Liberia. Nor would Garvey have been successful in entering non-English-speaking Africa. For his works had been banned in such places as Dahomey, where his followers had staged an abortive rebellion. In the Congo under Belgian rule Black missionaries had been blamed for encouraging the "problem" of Kimbanguism (so-called after Simon Kimbangu, a nationalist preacher), by distributing Garvey's paper, the *Negro World*.[23]

The reluctance to allow unrestrained entry of Black missionaries into Africa was of respectable vintage. One of the earliest cases had been that of the celebrated Olaudah Equiano, the ex-slave who become England's foremost Black abolitionist. In 1779, at the suggestion and with the backing of his influential English friends, he applied to the "Right Reverend Father in God, Robert, Lord Bishop of London" to be allowed to carry the message of the Scriptures to the people from whom he sprang, and whom he knew well. Equiano described the result of his audience with the reverend gentleman:

> He received me with much condescension and politeness; but from certain scruples of delicacy, and saying the Bishops were not of the opinion of sending a new missionary to Africa, he decided not to ordain me.[24]

With the emancipation of slaves in the West Indies and the resultant upsurge of interest, the pattern of discreetly screening or discouraging Black applicants seems to have taken on all the characteristics which were to attract greater attention in the twentieth century.

Thus, in 1840 the British home committee of the Baptist Missionary Society vetoed the plea of their representative in Jamaica, William Knibb, that Jamaicans, who had been clamoring for an opportunity and donating large sums for missionary activity, be sent to Africa. Knibb's persistence later succeeded. In the following year, 1841, the Scottish parent body of the United Presbyterian Church, facing similar enthusiasm, refused to approve a scheme to settle Jamaican Christian families in West Africa. Three years later, in 1844, the body approved of the scheme, this time with white persons instead. The white families were allowed to take along two West Indians on probation. Their stay was to be extended only if they proved amenable to their white superiors. Parallel pressures against sending West Indians to Africa at this time also came from the planter class, who feared a shrinkage in their labor force.

The policy then, as later, was to refrain from allowing indiscriminate entry to New World Black people. When they were allowed in they were to go as subordinates, on probation, and only after such time as they had shown themselves to be what the colonial ecclesiastical and governmental authorities considered the right caliber.

The English Archdeacon Holkertón of the West Indian island of Antigua expressed this idea clearly in 1839: "when you forward them [Black missionaries] from England, send as their superintendant, one of ourselves, a minister who shall direct their energies, bear with their weaknesses, . . ." Four years later, we are informed, this gentleman had become opposed to West Indian missionaries under any circumstances.[25]

Meanwhile, the same process was discernible in the United States.

In 1825, for example, the American Board of Commissioners appointed a Black Presbyterian to Liberia. The project was dropped "for some unspecified reason." Eight years later the project was consummated, this time with a white missionary couple instead. A year later, a Black female teacher-assistant was added.[26] In 1887, an Afro-American graduate of Hampton and Tuscaloosa Theological Institute applied to his church, the Southern Presbyterians, for missionary work in Africa. He was refused. In 1890 a white volunteer came forward. So the church sent them both.[27]

By the turn of the twentieth century, with Afro-American missionaries implicated in "Ethiopianist" activities all over South and Central Africa, the century-old conditions for the entry of Black missionaries were re-stated several times, but never so clearly as at an international conference of missionaries concerned with Africa, held at Le Zoute, Blegium in 1926. The relevant resolutions passed by this conference are so remarkable that they must be quoted in full.

American Negroes and Africa

1. Findings as to Facts
    (a) There are no legislative restrictions specifically directed against the American Negro, but most African Governments are opposed to, or place difficulties in the way of, the sending of American Negroes to Africa.

2. Opposition to the sending of American Negroes to Africa is due mainly to these factors:
    (a) The unrest caused by certain movements believed to be dangerous to order and government and to be encouraged from America.
    (b) The antagonism to Government in past years of certain American Negroes in Africa resulting in serious disturbances in some cases.
    (c) The failure of certain American Negroes in Africa in past years.

3. Owing to the effect of one or more of the reasons above-named, most African missionaries consulted do not think the present time auspicious for pressing upon Government such a general change in policy as would mean the sending of a large number of American Negroes to Africa in the immediate future, although strongly believing that efforts should be made to increase gradually the number of such missionaries.

4. There are at present working in various parts of Africa American Negroes of the highest characters and great usefulness, whose fine spirit and devoted work will in the course of a few years greatly increase the respect in which American Negro missionaries are held, and make easier the security of permission for the entrance of additional missionaries.

5. There is a natural and laudable desire on the part of a large number of American missionary societies, both white and Negro, to send additional American Negroes as missionaries to Africa—thereby giving the educated Negro an outlet for his zeal to render unselfish service, and aiding in a natural and important way the cause of African evangelization, education and general welfare.

2. Recommendations

In view of the above findings the Conference adopts the following resolutions:

1. That the Negroes of America should be permitted by Governments, and encouraged by missionary societies, to play an important part in the evangelization, medical service and education of Africa, and that the number of their missionaries should be increased as qualified candidates are available for needed work, and as their representatives already in the field still further succeed in gaining for their people and their societies that public confidence which is essential.

2. That every practical form of assistance should be given in the spirit of Christian fellowship, as to colleagues of the same missionary status, by white missionaries to qualified American Negroes working in Africa, and that the same spirit of co-operation should be expected by white missionaries from American Negro missionaries.

3. That Governments should be supported in requiring that American Negroes wishing to enter Africa for missionary purposes should go out under the auspices of responsible societies of recognized and well-established standing; and that owing to the difficult and delicate inter-racial situation in Africa, exceptional care should be used in the selection of men and women of strength of character and a fine spirit of co-operation able to meet the same tests as white missionaries.

4. That in the interest of comity and co-operation American Negro missionary societies not now represented in Africa should work as far as possible through well-established societies already in Africa, and that, in accordance with the general rules of missionary procedure, they should give special attention to unevangelized districts.

5. That when missionary societies of established reputation are unable to secure the admission of American Negroes needed for important work and qualified to perform it, the matter may properly be taken up with the International Missionary Council for the use of its friendly offices.

6. In adopting these resolutions the Conference recognizes that the

above recommendations are not ideal or a complete solution of the problem under consideration, but believes that they represent the "next steps" which may be wisely taken, and that they should, in the providence of God, gradually bring about a highly significant and important contribution by the Negroes of America to their distant kindred in Africa.[28]

This resolution had come about as a result of a plea to the conference by Dr. John Hope, President of Morehouse College in Atlanta. Dr. Hope pointed out that five hundred Black graduates a year were being turned out by Southern colleges and that "those who have a desire to give service in Africa ought to be given a chance"[29]. This was, then, a genteel plea for a relaxation of missionary discrimination.

It is clear from the resolution with its reference to a gradual relaxation "as qualified persons are available" that Dr. Hope was firmly rebuffed.

However diplomatic and restrained the language of the "findings as to facts" and accompanying resolution, one thing is exceedingly plain. That is, that despite the subtle attempt to pass the buck to governments, this was no pious entreaty from a bunch of holy but impotent churchmen. There is, in this document, a certain authority, a certain self-assurance which suggest that its drafters had every reason to believe that they were formulating policy which would be respected by their governments.

The personnel of the committee which drew up the document bears this out.[30] It was a large committee, and included the most high-powered politico-missionary personalities in the Western World. This says something for the importance which Christendom attached to the Afro-American missionary question. The chairman was Dr. Anson Phelps-Stokes, secretary of the Phelps-Stokes Fund, which in almost two decades had established itself as an international authority on "Negro Education" in the United States and Africa. It had played a large role in internationalizing the Christian industrial education for Black people popularized in Hampton and Tuskeegee Institutes in the American South. And so great was the Fund's international reputation that it had been commissioned by the British government to participate in educational commissions to Africa.

Also in the committee was Dr. Thomas Jesse Jones, executive director of the Fund and, in the eyes of Western governments, the foremost authority on educational and philanthropic matters concerning Black people in the United States. Jones, a few years earlier, had had occasion to defend himself against those who attacked "home missions" on the "ground of the supposed blindness of missions to the right of Negro self-determination and self-expression."[31]

The committee included, too, Dr. C. T. Loram, who had been commissioned by the South African government to survey African education in that country.

Most illustrious perhaps, was none other than Sir Frederick Lugard, British imperialist extraordinary, subjugator of Uganda, creator and first Governor-General of Nigeria, and apologist of the "dual mandate" concept adopted as a creed by the British Colonial Office.

The committee included, too, J. H. Oldham, a sort of British equivalent of T. Jesse Jones, and editor of the influential *International Review of Missions*, in which all the big names, including Booker T. Washington, had published.

Jones and Oldham sat together on a British Government clearinghouse committee financed partly by the Phelps-Stokes and Rockefeller Funds which sent hundreds of missionaries working in Africa to the Southern United States for first-hand experience of "Negro Education,"[32] even as they thwarted the attempts of Afro-American missionaries to enter Africa.

Also on the committee were at least two Afro-Americans in the persons of Dr. John Hope and Mr. Max Yergan, a well-known missionary. The study of the conference does not indicate what their attitude to the final report was, or whether there had been any dissenting voices. In any case, they were vastly outnumbered. Yergan's presence on the committee is particularly interesting, since an international storm had arisen five years earlier over his exclusion from South Africa, due to the machinations of none other than T. Jesse Jones himself.[33]

So, at a time when the Pan-Africanism of Marcus Garvey and W. E. B. DuBois was running high, a group of high-powered white politico-missionaries was able to sit down and calmly determine the conditions under which the potentially significant contributions of an important sector of the Afro-American population would be maintained at a tractable trickle.

This, then, was the stark political reality. The ancient Pan-Africanist sentiments of Afro-Americans; the enthusiasm of large numbers of Africans; the support of sympathetic white missionaries; the lip-service of less sincere white churchmen; all spoke to the question of who loved Africa. But the real world answered with another question—that of who ruled Africa.

Notes

1. Henry Koster, *Travels in Brazil,* quoted in Lewis Hanke, ed., *History of Latin American Civilization,* Vol. II (Boston: Little Brown & Co., 1967), p. 160.
2. C. P. Groves, *The Planting of Christianity in Africa, Vol. II, 1840–1870* (London: Lutterworth, 1964), p. 24 ff; A. Barrow, *Fifty Years in Western Africa: being a record of the West Indian Church on the Banks of Rio Pongo* (London, 1900).
3. C. P. Groves, *op. cit.,* p. 32.
4. Thomas Jesse Jones, *Education in Africa* (New York: Phelps-Stokes Fund, 1922), p. 166.
5. Black churchmen were sometimes appointed to diplomatic positions in Liberia by the U.S. government. During the 1890s for example (1895 to 1899) a bishop of the African Methodist Episcopal Church was U.S. Consul General to Liberia. See William H. Heard, *From Slavery to the Bishopric in the A.M.E. Church* (Philadelphia: AME, 1924), p. 48.
6. The Rev. Bishop H. M. Turner, DD, "Essay: The American Negro and the Fatherland," in J. W. E. Bowen, DD, ed., *Africa and the American Negro: Addresses and Proceedings of the Congress on Africa, Held under the Auspices of the Stewart Missionary Foundation for Africa of Gammon Theological Seminary in Connection with the Cotton States and International Exposition, December 13–15, 1895* (Miami: Mnemosyne Publishers Inc., 1969, first published 1896), p. 195.
7. *Ibid.*
8. Heard, *op. cit.,* pp. 55–56.
9. The date may be incorrect. See George Shepperson and Thomas Price, *Independent African* (Edinburgh: The University Press, 1958), p. 454, n. 1.
10. Rev. Charles S. Morris, *Ecumenical Missionary Conference, Vol. I* (New York: 1900), p. 471.
11. *Ibid.,* p. 470.
12. *Ibid.,* pp. 469, 470.
13. Shepperson and Price, *op. cit.* They also deal extensively with Joseph Booth's career.
14. *Ibid., passim.*
15. Professor E. L. Parks, DD, "The Stewart Missionary Foundation for Africa and the Purpose of the Congress," in J. W. E. Bowen, ed., *Africa and the American Negro, op. cit.,* p. 10.
16. His Excellency, The Honorable W. Y. Atkinson, "Address of Welcome," *Africa and the American Negro, op. cit.,* p. 15.
17. *New York Times,* January 10, 1930, p. 2.
18. Clarence Clenenden, Robert Collins and Peter Duignan, *Americans in Africa, 1865–1900* (Stanford University, 1966), p. 63.
19. L. J. Coppin, *Unwritten History* (Philadelphia: AME, 1919), p. 314.
20. Quoted in Robert I. Rotberg, *The Rise of Nationalism in Central Africa* (Cambridge, Mass.: Harvard University Press, 1967), p. 140.
21. *Americans in Africa, op. cit.,* p. 63.
22. Quoted in Bengt Sundkler, *Bantu Prophets in South Africa* (London: OUP, 1961), p. 58.
23. Jabez Ayodele Langley, "Garveyism and African Nationalism," *Race,* XI, 2, (October, 1969) p. 169.

24. *The Life of Olaudah Equiano or Gustavus Vassa, the African,* in Arna Bontemps, *Great Slave Narratives* (Boston: Beacon Press, 1969), pp. 177–179.

25. C. P. Groves, *op. eit.,* p. 27; for other references to the West Indies, see *ibid.,* pp. 24–39.

26. Clarence Clenenden *et al, op. cit.,* pp. 67, 68.

27. *Ibid.,* p. 63.

28. Edwin W. Smith, *The Christian Mission in Africa, A Study Based on the Work of the International Conference at Le Zoute, Belgium, September 14th to 21st, 1926* (London: International Missionary Council, 1926), pp. 122–124.

29. *Ibid.,* pp. 100–101.

30. *Ibid.,* p. 176.

31. T. Jesse Jones, *Education in Africa* (New York: Phelps-Stokes Fund, 1922), p. 88.

32. For a detailed treatment of this subject see K. J. King, "Africa and the Southern States of the USA," *Journal of African History,* X, 4 (1969).

33. K. J. King, "The American Negro as Missionary to East Africa," *African Historical Studies, III, 1 (1970).*

3

Revolutionary Upheaval in Trinidad, 1919: Gleanings From British and American Sources*

Large numbers of oppressed Black people in Trinidad and Tobago participated in a series of violent challenges against British colonialism in December of 1919.[1] The disturbances grew out of a strike by dock workers in Port-of-Spain. The intensity of the December outbreak and the widespread manifestations of hostility against whites seem to have caught some members of officialdom offguard. Yet, racial tensions had been simmering for some time, and in the months before December there were ample evidences of the trouble to come.

A key element in the atmosphere of resentment against the British colonials in particular and white people in general was the returning soldiers of the British West Indies Regiment (hereinafter B.W.I.R.) who had rallied to the call of Empire during World War I. The beginning of the war had found Blacks among the most eager to fight. They besieged the British government with requests to enlist and, in the face of official demurrals, some even made their way to England at their own expense. When eventually their requests were heeded, they consistently overwhelmed the authorities with more recruits than were needed.[2]

Yet, between the time of their enlistment in the B.W.I.R. and 1919 the soldiers had suffered massive blows to their dignity and their physical well-being. They had seen white and light-skinned West Indians accepted as fighting men while their own requests were met with procrastination; they had been confined for most of the war to fatigue

*Originally published in 1973

47

duty, menial labor, carrying ammunition under heavy fire and garrison duty; they had seen comrades die from neglect in white-run hospitals; they had been subjected to every kind of petty racial abuse; their remuneration and benefits were usually inferior to those of white troops; and, with the war's end, even those benefits promised them were not forthcoming. And to further exacerbate matters, some of the returning soldiers had been involved in riots in Cardiff, Wales, during which British mobs had vented their racist fury against the tiny Black population.[3]

Upon returning home to Trinidad, the veterans immediately organized The Returned Soldiers and Sailors Council and Organization which held public meetings and propagandized their grievances to the people.[4] This organization may have been an offshoot of the Caribbean League which was formed by West Indian soldiers in Taranto, Italy, after their mutiny at that place. The League was Pan-West Indian in character and planned to strike for higher wages and demand self-determination for Black people by any means necessary, on their return to the islands. Its existence was leaked to Major Maxwell Smith, commanding officer of the 8th Battalion, B.W.I.R., who is credited with having hastened its demise.[5]

By 1919 Maxwell Smith, now lieutenant colonel, was ready to confess his inability to stop the flow of ideas, whatever may have been his role in causing the physical disintegration of the Caribbean League. In a letter dated July 22, 1919, he reminded the Commandant of Local Forces in Trinidad that he had exposed the Caribbean League to the Secretary of State for the Colonies during his active service in Italy. He stated "that the feeling of the black man against the white, to which I alluded in that communication and which at that time was limited almost entirely to Jamaican troops, has spread, not only to many of the returned soldiers from this Colony, but also to the black population of Port-of-Spain generally." He testified to the possession of "abundant evidence."[6]

In order to appease the soldiers, the authorities made the empty gesture of inviting them to participate in a parade to mark the peace celebrations, which took place at the Queens Park Savannah on July 19, 1919. They were to be given the dubious privilege of leading the parade. Only 132 fell in. A "considerable number" turned up to watch, some in uniform and others in civilian attire. Those in mufti heckled the non-participants in uniform and they all booed as the participants marched past. A worried Inspector General of Constabulary confided to the local Colonial Secretary that the reason for the poor turnout was that the soldiers were disappointed at not being armed for the occasion, since "some who had possessed themselves of ammunition whilst on active service intended to load with ball cartridges during the feu de joi and shoot down all the officers."[7]

Meanwhile, other efforts to appease the soldiers were redoubled. The Discharged Soldiers Central Authority, for example, a local committee appointed by governor Sir John Chancellor, attempted to find jobs for unemployed soldiers and administered a land settlement scheme whereby veterans who were familiar with agriculture could be apportioned five acres which would assume the character of a free grant when cultivated. The acting governor in September prematurely complimented this committee for lessening the tension and concluded that "for the present there is no cause for alarm."[8] Nevertheless by this time British Military Intelligence seems to have been investigating the situation anyway.[9]

Another important element in the situation was the workers. For many months before December they had probed the government with a series of strikes. As early as May the American Consul in Port-of-Spain, Henry D. Baker, had informed his superiors in the U.S. State Department of serious work stoppages by stevedores, railway workers and tramcar operators. He noted their impoverished condition.[10]

But the soldiers and workers were not the only agents at work sowing the seeds of the race consciousness which was to erupt in December. They had powerful allies in the *Argos,* a militant local paper, and *The Negro World,* organ of Marcus Garvey's Universal Negro Improvement Association and African Communities League, with headquarters in Harlem, U.S.A.

In July a group of the leading white citizens had fulminated concerning the *Argos*—"The impunity with which this irresponsible publication has for a long time past been permitted to circulate all kinds of revolutionary, seditious and mischievous literature is regarded as a scandal by all the serious members of this community . . . [it is] owned by a Chinaman of no particular persuasion and run by four or five 'coloured gentlemen' of the most pronounced type of hater of the white man."[11]

This invective was re-inforced by economic sanctions against the paper, in the form of a withdrawal of advertising, which circumstance had, in the opinion of the Inspector General of Constabulary, caused the editors to be "brought to their senses." If this shock should prove to be temporary, the Inspector General suggested deportation of some of the paper's personnel, including a Mr. Lee Lum, and a Mr. Dick Wharton, "a most mischievous and anti-white individual."[12] By September, too, the acting governor had been authorized by the imperial Colonial Office to pass a seditious publications ordinance to deal with the *Argos* if necessary.[13]

The *Negro World* played a similar role in preparing the population for the events of December. Indeed, many of the December strikers were adherents to Garveyite principles and their organization, the Trinidad Workingmen's Association, maintained close ties with Garveyism until the 1930s. As early as June the acting governor of Trinidad confided to the governor of British Guiana that he was surreptitiously, and illegally, seizing copies of the paper entering the island.[14] The paper continued to be smuggled in anyway, as American Consul Baker complained to the State Department in October. He went so far as to forward to Washington some of the wrappers in which copies of *The Negro World* had been mailed to Trinidad. These bore the name of Marcus Garvey as the sender and were addressed to persons in various parts of the island. The wrappers, Baker explained ominously, "show how the United States mails are being used for the purpose of forwarding to a friendly country, papers directly inciting the negro population to acts of murder and anarchy."[15]

Actions by the *Negro World* and the *Argos* were not unrelated, as Baker, apparently an avid reader of both, well knew. In February of 1920 for example, an *Argos* article proffering felicitations to two young Trinidadians hoping to qualify for employment in Garvey's Black Star Line in New York sent Baker scurrying to the local police authorities for more information on these two potentially undesirable immigrants to the United States.[16]

Yet another factor playing upon the situation in the months preceding December was the question of racism in Britain. On the 17th of July persons involved in the Cardiff riots in Britain had returned home and the *Argos* had taken the opportunity to familiarize the populace with the atrocities which had been visited upon the Black population in Britain.[17] So that when, during the peace celebrations in July, several British sailors from the H.M.S. *Dartmouth* "were wantonly and severely assaulted, as were several other European members of the community" and "very lewd and disparaging remarks were freely made about the white race and about their women folk," and the Deputy Inspector General and an Inspector Carr of The Constabulary were stoned, the blame was placed on the *Argos*. The offending article had described how a white mob in Cardiff had attacked a Black man's funeral, cut off the corpse's head, and used it as a football.[18] It is interesting to note that veterans and other Black people were reacting against the same mix of events at the same time (during the peace celebrations) and in a similar fashion, in Jamaica and in British Honduras.

On the 24th of July, two days after some of the above attacks on whites, a delegation consisting of the mayor of Port-of-Spain, a city councillor, and two Black solicitors was moved, either by fear or approbation, to appeal to the acting governor to request the release of the Trinidadians who were among a batch of military prisoners who had been landed intransit to Jamaica.[19] The prisoners were duly released. In advocating release of the prisoners to his superiors in London, the acting governor explained that "a very strong feeling was at once aroused amongst the black section of the community and threats were openly made, not only by the usual idlers and loafers and irresponsible persons, but by black and coloured men of some standing and influence, that the whites should be killed."[20]

Not unnaturally the resident white community felt greatly threatened and at times were reduced to a state bordering on hysteria. Nowhere is this better illustrated than in a "confidential and urgent" letter written on July 30 by a committee of the most influential white citizens to the Colonial Secretary. The signatories were six persons, most of whose names are still well-known in the island half a century later—George F. Huggins, C. de Verteuil, J. A. Bell Smythe, A. S. Bowen, A. H. McClean, and H. H. Pasea.

The letter pointed out that while the 1903 taxation riots had found men of all classes and colors on both sides, the present situation was "of a far more dangerous kind" since "a substantial minority of the black population openly proclaims that it has no further use for the white man, and means to eliminate him." The letter went on to state that "the palpable absurdity of such an idea in no way robs it of its danger or diminishes its attractiveness to the negro mind." The signatories advised the suppression of the *Argos*, "this poisonous organ," the arming of the white population, the establishment of "a body of white regular troops however small"; and they warned against the emergence of the "creole coolie," as they termed the new Indian who could not be manipulated as a buffer against the African, but who might even join the African against a common oppressor. On this question of the

"creole coolie" this committee of worried white residents expressed
itself as follows:

> One point more, in the years gone by the large East Indian indentured
> population, numbering many thousands and largely under the control of
> their respective plantation owners, managers and overseers, was looked
> upon as a substantial safeguard against trouble with the negroes [sic] and
> *vice versa*. With the abolition of immigration such a counterpoise has
> ceased to exist and the "creole coolie" [sic] will either remain an inter-
> ested spectator or join the mob.[21]

The fears of these white capitalists (Huggins was president of the
Chamber of Commerce) seem not to have been unfounded, for as has
usually happened during periods of revolutionary upheaval in
Trinidad, the Indian rural laborers seem to have taken advantage of the
general ferment to strike some blows of their own against the common
foe.[22]

This letter was too much even for the white Inspector General of
Constabulary. "If the white people in the Colony would only cease
cackling and spreading and enlarging on the wild rumours going
around, the situation would soon be clear," he wrote. Arming all the
whites would, among other things, in his estimation cause resentment
among the loyal colored and Black folk. He was nevertheless equally
hostile to the *Argos* and preferred two gunboats to a small force of
white troops, for, "as is well known the presence of a Man of War
within easy reach is very comforting to the Community as a whole and
has a very restraining influence on the lawless."[23]

This question of the relative merits of a permanent body of white
troops or a British gunboat or two to ward off the impending catas-
trophe continually plagued the minds of colonial officials in the months
before December.

On July 22, Lt. Colonel Maxwell Smith, he who had helped to
expose the formation of the militant Caribbean League among the
B.W.I.R. soldiers in Italy, suggested two permanent companies of
white regular troops and, pending their arrival, a gunboat to remain on
duty in the island.[24] The Inspector General of Constabulary, however,
thought the time unripe, since the local Black constabulary were "thoroughly loyal," an opinion which was to be jolted by the events of
December.[25] On July 29, the acting governor telegraphed the naval
commander-in-chief in Bermuda requesting that the H.M.S. *Cambrian* should remain awhile in Trinidad. He explained to the Secretary

of State for the Colonies in London that he had not sought his prior authority for this drastic move since the West Indian and Panama cable was broken and the times were perilous.[26] On 7 August he elaborated on his preference for a gunboat over a permanent white garrison to the Secretary of State. On the 5th of September the Secretary of State, Viscount Milner, was advised by one of his staff that white troops were much more urgently needed in Belize, British Honduras, where the threat to British colonialism was more serious.[28] On September 10 Milner authorized, *ex post facto*, the stationing of the H.M.S. *Cambrian* in Trinidad, while rebuking the acting governor for having short-circuited the proper channels.[29]

Throughout the period of tension before December, the British colonialists, while prudently taking military precautions against a possible outbreak, still clung to the timeless myth of a minority of agitators stirring up a contented population. The colonialist mentality could not, or would not then, conceive of an oppressed people wanting to be free. This view is summed up in the opinion of the acting governor who in August thought that the majority of "responsible black and coloured people" were against the manifestations of racial feeling. He continued, in a fashion typical of people in his station in life, that "There is undoubtedly, more especially in Port-of-Spain, a class which would be glad to seize any opportunity, if any pretext presented itself, of causing any outbreak, but there is no evidence that this attitude is general."[30] One week earlier he had come close to arguing the opposite when confronted with a demand for the release of military prisoners.

On December 1st the fury of the Black workers and their supporters erupted and within three days British colonialism in Trinidad was brought to its knees. For three weeks previously a strike by dock workers had been successfully broken by workers imported for the purpose from Venezuela, Barbados and rural Trinidad. But now the strikers turned violent.[31] The power of the people was such that with more sophisticated planning and a more self-conscious realization of their own strength they may have toppled British rule. On December 4th, in a terse telegram, governor Sir John Chancellor confessed to the Secretary of State for the Colonies how close colonial rule in the island had come to disaster: the populace had forced the closing of businesses and the halting of traffic in the business and administrative district; the Inspector General of Constabulary had declared that he could no longer ensure the safety of the town unless concessions were made to the strikers; the authorities were afraid to open fire on rioters in Port-of-Spain lest there be reprisals against whites living in the country districts; a committee from the Chamber of Commerce had expressed its worry; and a warship, the H.M.S. *Calcutta*, complete with an admiral on board, had arrived. It was in this context that the governor gave one of the most important indications of his weak position. He explained, "I accordingly induced shipping agents on grounds of public policy to meet the representatives of strikers and try to come to an agreement. They reluctantly consented and have granted an advance of wages which has satisfied stevedores who are returning to work."[32] The reluctance of the employers is not difficult to explain. This was two decades before trade unions among Black colonized workers in British Africa and the West Indies began to receive any significant legal recognition. The American Consul, Baker, reminded the State Department that this 25 per cent wage hike represented "apparently the first instance of any Labor Union in the British West Indies ever having received recognition from employers."[33]

By the end of the first week in December the most precarious point seemed to have been passed, thanks to prompt concessions to the Port-of-Spain stevedores. By this time, however, the disturbances had spread to rural Trinidad and to Tobago, in which latter place the police had fired into a crowd, inflicting several casualties, and killing one Nathaniel Williams whom they identified as the "chief ringleader."[34]

The concessions given to the strikers had, of course brought criticism upon the British administration from local white businessmen. The American Consul, Baker, from his membership in the whites-only Union Club, could glean the confidential information that the Chamber of Commerce had threatened to send a telegram to the Secretary of State for the Colonies in London, complaining about the local administration's defeat at the hands of the populace. The governor was moved to apologize and the telegram, which would have adversely affected the governor's career, was not dispatched.[35]

The extent of the mollification was, however, limited, for on December 6th the Chamber of Commerce issued an "Ultimatum to Anarchy" wherein the authorities were again censured for their capitulation; and the threat of a resort to higher authority was reiterated.[36] The vice-president of the Chamber, Edgar Tripp, was vehement in regarding the decision as "one of the most humiliating surrenders to brute force that had ever been known in a British Coloney."[37]

The events of the first few days of December, and especially the apparent reluctance of the Black police in Port-of-Spain to confront the rioters, caused a realization of the fear expressed during the preceding months concerning the scarcity of white troops. As early as December 1 the Mounted Volunteers of Trinidad, composed mostly of white businessmen, were called out to guard banks, the treasury building, and the electric power plant.[38] This was followed by the formation of a volunteer force known as the Colonial Vigilantes. By December 11 Baker reported two hundred and seventy members of this force who were recruited, not surprisingly, mostly from the Union Club. Baker described the racial composition of this group as an organization that is "composed entirely of white persons, or of those who belong predominantly to the white race, and could be relied upon in the event of any negro uprising."[39] A few weeks later regular white troops did arrive, in the persons of the Royal Sussex Regiment, who were brought in from Jamaica.[40]

There was yet a third important element in Trinidad's white community which had a vested interest in a speedy return to normalcy. This was the colony of American businessmen and supervisory personnel and their dependents. Many of these were concentrated far from Port-of-Spain in the oil fields in the southern part of the island and in the vicinity of Brighton, where the General Asphalt Company of Philadelphia worked the island's deposits of this natural resource. Indeed, the number of Americans in the area and the frequent appearance of American vessels at the port of Brighton were sufficient to explain the existence of an American consulate there.[41]

Not long after the outbreak of December the General Asphalt Company infiltrated a trusted Black into the Trinidad Workingmen's Association to ascertain what plans the Black workers had for the company. This Black worker reported an imminent strike, whereupon the company's local manager, a Mr. Munoz, communicated his intelligence to the governor. The latter, presumably fearing a second defeat, hastily provided twenty-five rifles together with eleven rounds of ammunition each to the company, for the immediate start of a vigilante group among the Americans in the area. The company steamer *Viking* came to Brighton prepared to evacuate Americans if necessary. And Consul Baker in Port-of-Spain inquired of the State Department whether it would be kind enough to send some American naval vessels. He added that he would not suggest the landing of American marines without the consent of local authorities.[42] The Secretary to the Navy, however, thought that American vessels would not be necessary in view of the strengthening of British naval and other forces in the area and that it would be preferable for such a request for "humanitarian" assistance to come from the British themselves.[43]

Meanwhile, the American vigilantes had joined the Colonial Vigilantes, the latter commanded by Major A. S. Bowen, who was assisted in his command by, among other persons, Mr. Joseph Scheult, secretary of the Union Club, in which, Consul Baker explained, "almost all white persons of prominence in Trinidad are members." Baker himself regretted that he could not join the vigilante group "because of my official position."[44] These American vigilantes under British command soon encountered a peculiar problem. For their republican and patriotic sentiments would not permit them to swear an oath to "our Sovereign Lord the King." This was amicably modified to "His Majesty the King" and white solidarity was maintained.[45]

An interesting component of the local white reaction to the events of December was the attempt (first manifested before December) to exonerate "our Negroes" and place all the blame on foreign anarchist propagandists and "small island" immigrants from neighboring colonies. The white-owned *Trinidad Guardian* of December 7th proffered the following piece of gratuitous information: "It is a dreadful thing that an ignorant and naturally peaceful people should be so shamefully misled and deluded by a handful of gimcrack anarchists."[46] The *Trinidad Guardian* and the Chamber of Commerce called for the deportation of these "scum of the wharves of the West Indies" and Edgar Tripp went so far as to assert that not a single rioter was born in Trinidad.[48]

In view of these pronouncements, American consul, Baker, hastened to assure the State Department that America would be spared the revolutionary sentiments of such deported persons. He would simply refuse a visa to any such person who applied for entry into the United States. And since he traced much of the Trinidad unrest to Marcus Garvey's *Negro World*, he "sincerely" hoped that the State Department would move against this paper, preferably by having the Post Office deny it use of the mails. He once more reminded Washington that the *Negro World*, more than other revolutionary organs, was "responsible for the rapid growth of class and race feeling, and of anarchistic and Bolshevist ideas among the ignorant population" in Trinidad.[49]

The events of 1919 in Trinidad were duplicated, to a greater or lesser degree, in British Honduras, Jamaica, Grenada, and elsewhere in the Caribbean. And the revolutionary upheaval among Black people in the

Caribbean was in turn only a part of the world-wide post-war struggles of African peoples for self-determination and freedom from bondage. The Black proletarians of Port-of-Spain were infected by the same spirit as the New Negro who fought back, during the same period, in places like Chicago in the United States and Cardiff in Britain.

Notes

1. See W. F. Elkins, "Black Power in the British West Indies: The Trinidad Longshoremen's Strike of 1919," *Science and Society*, XXXIII, 1, Winter 1969, pp. 71–75.

2. The ordeal of the Black West Indian soldiers is documented in C. L. Joseph, "The British West Indies Regiment 1914–1918," *The Journal of Caribbean History*, Vol. 2, May 1971, pp. 94–124, and W. F. Elkins, "A Source of Black Nationalism in the Caribbean: The Revolt of the British West Indies Regiment at Taranto, Italy," *Science and Society*, XXXIII, 2, Spring 1970, pp. 99–103.

3. Public Record Office, London, C.O. 295/521, Acting Governor of Trinidad, W. M. Gordon to the Right Honourable Viscount Milner, G.C.B., G.C.M.G., etc., etc., etc., etc., Secretary of State for the Colonies, (London), 29 July 1919, Secret.

4. C.O. 295/521, G. H. May, Inspector General of Constabulary to the Colonial Secretary, 29 July 1919.

5. Joseph, *op. cit.*, p 120; Elkins, "A Source of Black Nationalism . . ." *op. cit.*, p. 102, and sources quoted therein.

6. C.O. 295/521, Lt. Col. Maxwell Smith, Dispersal Area Commandant to the Commandant, Local Forces, 22 July 1919.

7. C.O. 295/521, May to Colonial Secretary, 29 July 1919.

8. C.O. 295/522, Gordon to Milner, 10 September 1919.

9. C.O. 295/521, minutes of 4 and 10 September 1919.

10. National Archives of the United States, Records of the Department of State, R.G. 59, File No. 844 g.5045/-, Henry D. Baker, American Consul, Trinidad, to the Secretary of State (Washington) May 8, 1919.

11. C.O. 295/522, Messrs George F. Huggins, C. de Verteuil, Col. J. A. Bell Smythe, Major A. S. Bowen, Messrs A. H. McClean, H. H. Pasea to Colonial Secretary, 30 July 1919.

12. C.O. 295/522, May to Colonial Secretary, 5 August 1919.

13. C.O. 295/521, minute, 5 September 1919.

14. C.O. 295/521, Gordon to Governor of British Guiana, 10 June 1919.

15. National Archives of the United States, Records of the Post Office Department, Office of the Solicitor, Correspondence, Reports and Exhibits Relating to Transmittal of Mail Violating 1917 Espionage Act, 1917–1921. R.G. 28, Box 56, Unarranged, File No. 500, Baker to Secretary of State, October 5, 1919; the question of the wrappers is also discussed in *ibid*, Otto Praeger, Acting Postmaster General to Secretary of State, October 30, 1919.

16. National Archives, Records of the American Consulate, Port-of-Spain, Correspondence for 1920, R.G. 84, 840.1/2052, Baker to Inspector Costello, Constabulary

Headquarters, Port-of-Spain, February 16, 1920, enclosing a clipping from the *Argos*, February 13, 1920; the correspondence continues in R.G. 84, 840.1/2053 and R.G. 84, 840.1/2054.

17. C.O. 295/521, Gordon to Milner, 29 July 1919.

18. C.O.295/521, May to Colonial Secretary, 29 July 1919.

19. C.O. 295/521, Gordon to Milner, 29 July 1919.

20. *Ibid*.

21. C.O. 295/522, George F. Huggins, *et. al.*, to Colonial Secretary, 30 July 1919.

22. R.G. 59, 844g. 5045/3, Baker to Secretary of State, December 5, 1919. Baker refers here to an overseer being beaten at Caroni Sugar estate; a few days later he reported that several deaths occurred following riots by sugar workers—R.G. 59, 844g. 00/-, Baker to Secretary of State, December 9, 1919.

23. C.O. 295/522, May to Colonial Secretary, 5 August 1919.

24. C.O. 295/521, Smith to Commandant of Local Forces, 22 July 1919.

25. C.O. 295/521, May to Colonial Secretary, 29 July 1919.

26. C.O. 295/521, Gordon to Milner, 29 July 1919.

27. C.O. 295/522, Gordon to Milner, 7 August 1919.

28. C.O. 295/521, minute, 5 September 1919.

29. C.O. 295/521, Milner to Gordon, 10 September 1919.

30. C.O. 295/522, Gordon to Milner, 7 August 1919.

31. R.G. 59, 844g. 5045/3, American Consul Baker to Secretary of State (Washington) December 5, 1919.

32. C.O. 295/523, Chancellor to Secretary of State, December 4, 1919 (telegram).

33. R.G. 59, 844g. 5045/3, Baker to Secretary of State (Washington), December 5, 1919.

34. *Trinidad Guardian*, December 10, 1919, clipping enclosed in R.G. 59, 844g. 00/2, Baker to Secretary of State, December 10, 1919.

35. R.G. 59, 844g. 5045/3, Baker to Secretary of State, December 5, 1919.

36. Quoted in R.G. 59, 844g. 5045/2, Baker to Secretary of State, December 8, 1919.

37. This paraphrase of Tripp's statement is from Baker, *ibid*.

38. R.G. 59, 844g. 5045/3, Baker to Secretary of State, December 5, 1919.

39. R.G. 59, 844g. 00/1, Baker to Secretary of State, December 11, 1919.

40. R.G. 59, 844g. 00/6, Baker to Secretary of State, January 24, 1920.

41. The records of the American Consulate at Brighton, unlike those of Port-of-Spain are mostly mundane and devoid of social commentary. They are in Record Group 84, National Archives.

42. R.G. 59, 844g. 00/-, Baker to Secretary of State, December 9, 1919.

43. R.G. 59, 844g. 00/5, Secretary of the Navy to the Secretary of State, January 13, 1920.

44. R.G. 59, 844g. 00/1, Baker to Secretary of State, December 11, 1919.

45. R.G. 59, 844g. 00/4, Baker to Secretary of State, December 19, 1919.

46. Quoted in R.G. 59, 844g. 5045/2, Baker to Secretary of State, December 8, 1919.

47. R.G. 59, 844g. 5045/2, Baker to Secretary of State, December 8, 1919.

48. *Ibid*.

4
Marcus Garvey and the West Indies*

There have been several movements to federate the British West Indian Islands, but owing to parochial feelings nothing definite has been achieved. Ere long this change is sure to come about because the people of these islands are all one. They live under the same conditions, are of the same race and mind and have the same feelings and sentiments regarding the things of the world.

—*Marcus Garvey, 1913*

The Honorable Marcus Mosiah Garvey (1887–1940) is undoubtedly one of the most important figures in West Indian history. At a time when African peoples all over the world were colonized, disfranchised and subjugated, he provided hope and helped sow the seeds for nationalist struggles in Africa, Afro-America, the West Indies and elsewhere. His Universal Negro Improvement Association (UNIA), founded in Jamaica in 1914 and re-established in the United States around 1917, in the process became the largest Pan-African movement in history. By the mid-1920s it boasted approximately 1,120 branches in over 40 countries.

Within the West Indies, Garvey's UNIA stands out as one of the few Pan-Caribbean political movements in our history, and probably the most successful. For there were UNIA branches in Cuba, Trinidad, Jamaica, the then British Guiana, the Dominican Republic, Barbados, the then British Honduras, the Bahamas, Antigua, Bermuda, Dominica, Suriname, Grenada, Haiti, Nevis, Puerto Rico, St. Kitts, St. Lucia, St. Thomas and St. Vincent. This was therefore a genuine Pan-Caribbean mass movement, cutting across political and linguistic barriers. Cuba had more branches (52) than any other territory in the West Indies, and indeed more than any country other than the United

*Originally published in 1978

States. Trinidad had at least 30 branches. Jamaica had 11, British Guiana 7 and the Dominican Republic 5.

In addition to the large number of branches in the West Indies proper, West Indian emigrant workers made up a very large percentage of UNIA members in such Latin American countries as Panama, Costa Rica, Honduras, Colombia, Guatemala and Nicaragua. Many West Indians also joined the movement in other countries, especially in such United States cities as New York, Boston, and Miami, which were major destinations for West Indian emigrants.

The rapid spread of Garvey's movement may be attributable to several factors. For one thing, the World War I period was a time of worldwide radicalism. African peoples were also at their most desperate point in history and so needed vigorous leadership. Garvey himself was also a tireless and exceedingly able organizer, in addition to being an exceptional orator and a strongly charismatic figure. His ideological position also appealed to masses of people. He urged Black people to be self-reliant, to put their racial interest first in a world which universally oppressed them, and to strive to build a strong nation in Africa, strong enough to compel world respect and lend support to African people everywhere.

The UNIA's impact on West Indian affairs was almost immediate. Garvey's agents traversed the area establishing branches and spreading the word of nationalism and anti-colonialism. Some were deported from, and/or refused permission to land in certain territories. The UNIA weekly newspaper, the *Negro World* was widely distributed in the area practically from its inception late in 1918. Several of the British colonial governors responded by banning it, illegally in 1919, and from 1920 on by means of hastily introduced Seditious Publications Ordinances. Despite these measures the paper found its way in, sometimes through the mails, sometimes smuggled in by seamen. Copies intercepted by the authorities were burned.

By 1919 the UNIA in the West Indies was firmly entrenched enough to figure prominently in the labor riots and racial unrest that swept the area. The British colonialists blamed the *Negro World* for the upsurge of race consciousness which formed a backdrop to the disturbances. In Trinidad, many of the leaders of the Trinidad Workingmen's Association, the major organization involved in the stevedores' strike of December 1919, were also members of the UNIA. It was reported that Garvey's editorials were read aloud at their meetings. In British Honduras, S. A. Haynes, one of the major figures involved in the riots, was a Garveyite. He later became a high-ranking UNIA official in the United States.

After 1919 the UNIA maintained its links with the budding West Indian labor movement. A. Bain Alves of Jamaica, members of Hubert Critchlow's British Guiana Labor Union and D. Hamilton Jackson, leader of the St. Croix Labor Union, were among those who established contact with the UNIA in the 1920s. Indeed, Basil Brentnol Blackman, former secretary-treasurer of the Caribbean Congress of Labor, once said that most of the working class leaders coming to power in the 1930s in the West Indies had been influenced by involvement at some level in Garvey's UNIA. Garvey himself founded a Jamaican Workers and Laborers Association after his deportation from the United States in 1927.

Garvey's impact generally on progressive elements in the West Indies, both within and without the labor movement, can be said to have been substantial. Grenada's T. A. Marryshow wrote favorably of him in his *West Indian* newspaper; in Trinidad the *Argos* and the *Labour Leader* (organ of the Trinidad Workingmen's Association) regularly supported him; in Barbados Clennel W. Wickham endorsed Garveyism in the pages of the *Barbados Weekly Herald*.

By the 1920s the UNIA had become, in several greater Caribbean territories, the virtual representatives of the Black population. At a time when most Black people in the area were denied the right to vote, and in an age mostly predating mass political parties, the UNIA often performed the function of quasi-political party as well as mutual aid organization. It was a major, sometimes *the* major, organized group looking after the interests of the mass of Black people. In 1923 the British government seriously considered recognizing the Cuban UNIA as the body representing the British West Indian population in that island. To this day in Costa Rica the UNIA enjoys a position of importance among the Black section of that country.

And when mass-based party politics did come to the West Indies, Garvey and the UNIA were again in the vanguard. For Garvey's Peoples Political Party, formed in Jamaica in 1929, was a pioneer in its class, at least for the British West Indies. A West Indian federation with dominion status was among its aims.

Garvey, in his travels in the West Indies, fared little better than his lieutenants, being occasionally barred from some areas. At various times he was refused permission to land in Bermuda, Cuba, the Canal Zone and Trinidad. Yet on other occasions he was received by such persons as the governor of Oriente province in Cuba, the president of Costa Rica and the governor of British Honduras. His most extensive trip to the British Caribbean came in 1937, three years before his death. On that occasion he was prevented by the British authorities from holding open air meetings in Trinidad. Nor was he permitted to refer to the labor struggles which had erupted there. Indeed, were it not for the personal intervention of Captain A. A. Cipriani, he may not have been allowed to land at all.

Garvey is yet to be given full credit for his tremendous contribution to West Indian history. He did more than any other single individual to stimulate the anticolonialism, racial pride and working class consciousness that laid the groundwork for the struggles of the late 1930s and thereafter. No one can equal him in his successful effort to demonstrate the historical and cultural unity of the Caribbean.

Many of the persons who followed Garvey are still alive in the West Indies. I have myself spoken with Garveyites in Jamaica, Tobago, Dominica and Trinidad. It was in Tobago that I recently saw my first Black Star Line (Garvey's steamship company) stock certificate, proudly showed to me by a man who joined the UNIA in Cuba in 1920.

Garvey is of course now a national hero in Jamaica. He should be a national hero everywhere in the Caribbean (and in many other places too). On recently returning to Trinidad after an eight year absence I was pleased to see that interest in him is again growing. A large photograph of him was displayed in Independence Square, and in Woodford Square, the people's historian Clemey George sang his praises to large and attentive crowds.

5
Marcus Garvey and Trinidad, 1912–1947*

Marcus Mosiah Garvey was born in 1887 in rural Jamaica. By the end of World War I he was well on the way to becoming the most loved, most feared and most hated Black man in the world. The years of his greatest triumph (1916 through 1927) were spent in the United States. That he organized the largest Black mass movement in the history of that country is well known. That he was the most potent force in his time for the forging of a spirit of Pan-African oneness among Black people everywhere, is widely acknowledged. What is yet to be fully appreciated is the tremendous influence exerted by Garvey on the development of working class militancy and Black nationalism in the West Indies. Garvey's organization, the Universal Negro Improvement Association (UNIA), was formed in Jamaica in 1914. By the early 1920s it existed all over the Caribbean—Jamaica, Cuba, Santo Domingo, the U.S. Virgin Islands, Trinidad, British Honduras, Grenada, British Guiana, Suriname, St. Lucia, Barbados, these were but some of the places which boasted UNIA branches. In addition, some of the most loyal units of Garvey's worldwide organization were to be found among the many groups of West Indian exiles and immigrants in such greater Caribbean territories as Costa Rica, Honduras, Guatemala, Nicaragua, and Panama. In the United States, substantial numbers of UNIA members in such places as New York City and Florida were from the islands, and in other areas, though less numerous, they were often prominent.[1] Garvey's followers were everywhere composed overwhelmingly of proletarians and peasants. And among his followers and those influenced one way or another by the UNIA there appear some of the most important labor leaders in the West Indies in the period from World War I through World War II. Among these are Captain A. A. Cipriani of Trinidad, A. Bain Alves of Jamaica,

*Delivered as a conference paper in 1973 and revised subsequently

D. Hamilton Jackson of the U.S. Virgin Islands, and Hubert Critchlow of what was then British Guiana. One long-standing participant in the West Indian labor leadership has suggested that most of the major labor leaders who came to prominence in the British West Indies as late as the 1930s were profoundly influenced by Garvey.[2] This paper will confine itself to a demonstration of some of the often intimate links which developed between Garvey and large numbers of Black people in and from Trinidad. On occasion, as will be seen, the radical nature of Garvey's program of African liberation, economic emancipation, race pride and anti-colonialism, could also lead to collaboration with radical representatives of Trinidad's Indian, Chinese and white communities.

It is impossible to pinpoint Garvey's first contact with Trinidadians. Certainly, by the time of his wanderings through Central America (1910–1912) there were emigrants from Trinidad among the communities of West Indian laborers he worked amongst. It was during this sojourn, round about 1912 in Panama, that he met J. Charles Zampty. Zampty, a native of Belmont,[3] Port-of-Spain, had recently come to Panama in search of work on the Panama Canal. This brief meeting took place, significantly, in the context of a labor union, for the occasion was an address by Garvey to the Colón Federal Labor Union, composed mostly of Black workers. Zampty migrated to New York in 1918 and immediately became a member of the one year old New York UNIA. In 1919 he moved to Detroit in the hope of finding work with the Ford Motor Company and shortly afterwards became one of the founders of the Detroit UNIA. In 1922 he accompanied Garvey all over the United States, acting as UNIA auditor. In 1977, two generations later, he is still a member of the Detroit UNIA and Auditor-General of the organization on the international level.

By the time that Zampty was joining the New York UNIA late in 1918, Garvey was already in the process of disseminating his propaganda throughout the Caribbean. Zampty himself had read copies of Garvey's paper, the *Negro World*, on the Panama Canal, where they were distributed by Japanese sailors. By late 1918 and early 1919, the paper was being circulated in Trinidad. "NEGROES GET READY," its masthead proclaimed, in huge letters which dwarfed the headlines. Among the Trinidadians who were most ready were the militant members of the Trinidad Workingmen's Association.

Formed by Alfred Richards in 1897, the Workingmen's Association could already boast a respectable record of agitation on behalf of workers. But its major exploits were still to come. And the propaganda of

Marcus Garvey was to play an intimate role in the organization's development from this period on. Within a remarkably short space of time the top leadership of the Association would largely overlap with the top leadership of the UNIA in Trinidad, and members of the Association would play important roles at the UNIA headquarters in Harlem.

One of the main figures behind the resurgence of the Association in 1919 was W. Howard Bishop.[4] He later edited the Association's organ, the *Labour Leader*, and was for long a major figure in Trinidad Garveyite circles. Articles from his *Labour Leader* were sometimes reprinted in the *Negro World*.[5] He may have been responsible for the appearance in the *Negro World* as early as June 15, 1919, of the text of a memorial from the Workingmen's Association to the British government. When he died in 1930 the Trinidad UNIA was represented at his funeral by its president, E. J. Louis, and Garvey's Jamaican *Blackman* newspaper (by this time Garvey had been deported from the United States) lamented the loss of a friend. At his death he was general secretary of the Workingmen's Association.[6]

The activities of Bishop and his colleagues in 1919 centered around several strike actions which involved workers in a variety of occupations. This trade union type activity was enacted, however, against a context of agitation for representative government and social justice for the oppressed Black masses. In all of these areas Garvey's *Negro World* provided powerful supportive propaganda.

The colonial authorities first became aware of Garvey's efforts in the island in February 1919. Then it was discovered that UNIA agents were soliciting memberships and selling the *Negro World*.[7] The government immediately declared war on the publication. Copies of the paper shipped as freight were seized under the provisions of an Ordinance No. 25 of 1909, while those entering through the mails were confiscated under a War Censorship Ordinance No. 38 of 1914. Seizure under the 1909 ordinance was illegal, a fact readily admitted by the acting governor, since the proclamation required by the ordinance had not been issued.[8] The Colonial Office was quite happy to condone the suppression of "publications inciting to race hatred," as one official put it, provided they were "likely to lead to violence."[9] The *Negro World* was obviously considered within this category.

Sharing this view of the *Negro World* was the American Consul in Port-of-Spain, Henry D. Baker. Baker, an energetic and apparently efficient character, dabbled incessantly in the internal affairs of

Trinidad, and on occasion gave the appearance more of an unofficial governor of the island than a mere diplomat. The British governor held him in enough deference to pass over to him confidential documents in which he might be interested, and Baker did not hesitate to directly request confidential information from the British police authorities in the island when he felt like it. He also belonged to the white Union Club, a favorite haunt of the local white overlords. From this informal perch he could observe intimately the attitudes and intentions of a powerful section of the Trinidad community. Baker repeatedly suggested to the U.S. State Department after the riots of December 1919, that the *Negro World* was "responsible for the rapid growth of class and race feeling, and of anarchistic and Bolshevist ideas among the ignorant population here."[10] In October 1919 he went so far as to remit back to the Post Office Department in Washington wrappers in which Garvey had posted copies of the paper to individuals in the island. He claimed that thousands of copies were arriving in Trinidad with every mail.[11] Despite the efforts of the British authorities and of Baker himself, a large number of copies continued to circulate through the island, a fact which Baker admitted. And it would appear that they were on occasion sold quite openly.[12]

Baker's reference to the *Negro World* link with socialism in Trinidad was corroborated by W. A. Domingo, editor for a few months in 1919 of Garvey's paper and himself a socialist. In an article published in July 1919 while he was editor, he had deplored the ignorance of socialism manifested by New World Black people. The only exceptions of which he was aware were some small groups in the United States, and "a relatively well-organized group in the island of Trinidad, British West Indies."[13] This may well have been a reference to the Trinidad Workingmen's Association, some of whose material had already appeared in the *Negro World*. For the Association maintained close ties with the British Labor Party, which considered itself socialist.[14] Garvey himself, though eschewing socialistic doctrines concerning the primacy of class over race, nevertheless remained a lifelong admirer of both the British Labor Party and Lenin, so the Association's simultaneous espousal of socialism after a fashion and Garveyism, was in no way incompatible with the tendencies of Garvey himself.[15]

Garvey's links with the Trinidad populace in 1919 were not confined to the Workingmen's Association. Other persons obviously read his paper, and Black soldiers returning from the war, some of whom undoubtedly found their way into the ranks of the Association, were said to be bringing back copies picked up while on duty overseas. The *Argos,* a local paper owned by a Chinese immigrant (Mr. Lee Lum) but edited by Black radicals, was also a potent vehicle for the spread of Garvey's ideas. Their espousal of representative government for the Black race was a cause of some concern alike to the British authorities and the local white elite. One *Argos* reporter, Charles A. Petioni, moved to the United States and participated actively in the New York UNIA. He was a signatory to Garvey's important Declaration of Rights of the Negro Peoples of the World in 1920.[16]

1919 was a year of continuous labor and racial unrest in Trinidad, marked by, among other things, anti-white feeling, assaults on white people, bitterness among returned much-discriminated-against Black soldiers, and the dissemination of Garveyite and other Afro-American ideas. All of this culminated in serious riots early in December of that year. The rioting grew out of a strike by stevedores in Port-of-Spain and spread to other parts of the island and to Tobago. Many of the workers involved, the stevedores especially, were represented by the Workingmen's Association, which succeeded in obtaining a 25 per cent wage increase.[17] Consul Baker placed much of the blame for these events on Garvey.[18]

If Baker and the British administration needed any corroboration for Garvey's connection with the 1919 unrest it came shortly after the December riots in the form of a letter from Samuel Augustus Duncan. Duncan, a naturalized American from St. Kitts, had been the president in 1918 of the newly formed New York Branch of the UNIA. From this position he was ousted by Garvey, who objected to the nascent organization being used as a party-affiliated club by New York Republicans and Socialists. Duncan's response was to write a large number of British governors of West Indian and African colonies charging Garvey's "subtle and underhand propaganda" with responsibility for, among other things, "the recent bloody strikes in Trinidad."[19] The Governor of Trinidad, Sir John Chancellor, received a copy of Duncan's letter and passed it on to Baker, who advised his superiors in the State Department that "this propaganda from New York should not be tolerated by our government."[20]

The Trinidad government meanwhile embarked on a campaign of repression against Garvey and his associates in the Workingmen's Association. James Braithwaite, secretary of the Workingmen's Association, sometime president of the Port-of-Spain UNIA,[21] and a leader of the December strike, was fined, together with his principal aides, five pounds with an alternative of thirty days in jail, for calling the strike. On appeal to a higher court the latter not only agreed with the original verdict but took away the option of a fine and made the jail sentence mandatory. An ordinance was also introduced making striking illegal. [22]

But imprisonment was not the most serious sanction employed against the Garveyite leaders of the Workingmen's Association. Some were deported. Among these was an assistant secretary of the Workingmen's Association, Ven Edward Seiler Salmon. Salmon's interesting career in the Black struggle included labor agitation against the United Fruit Company in British Honduras and membership in the African Orthodox Church, which was closely related to the UNIA. [23]

Of the deportees, one, John Sydney de Bourg, went on to become a member of the UNIA hierarchy in the United States. Born in Grenada, de Bourg came to Trinidad at the age of thirty and had lived there for thirty-seven years at the time of his expulsion by the British. [24] He had held various high positions in the Workingmen's Association, having been a member of the executive committee since at least 1906. In 1914 he had led a radical coup within the organization which resulted in the eventual ouster of Alfred Richards, the more moderate incumbent president. [25]

Following his deportation from Trinidad, de Bourg sojourned briefly in Grenada and proceeded to New York where he arrived on July 28, 1920. The purpose of his visit was to attend Garvey's First International Convention of the Negro Peoples of the World, where he was part of the Trinidad delegation. DeBourg's entry into the United States represented a victory, unwitting or otherwise, over Consul Baker. For Baker, early in 1919, had begun selectively refusing visas for entry into the U.S. to Trinidadians he considered undesirable. The action was condoned by the State Department which advised him to obtain the co-operation of neighboring consuls. In December, following the riots, Baker had reaffirmed his position, informing the State Department that he would refuse a visa to any of those who might be deported from Trinidad. [26]

Having successfully negotiated the visa hurdle, de Bourg and his colleagues proceeded to make a favorable impression on the convention. De Bourg's name appears among the signatories to the celebrated Declaration of Rights of the Negro Peoples of the World adopted by the conference, and, with the backing of Garvey himself, he was elected Leader of the Negroes of the Western Provinces of the West

Indies and South and Central America, with an annual salary of $6,000.[27] An official at the British Colonial Office, examining the UNIA Declaration of Rights a few months after the conference, expressed some alarm at the role of the Trinidad delegation. He wrote, "I recognize such old friends from Trinidad as de Bourg, McConney and Braithwaite among the signatories. It's the signatories rather than their publications which are dangerous."[28]

DeBourg spent most of the next two years travelling widely on behalf of the UNIA. He delivered speeches, helped resuscitate failing branches, sold stock in Garvey's Black Star Line Steamship Corporation and negotiated with governmental authorities on behalf of UNIA members. These activities covered places as far afield as Brooklyn, New York; Louisville, Kentucky; Camaguey, Cuba; Jamaica; and San Juan, Puerto Rico.[29] In 1921 he toured the West Indies with Garvey. Of great assistance to de Bourg in his UNIA work was his experience in the leadership of the Workingmen's Association. For in 1922 we find him negotiating on behalf of the UNIA members in San Pedro de Macoris, Santo Domingo, with plantation owners and officials of the U.S. military administration which was then occupying the island. With the former he negotiated for a schoolroom and other fringe benefits for UNIA use, and from the latter he recovered confiscated UNIA property.[30] For his UNIA work de Bourg was elevated to the UNIA aristocracy of merit. He was made a Knight Commander of the Nile and Duke of Nigeria and Uganda, and received the Gold Cross of African Redemption.[31]

De Bourg eventually fell out with Garvey, testified against him during his celebrated 1923 trial, and was awarded $9,781 in a suit for back pay against the UNIA.[32] Garvey lamented de Bourg's treachery, claiming that de Bourg had proved a failure as a fund-raiser, an important part of his job, having raised only $200.00 in sixteen months of active UNIA employment.[33] Garvey wrote,

> There was one old man from Trinidad, over sixty years of age, who came to the convention with tears in his eyes. He made a pitiful plea to the convention for help. He stated that he was once a man of means in the Island of Trinidad, but that he fought the battles of the poor blacks and was hounded by the British, who impoverished him and drove him out of the country. His story was plausible. He appeared poorly attired and suggested that he was really in need of help. I, myself, suggested this man for the position of leader of one of the Provinces of the West Indies at

a salary of $6,000 per annum. I personally did everything to help the old man, yet he was the principal enemy witness against me for the Government in 1923. . . .[34]

The presence of de Bourg and his colleagues at Garvey's 1920 convention was evidence of what had by this time become a fairly widespread adherence to Garvey's ideas by the Black masses in and out of the Workingmen's Association. Governor Chancellor reported during the year that "at the meetings of the 'Workingmen's Association,' and elsewhere, verbatim quotations from the 'Negro World' and the writings of Marcus Garvey are used by negro speakers." He mentioned also that shares in Garvey's Black Star Line were held in Trinidad.[35] Earlier in the year Baker had requested confidential information from the local police on two young Trinidadians who were planning to work for the line. One, Randolph Flanner, an ex-employee of the Trinidad Government Foundry, was already in New York and expected to be shortly appointed third engineer on the line's *Phyllis Wheatley*. The other, Allan Berridge, son of a Town Hall clerk and also a foundry employee, was about to leave for New York where he hoped to study mechanical engineering with a view to also joining the Black Star Line. The police authorities assured Baker that they were both of good character.[36] This attraction of the Black Star Line for Trinidadians, as for Black people elsewhere, was enhanced by the discriminations which Black passengers were forced to endure on white-owned ships. In a typical account a writer to the *Negro World* in 1920 catalogued the racist practices of the Trinidad Shipping and Trading Company Ltd. and the British ship "Maraval" plying between Trinidad, Grenada and New York. Among other things Black first class passengers were required to eat after the white passengers.[37]

In order to further try and stem the onrush of Garveyite influence the Trinidad government in April 1920, in concert with several other West Indian governments, passed a Seditious Publications Ordinance, aimed especially against the *Negro World* and *Crusader* (yet another New York publication published by yet another West Indian-American, Cyril Briggs). The Colonial Office had authorized the passage of this bill in 1919, with a view, at that time, to dealing in a legitimate fashion with the *Argos* and the *Negro World*.[38] (The latter, as already mentioned, was being illegally destroyed since early 1919.) The procedure both before and after the Seditious Publications Ordinance was to search Black crews as well as the ships themselves if they came from New York. A police inspector checked the mails for those entering by that route.[39] In a typical operation the police in August 1920 discovered a large cache of the *Negro World* hidden in between a cargo from New York. Among the find (and confiscated in the mail also at about the same time) were a large number of leaflets, including a pamphlet specially addressed by Garvey to the people of Trinidad.[40] With the passage of the new ordinance the authorities also intensified their efforts against those papers which still eluded the police net and found their way into the island. Houses were searched by detectives. Indeed as late as 1931 Albert Gomes, then editor of the radical *Beacon* magazine, was visited by a detective with "an apologetic mien, a roving eye, [and] a notebook" who was searching for Communist and more especially for Garvey's papers.[41]

Consul Baker, of course, applauded the action of the British over-lords, and the *Argos*, not surprisingly, protested the Seditious Publications Ordinance.[42] A wide cross section of opinion in fact opposed the ordinance, but not always because of any love for Garvey. Thus the *Port-of-Spain Gazette* argued that the bill was worded so broadly as to make any criticism of government vulnerable. Also opposing the measure was the *Teachers's Journal*.[43] And in England at the annual conference of the Labour Party Mr. Ben Spoor, a member of parliament from Durham, introduced a resolution against restrictive legislation in the colonies in general and requesting the withdrawal of this ordinance in particular. Spoor and others pointed out that the "so-called negro population" (as one delegate put it), were still treated like slaves and subjected to tyrannical government, and that if labor was to advance in England it would have to advance in the colonies too. One delegate, presumably expressing the sentiment of many present, feared the effect the ordinance would have on the English labor paper, the *Daily Herald*.[44] And a popular calypsonian denounced the blatant class nature of this legislation and the tyranny of British rule. He sang,

> Class legislation is the order of this land;
> We are ruled with the iron hand.
> Class legislation is the order of the land;
> We are ruled with the iron hand.
> Britain boasts of equality,
> Brotherly love and fraternity,
> But British colours have put we,
> In perpetual misery in this colony.[45]

The sentiments of the masses, as expressed in this calypso, contrast with those of the local white businessmen, whose organ, the *Trinidad*

Guardian, applauded the measure, arguing that the only persons with any cause for objection ought already to have been in jail.[46]

1920, therefore, was a year of advance and consolidation for Garvey's ideas among Trinidadians at home and abroad. One discordant note was provided, however, by a Trinidadian in New York who fell in among Garvey's enemies, and who for a while tried to operate a rival organization under Garvey's nose in Harlem. The person in question was F. E. M. Hercules, whose history of participation in race struggles certainly rivalled Garvey's. His record included formation of a Young Men's Coloured Association while still a schoolboy in Trinidad, and important roles in the Society of Peoples of African Origin and the African Progress Union in England around the period 1918–1919. In 1919 he had toured the West Indies propagandizing Black people to an awareness of their oppressed condition and doing what he could to encourage self-reliance and resistance.[47]

In Harlem early in 1920 Hercules began holding weekly meetings of his newly-formed African International League. The League's program did not look too different from Garvey's, featuring as it did economic self-reliance and Pan-African co-operation. His meetings were well-attended by Garvey's Black enemies and were regularly and favorably reported in the *Emancipator* of W. A. Domingo, Jamaican ex-editor of the *Negro World*, now turned anti-Garvey propagandist. In March the *Emancipator* published a thinly-veiled Hercules criticism of "a certain would-be imperialist organization" (undoubtedly the UNIA) which wrongly, in his opinion, wished to set up its headquarters in Liberia.[48] Hercules, however, slid into relative oblivion, while Garvey proceeded from strength to strength.

1921 saw a further deepening of the links between Trinidad and Garvey. Eugene Corbie, a Trinidad student at the City College of New York and a UNIA member, early in 1921 attempted to set up a music bureau in connection with the UNIA. The bureau would encourage and consolidate the efforts of Black artistes.[49] Corbie had a brilliant academic career at City College and won wide acclaim for his prize winning performances in inter-collegiate oratorical contests. Trinidadian George Padmore considered Corbie one of the "two most outstanding coloured youth leaders in college circles" in the United States, the other being Padmore himself.[50]

But perhaps the most noteworthy, and certainly the most colorful link between Garvey and Trinidad in 1921 came in the person of

Hubert Fauntleroy Julian, or, as he quickly became known, the Black Eagle. Julian, an intrepid and flamboyant immigrant from Trinidad, is reputed to have been the first Black person to qualify as a pilot in North America. He entered the United States from Canada in March 1921, headed for Harlem and soon met Garvey. According to Julian they "quickly became close friends." For Garvey's 1922 convention they secretly agreed upon a publicity stunt which would both advertise the UNIA and gain Julian the entree into influential circles which he desired. He flew a Curtis biplane back and forth over the convention parade. Due to the absence of restrictions against low-flying at that time he could get near enough to the marchers to create considerable interest. To heighten the effect, the plane was inscribed with UNIA slogans. Later that night Garvey introduced Julian to a mass meeting as the mystery pilot, taking the opportunity to hold up Julian as an example of what the Black man could achieve, given an equal opportunity.[51]

By June 1921 the Black Star Line was announcing that its ship, the *Phyllis Wheatley*, would call at Trinidad on its way to its maiden West African voyage,[52] and on the line's *S.S. Kanawha* transporting Garvey's party in the West Indies there was at least one crew member from Trinidad, namely Joshua Parris, a fireman. Parris had previously been fourth engineer on the line's *Yarmouth*.[53]

1921 was also the year in which Garvey, as a preliminary step to moving his headquarters to Liberia, set up a legation there. As resident secretary of the legation he named Cyril A. Crichlow, a naturalized American citizen from Trinidad. The post carried a salary of $2,500 per annum. Crichlow was co-proprietor of the Crichlow-Braithwaite Shorthand School in Harlem, apparently the leading Black business school in New York City. He himself had for some time been the UNIA's "official reporter," which post involved taking down verbatim shorthand notes at UNIA meetings. In 1920 he had been among the signatories to the Declaration of Rights of the Negro Peoples of the World. In Liberia Crichlow soon ran afoul of the Liberian UNIA potentate, Gabriel Johnson, who saw Crichlow's position as an attempt to usurp his own power. In his conflict with Johnson, Crichlow took the extraordinarily asinine step of turning to the U.S. minister in Monrovia for support. In the process he turned over confidential UNIA documents to this representative of the U.S. government and thereby contributed more than his share to the unsuccess of Garvey's Liberian plans. To add to his discomfiture he fell ill. His stay in Liberia lasted from March 18 to August 6, 1921. He sued Garvey on his return for $1,237.99, claiming arrears of pay. A court awarded him $700.00 since he had not fully performed his contract.[54]

Meanwhile in Trinidad in 1921 the British colonialists continued to do what they could to humbug the UNIA. Their big achievement for the year consisted in denying entry to the Rev. Richard Hilton Tobitt, a UNIA commissioner who was visiting branches in the Caribbean area. Tobitt was nonetheless allowed into places such as Barbados and British Guiana, and a few years later while again on UNIA business, was received by the governor of Suriname and given the freedom of that country.[55] Tobitt's exclusion from Trinidad was also an oblique attack by the government on the Workingmen's Association whose "leading members", the *Port-of-Spain Gazette* reported, had arranged a "sumptuous breakfast" for him.[56] Tobitt complained to Winston Churchill at the Colonial Office about the arbitrary action of the Trinidad government. Churchill refused to intervene.[57] Local UNIA members remained undaunted. Robert E. R. Fletcher, assistant-secretary of the Port-of-Spain division, condemned the British authorities for inciting racial hatred and declared that the Black masses would not be intimidated, for "We feel that the same vision that the other Negro peoples of the world have caught sight of we, too, have caught sight of. . . ."[58]

The government exclusion of Tobitt served only to confirm what was by this time a fairly obvious fact, namely that Trinidad, of all the British possessions, seemed to be the most repressive against the UNIA. The exclusions, jailings, shootings, deportations, initial illegal burnings of the *Negro World*, house searches, ordinance against striking, prompt passage of the Seditious Publications Ordinance, and other similar measures all added up to an extremely repressive package. None of these measures taken individually was of course peculiar to Trinidad, but Trinidad has a good claim for first place for the comprehensiveness of its hostility to the UNIA. Of the British possessions and dominions, Bermuda, with its large and proverbially reactionary white population, came closest to Trinidad in anti-UNIA endeavor. South Africa, which possessed the largest number of UNIA branches on the African continent, is not excepted from these comparisons.[59] The infamy of Trinidad's government had by 1922 become so notorious that a West African newspaper, the *Gold Coast Leader*, could editorially speak of "the obstructionist parts of the West Indian Colonies, such as Trinidad."[60]

That Trinidad's reputation was well-merited was further evidenced by two events in 1922 and 1923. The first involved a projected world tour by Garvey. Garvey's announcement threw the British Colonial Office into a dither. A flurry of correspondence ensued between London and all British governors in Africa and the West Indies. The Colonial Office wanted, if possible, to agree on some pre-arranged strategy for dealing with the visit if it materialized. Of the British West Indian colonies, British Honduras, the Leeward Islands, Grenada, Jamaica, British Guiana and initially Barbados, all accepted the Colonial Office suggestion that it would be preferable to let Garvey in and then try and treat him as of no consequence, rather than risk unrest by refusing him entry. Trinidad and Bermuda insisted on prohibiting his entry.[61]

The second event concerned the ban on the *Negro World*. By 1922–1923 some West Indian governments had lifted the ban on the paper due to a combination of public protests and the belief in some gubernatorial quarters that the tone of the paper had mellowed since 1919. Jamaica and Barbados were among the areas now admitting the paper.[62] In this situation the governor of British Guiana communicated his desire to lift the ban to the Secretary of State for the Colonies, Winston Churchill. He however expressed reservations about admitting it into British Guiana while it was still seditious in nearby Trinidad.[63] The governor of Trinidad, in response to an inquiry from Churchill, declared it his intention to keep the ban in Trinidad. He added that he had recently refused a petition from the Trinidad UNIA to repeal the Seditious Publications Ordinance and withdraw the proclamation prohibiting entry to the paper, "owing to the objectionable character of the matter" still appearing in it.[64]

The extreme anti-UNIA stance of the Trinidad government can no doubt in large part be explained by the presence there of one of the more rabidly obscurantist white minorities in the islands. And their reaction was matched by their influence and vocality. They ran the Chamber of Commerce, selected candidates during the war for their white Merchants and Planters Contingent, controlled their own newspaper, and were in no way awed by British governors. During the 1919 unrest, for example, they bombarded the governor, the public and the Colonial Office with alarmist and sometimes openly racist petitions and statements of all kinds. And when the governor at one point capitulated to the strikers they threatened to report him to the Colonial Office and exacted an apology from him.[65]

The attitude of the government can also be explained in part by the simple fact that the Trinidad UNIA, with its large membership, and its intimate link with one of the most powerful working class organizations in the British islands at the time, was a force not to be taken lightly. By the early 1920s Trinidad was the most thoroughly organized UNIA stronghold in the British West Indies, and of the non-British islands only Cuba had a larger number of UNIA branches. De Bourg at the 1922 convention in New York gave a figure of thirty-three for the association's branches in the island.[66] The following year UNIA commissioner Tobitt gave the number as thirty-two and testified to the continued circulation there of the *Negro World* despite the opposition.[67] A UNIA headquarters compilation of 1927 named thirty divisions. They were spread all over the island, in large towns and rural areas alike. Branches were listed for Balandra Bay, Carapichaima, Caroni, Cedros, Chaguanas, Couva, D'Abadie, Enterprise, Gasparillo, Guaico, Iere Village, La Brea, Lily of the Nile [the headquarters division in Port-of-Spain], Los Bajos, Mucurapo (St. James), Marabella, Matura, Morne Diablo, Palmyra, Penal, Port-of-Spain, Princes Town, Rio Claro, St Mary (Moruga), Ste. Madeleine, San Fernando, Siparia, Tableland, Victoria Village and Williamsville. Cuba, according to the same compilation, had fifty-two branches and Jamaica ten.[68] Apart from the areas listed above this author has come across references to divisions in Brother's Road, New Grant, Cumana, Tabaquite and St. Joseph. And the absence of a division in an area did not necessarily imply an absence of UNIA members. Thus persons from Toco belonged to the division in nearby Cumana[69] and there were Garveyites in Mt. Stewart Village, Point-à-Pierre and Vistabella,[70] which places may or may not have had divisions of their own.

The Trinidad UNIA enjoyed a very active existence and ministered to many of the needs of its members. In addition to its obvious function of stimulating race pride and Black self-reliance, its effectiveness as a workers' organization was enhanced by the close association with the Workingmen's Association. And both the workers and peasants within it benefited from the fact that, like UNIA branches everywhere, they also doubled as friendly societies, paying death and other benefits to members.

Activities revolved here, as elsewhere, around the regular meetings of the association. The Lily of the Nile (headquarters) division possessed its own Liberty Hall[71] (as all UNIA meeting places the world over were called). Some divisions had to make do with the use of halls belonging to other institutions. Thus we find the Ste. Madeleine division using the Be of Good Cheer Friendly Society Hall, the Port-of-Spain division using the Ideal Hall on Tragarete Rd., and so on.[72] Many of the UNIA auxiliaries familiar to branches elsewhere also existed in Trinidad. These included the Black Cross Nurses, the Universal African Legions, Boy Scouts, Scout Girls, and UNIA choirs. Sometimes, instead of a lay chaplain, clergymen from the African Methodist Episcopal (A.M.E.) Church handled the religious aspects of meetings.[73] There was considerable interaction between members of different divisions. It was quite common for members to travel long distances by train to attend meetings of far away divisions. This would be especially true for a special event, such as the unveiling of a new charter or the dedication of a new Liberty Hall. Such interaction also existed between members from various countries in the area. Trinidad Garveyites crop up addressing UNIA gatherings in St. Kitts, British Guiana and Barbados, among other places.[74] Members from other islands also turned up at meetings in Trinidad.

This interaction extended also to the parent body in Harlem, U.S.A., and took many forms. A large number of Trinidad members, for example, contributed to various funds being raised by the parent body in Harlem. Throughout the pages of the *Negro World* for 1922 there appear a fairly large number of Trinidadians among contributors to the convention fund and the Marcus Garvey defense fund. These persons represented divisions in St. Joseph, Princes Town, Port-of-Spain and La Brea, among other places. In one edition of the paper no less than fifty-five names from Palmyra, Mt. Stewart Village, San Fernando, Point-à-Pierre and Vistabella were listed as contributors to the defense fund.[75] In 1924 one Jonathan C. Watts of Princes Town donated $120 to Harlem headquarters.[76]

Close contact with the Harlem headquarters was also maintained by the sending of delegates to Garvey's international conventions. Their presence at the 1920 convention has already been noted. At the 1922 convention, apart from Trinidadians living in New York, Fitz Aaron Braithwaite was sent as a Trinidad representative, and returned home immediately after the event.[77] At the 1924 convention (there was none in 1923) a Trinidad delegate, I. Cipriani, was mentioned several times in reports of the deliberations.[78] The next convention at which Garvey presided was in 1929 in Jamaica. Here Miss Edith Devonshire, lady president of the Trinidad headquarters (Lily of the Nile) division played an active part, being elected to the convention's Social and Political Committee.[79]

For those who could not make it to Harlem, the Trinidad branches sometimes held a convention of their own to coincide with Garvey's. In 1921 the Carapichaima division hosted such a convention.[80] And in 1922 the Lily of the Nile division held a thirty-one day convention, coinciding exactly with that in Harlem. Over a thousand people attended the opening night festivities, during which a picture of Garvey was unveiled. Among the speakers was a lady president from Barbados and a Mr. Cyrus (possibly himself a Trinidadian) who was described as a founder of the New York division and on a visit to the island. Four hundred and sixty new members were added to the organization during this convention.[81]

Other special meetings celebrated such events a Ethiopia's admission into the League of Nations, Emancipation Day and the expected visit of Garvey's representative, Mme. M. L. T. de Mena.[82] There is no better way to capture the everyday flavor of the organization than by a brief description of an important, but fairly typical meeting. This particular meeting celebrated the unveiling of the charter for the Port-of-Spain division and was held at the Ideal Hall in Tragarete Road, Port-of-Spain, in March 1922. The huge, standing room only crowd included several members from country districts. The meeting started at 3 p.m. with a procession led by the UNIA Juveniles (both girls and boys) and the choir, under choirmaster Reginald Solomon. Next came the officers, including president Stanley Jones, vice-president Thomas O'Neale, chaplain Reginald Perpignac, the director of the Black Cross Nurses in Trinidad and Tobago, Mrs. Louise Crichlow and Percival Burrows, commissioner for Trinidad. They were followed by a detachment of Black Cross Nurses.

Commissioner Burrows then presided over the unveiling, which was performed by little Miss Nauma Braithwaite, dressed as an Ethiopian queen. Burrows next presented each officer with his emblem of office—a gavel to the president, Bible to the chaplain, and so on. The recipients included officers of the choir, nurses, Motor Corps, juveniles and the African Legion. A number of speeches followed, delivered by Mrs. Crichlow, Mrs. Isaac Hector, lady president of Chaguanas, Joshua Douglas, president of La Brea, who had travelled by boat and train to be present, and Joseph Charles, also of La Brea, who urged Black-owned businesses. These last three then left to catch a train back home. At least eight speeches followed, interspersed with a violin solo and a song. The feature address was by W. Howard Bishop of the Workingmen's Association, who spoke on the need for Black unity. This presentation was much applauded. The recessional hymn was sung as the procession made its way to the robing room, and the meeting ended with the singing of the Universal Ethiopian Anthem (adopted in the 1920 Declaration of Rights as the anthem of the Black race).[83]

The presence of W. Howard Bishop at this meeting is evidence of the continuing close relationship between the two associations. Meetings of the Workingmen's Association were regularly held at Liberty Hall in downtown Port-of-Spain. When in 1924 the British Guiana Labor Union leader Hubert Critchlow visited Trinidad on his way to a labor conference in England, he addressed a meeting sponsored by the Workingmen's Association at Liberty Hall. Critchlow's union not only enjoyed cordial fraternal relations with the Trinidad Workingmen's Association, but also maintained links with the UNIA in British Guiana.[84] At this 1924 meeting in Port-of-Spain's Liberty Hall Critchlow was given a mandate by the Workingmen's Association to lobby in England for trade union laws for Trinidad. The close association between organized labor and the UNIA is further evidenced by the fact that most of the Workingmen's Association dignitaries on the platform for the Critchlow speech were also high ranking Garveyites. These included W. Howard Bishop, general secretary of the Workingmen's Association; James Braithwaite, its ex-secretary and sometime president of the Port-of-Spain UNIA; and Fitz Aaron Braithwaite who, apart from being sometime treasurer and pianist of the Port-of-Spain division,[85] had represented Trinidad at Garvey's 1922 convention.[86] Captain A. A. Cipriani, the president of the Workingmen's Association and chairman of the meeting, also, as will be seen, maintained close ties with Garvey.

This Liberty Hall, at 28 Prince Street, Port-of-Spain, was the seat of the Trinidad headquarters division, the Lily of the Nile (not to be confused with the Port-of-Spain division).[87]

That there may, however, have been an occasional reservation about the Workingmen's Association connection is suggested in a very valuable account of five UNIA branches appearing in the *Negro World* of November 19, 1921. The account was written by J. R. Ralph Casimir, head of the Dominica UNIA and one of the most influential and hardworking UNIA figures in the West Indies, after a trip to Trinidad.

Casimir first visited Guaico, where the charter was unveiled during his stay on June 25, 1921. This branch had about a hundred members of whom only about twenty were financial. At Casimir's urging a unit of the Universal African Legions was formed here with four recruits under Mr. Elbert Morancie, an ex-corporal in the British West Indies Regiment.

Casimir next proceeded to the Tabaquite division, where he arrived on July 2nd. Here he was distressed to find that some of the officers had sent for Mr. Bishop and Mrs. Raviak of the Workingmen's Association for guidance in UNIA affairs. Mrs. Raviak informed Casimir that Bishop was a personal friend of Garvey, who had personally authorised him to propagate the UNIA message in Trinidad. The Garveyites in Tabaquite had also sent about $40.00 to James Braithwaite in Port-of-Spain, believing (wrongly, in Casimir's opinion) that he was head of the Trinidad UNIA.

On July 3rd Casimir visited Brother's Road, where he found a well-organized division containing about seventy-five members, despite being less than a month old. Casimir addressed them for three hours on organizational matters.

Penal was next, with a visit on July 10th. Here he reported one hundred and fifty members and was peeved at the Rev. A. E. Taylor of the A.M.E. Church for representing to the people that his was the church of the UNIA.

Casimir was most impressed by the La Brea division which he visited on August 7th. This division dated from around January 1921.

In his general remarks Casimir again criticized James Braithwaite, this time for collecting money allegedly for the Black Star Line without accounting for how it was spent. He was equally hostile to the "so-called" UNIA organizer Herman D. Thompson of St. Joseph who ordered UNIA supplies from New York and resold them at exorbitant profits. Thompson, he thought, belonged to the "old type of Negroes and is too bombastic." So it would appear that Trinidad, like the parent body in New York itself, was not without those who were willing to capitalize on the Black struggle for personal gain.

Presiding as UNIA commissioner over District No. 5 of the Foreign Fields, which included Trinidad, Grenada, St. Vincent, Brazil, Colombia and Venezuela, was Percival Leon Burrows.[88] As in the case of all UNIA commissioners, his job involved travelling to and overseeing the work of branches in the district, as well as acting as an ambassador on behalf of Black people. The document appointing him in 1922 read:

> Mr. Burrowes [sic] is authorized to supervise the various branches, divisions and chapters of the Universal Negro Improvement Association

and African Communities League. He is commissioned to represent the interest of all Negroes domiciled in the countries. In the matter of trouble and disturbances, he is authorized to take up the matter with the respective governments in protecting the interest of all Negroes.

The Universal Negro Improvement Association represents the interest of 400,000,000 Negroes the world over, and lends its moral, financial and political support to the actions of Commissioner Burrowes in the performance of his duties in connection with the Negro race.

We ask that all with whom he comes in contact exchange with him the courtesies due to a representative of a sovereign race.[89]

Burrows, like Zampty, de Bourg and Cyril Crichlow before him, moved on to occupy a top position in the UNIA international hierarchy. By August 1923 we find him presiding at Liberty Hall in Harlem (Garvey was in jail following his trial) and he shortly thereafter became secretary general of the association.[90]

Burrows by no means completes the list of persons connected with the Trinidad UNIA who achieved high office at the Harlem headquarters. The *Negro World* in 1925 reported that one Francis X. Quattell had been transferred from the Port-of-Spain division to Harlem, where he addressed a Liberty Hall meeting, but little is heard of him thereafter.[91] Much more important was Hucheshwar G. Mudgal, editor of the *Negro World* during some of its later years after Garvey's expulsion from the United States. Mudgal was born in India and emigrated to Trinidad before moving on to the United States. His connection with Garvey's publications began in 1922 when he took over the *Negro World* foreign affairs column vacated by Garvey's mentor, Duse Mohamed Ali. At this time he was also a foreign affairs columnist for Garvey's *Daily Negro Times*. After a period of apparent inactivity his foreign affairs articles reappeared on a regular basis in 1929 and he thereafter became the paper's editor. He busied himself debating the ideological correctness of Garveyism against Communists, and in 1932 produced a pamphlet, *Marcus Garvey—Is He the True Redeemer of the Negro?* In 1929 Mudgal was described as having an M.A. from Columbia University and being a Ph.D. candidate.[92]

But one of the most important United States based Trinidadians influenced by Garvey was George Padmore, who was never, as far as is known, a member of the UNIA. In 1928, about a year after Garvey's deportation, Padmore was responsible for a protest at the Howard University campus against a visit by the British ambassador to Washington, Sir Esme Howard. Lengthy mimeographed documents signed by Padmore as secretary of the International Anti-Imperialistic Youths' League accused the ambassador of complicity in Garvey's deportations from the U.S. in 1927 and Canada in 1928. Padmore was assisted in this endeavor by another Trinidadian student, Cyril Ollivierre.[93]

During the same year that Padmore was accusing the British ambassador of engineering Garvey's deportation from the U.S. and Canada, the British authorities in Trinidad were busy making plans to prevent Garvey's entry into Trinidad or expel him if he should somehow manage to land. Their plans had in fact started almost as soon as Garvey arrived back in Jamaica in December 1927. The governor, on hearing that "the notorious Marcus Garvey," as he put it, was contemplating a West Indian tour, immediately called together his executive council. This colonialist conclave unanimously agreed to prohibit Garvey's entry and the governor, again in his own words, "signed an order for use in case of need."[94] This was followed up with a law drafted especially for Garvey, empowering the governor-in-executive council to prevent the landing of, or expulsion of a person convicted anywhere of a crime for which sentence of imprisonment was passed, that person's British nationality notwithstanding.[95] Garvey addressed himself to this law some months later. He berated "the minority white colonists and the non-racial coloured class who have jointly lived off the ignorance and unfortunate condition of the black masses" and charged, correctly, that the law was passed for his benefit when it appeared that he might visit and confer with Black Trinidadians in an effort to better their condition.[96] Garvey was equally peeved by the fact that a section of the Black teachers came out against his visit on the ground that it might cause misunderstanding between the races. Garvey pointed out that the teachers themselves had lamented the poor economic situation of the Black section of the population, which made ludicrous their concern for understanding when other races were rich and happy. "In Trinidad," he declared, "the Negro teachers have openly declared themselves the enemy of the black masses." And from this circumstance he drew the important lesson that "We must adopt the internal boycott against traitorous Negroes as we shall do against our enemies of other races."[97]

Nine years later, in 1937, another projected Garvey visit to the West Indies found Trinidad still outdoing the other colonies in anti-Garvey hostility, as had usually been the case since 1919. This time Garvey obtained the support of Captain A. A. Cipriani. Cipriani, as the white leader of the Trinidad Workingmen's Association (in 1934 it became the Trinidad Labour Party), occupied a situation which was immensely unusual for one of his race in the island. During World War I he had been a captain in the British West Indies Regiment and apparently much disturbed by the multitudinous discriminations meted out to the Black rank and file. Back home from the war in 1919 he accepted leadership of the Workingmen's Association which was by this time, as has been seen, a Garveyite stronghold. His record of struggle on behalf of Black soldiers, the fact that his whiteness may have caused him to be perceived as less vulnerable to official harassment, and the fact that the largely non-Trinidad born leadership of the association not infrequently found itself the victims of deportation, may all have contributed to the choice of Cipriani as leader.

Cipriani thus found himself in control of a largely Garveyite organization in which a large number of his fellow leaders doubled as major UNIA figures. In this situation, then, it is not surprising that Cipriani and Garvey developed a mutual admiration for each other's political position. Garvey's *New Jamaican* newspaper, for example, went on record in September 1932 in praise of Cipriani. Apart from the obvious UNIA connection, the political ideas and careers of both men reveal many similarities. Cipriani served for many years on the Port-of-Spain City Council, Garvey on the Kingston and St. Andrew Corporation Council. Cipriani served in the Legislative Council, Garvey attempted unsuccessfully to do the same. Cipriani, as leader of the Trinidad Labour Party, pioneered modern party politics in Trinidad. Garvey did the same in Jamaica with his Peoples' Political Party. Both men campaigned for trade union legislation and such related measures as the eight hour day. Both had a peculiar fascination with the British Labour Party. And both were the targets of Communist attacks, so that George Padmore, during his Moscow years, could in the same paragraph attack "Negro capitalist misleaders, like Marcus Garvey" and "the white trade union faker, Captain Cipriani, in the West Indies" as "agents of imperialism."[98] Similarly when in 1930 Otto Huiswoud of the American Negro Labor Congress was expelled from Trinidad by the government he accused Cipriani, a "faker" and member of the "treacherous Amsterdam International," of being behind it.[99] Huiswoud was a Communist and long-standing foe of Garvey.

When Garvey decided, therefore, to include Trinidad on his West Indian itinerary for 1937 he immediately obtained Cipriani's assistance, since experience made him anticipate trouble from the Trinidad government. Cipriani conferred with the governor on July 5 and wrote

Garvey (now living in London) on the same day conveying assurances that he would be allowed to land. Garvey's precautions were well-advised, for officials at the Colonial Office, when they became aware of his intentions, did indeed suggest that he should be allowed into the other islands but kept out of Trinidad.[100] The reason for this attitude was that in 1937 Trinidad was in the throes of labor riots and unrest similar to that of 1919. The governor, Sir Murchison Fletcher, apparently unaware of Garvey's illustrious past, claimed to have heard Garvey's name for the first time at the outbreak of the 1937 unrest, when there was a rumor that he and Cipriani would appear in Trinidad together on July 3rd. Governor Fletcher nevertheless preferred to let Garvey in, lest making him a martyr at that particular time might turn out to be the greater of the two possible evils.[101]

On July 21 Garvey called on the Colonial Office. He showed officials Cipriani's letter and claimed that he would not stir up any trouble in Trinidad since in the present world conditions (presumably a reference to his fear of the greater evils of Nazism and fascism) he supported Britain. He went so far, according to the Colonial Office, as to deplore the recent outbreaks in Trinidad. He also agreed to a Colonial Offfice suggestion that he write to the West Indian governors concerning his good intentions. The Colonial Office expressed a belief in Garvey's sincerity.[102]

Garvey's unusual tractability here was in marked contrast to his earlier attitudes. By 1937 his organization was but a shadow of its former self and he had not only been deported from the U.S. but hounded out of Jamaica as well. In his time he had been kept out of the United States for five months (in 1921), practically deported from Canada (1928) and denied entry into Bermuda (1928) when he refused to give written assurances that he would not speak there. He had been jailed several times in the United States and Jamaica on palpably unfair grounds.[103] Now with his financial resources at a minimum and UNIA ranks across the world substantially reduced, Garvey may have considered it wiser to compromise in order to gain entry into Trinidad where he could perhaps rally his members and raise some money from public meetings. The Colonial Office statement that he deplored the Trinidad strikes was strange in the light of several articles of his in his *Black Man* magazine in 1938 in which he supported the strikers and rioters in Jamaica in particular and the West Indies in general. In similar vein with the Colonial Office remarks was a news release put out by the anti-Garvey Crusader News Agency in October 1937 accusing Garvey of attacking the strikers in the Trinidad press. According to this news release the local UNIA president, E. M. Mitchell, promised a cool reception for Garvey unless he could come up with "some satisfactory explanation of the remarks attributed to him."[104] Both the Crusader release and the Colonial Office remarks are further seemingly contradicted by the *Black Man* for August 1937 which reprinted an article in which Cipriani praised the governor for denouncing the "economic slavery" to which Trinidad's sugar workers were subjected.

In any event Garvey arrived in Trinidad on October 20 and was given a big welcome by the local UNIA who arranged a morning meeting for him at the Globe Theatre in Port-of-Spain. In the afternoon a concert was held at the same venue, followed by a Garvey speech. Garvey sailed the same night for British Guiana. He returned on October 26 and addressed UNIA meetings at the Gaiety Theatre in San Fernando, and in La Brea and Port-of-Spain. This very full day included a civic reception in his honor by the Port-of-Spain City Council, no doubt due to the efforts of Cipriani's Trinidad Labour Party which controlled this body. Less than a year previous to this the Labour Party's mayor, Alfred Richards (the same one who founded the Workingmen's Association in 1897) had arranged a similar civic reception on the Lighthouse Jetty for President Franklin D. Roosevelt of the United States who was in transit from a Pan-American Peace Conference.[105]

Despite Garvey's willingness to comply with all the Colonial Office stipulations concerning his visit, the governor of Trinidad still would take no chances. He was allowed to land only upon acceptance of the following written conditions:

a) that he would not hold any public meetings in any open space or park in this Colony;

b) that he would on no occasion or in any public utterance make any reference to or comment on recent disturbances in this Colony;

c) that he would not make any political speech or make any utterance which was calculated to cause disaffection among the people of the Colony or to promote ill will between the different races and classes resident in the Colony.[106]

One immediate casualty of these stringent conditions was an open air welcome meeting which Garvey's supporters had originally planned for a city park.[107] In the *Black Man* Garvey referred to his pleasant two days in Trinidad but said nothing of the restrictions placed on him.

During Garvey's last few years in London (he died there in 1940) the occasional contribution from such places as Belmont, La Brea and Port-of-Spain continued to trickle into his London headquarters.[108] He regularly indulged his love of public speaking at "Speaker's Corner" in Hyde Park at this time, where one of his most illustrious hecklers was Trinidadian Trotskyist C. L. R. James.[109] James nevertheless claims to have been influenced by Garvey during the events of 1919, when he regularly read the *Negro World*. Garvey's African theories, he alleges, "had no sense" but Garvey was preaching resistance, and that was positive.[110] James says that George Padmore, also still in Trinidad in 1919, was similarly influenced by Garvey,[111] which may explain Padmore's 1928 protest at Howard University, among other things.

In the United States, in the last decade of Garvey's life, at least one alleged Trinidadian was among those who tried to continue Garvey's work by founding new organizations based on his teachings. This particular Garvey disciple was one Antonio L. Paez who headed the International Negro Improvement Association of the World operating out of Chicago.[112]

Despite his experiences with the likes of de Bourg and Cyril Crichlow Garvey maintained throughout his career his affection for Trinidadians and an interest in the island's affairs. In 1930 his *Blackman* newspaper (not to be confused with the *Black Man* magazine), commenting on Trinidad's *East Indian Weekly*, praised the progressive nature of Trinidad's Indians and wished them well.[113] In 1933 his *New Jamaican* considered Trinidadians to be leaders in politics, business sense, sports and "general pluck."[114] And in 1939, while objecting to a British scheme to resettle Jews in British Guiana on the grounds of the racial strife that would ensue, he cited the case of Trinidad where, he said, their introduction had caused trouble and their merchants were humbugging local small businessmen.[115]

After Garvey's death in 1940 his followers in Trinidad maintained contact with Garveyites elsewhere, especially in the United States, for many years. This contact was facilitated by *The African*, a Garveyite journal which had subscribers in Trinidad and whose correspondence columns contained many letters from Trinidadians. A central figure in this continuance of Garveyite ideas three decades after they had first entered the island was David R. Modeste. In 1946 Modeste was holding Yoruba classes in Claxton Bay with the help of alphabet sheets and a primer donated by New York Garveyites. By 1947 he was reported as having sixty-two students in a Yoruba school in California, where he was helped by a Mr. G. Springer.[116] Modeste's contributions to African nationalism in Trinidad were manifold. He also taught Amharic and belonged to the Ethiopian Orthodox Church.[117] In 1947, too, the link between the UNIA and organized labor so evident in 1919 was still very much alive. For C. P. Alexander, then president of the Seamen and Waterfront Workers' Trade Union, was in touch with Garveyites during a visit to the United States and contributed an article on labor conditions in Trinidad to *The African*.[118]

Alexander's links with the movement thus illustrate again two linkages which reappear throughout this paper, namely the link between Garveyism and organized labor in Trinidad on the one hand, and that between African nationalism in Trinidad and in the United States (and elsewhere). This calls to mind the words of a secret British government document of 1919 which complained to the American authorities about the spread of Black militancy throughout the world. "It is certain," this document lamented, "that the various negro organizations in the United States will not leave the British colonies alone."[119]

Officers of the Trinidad UNIA about 1927

The names of several officers of the association have already been mentioned in the text and footnotes. The following list comprises those names mentioned in the membership cards for UNIA branches contained in the Central Division (New York) UNIA files housed in the Schomburg Collection at the Harlem branch of the New York Public Library. They are published here both as a tribute to these early toilers in the struggle for African liberation and self-determination and as a possible help to other researchers interested in this topic. The first name in each case is that of the president of the branch. The second is that of the secretary. Addresses are given where they appear on the cards.

Balandra Bay	Francis Lynch; George L. Martineau.
Carapichaima	Richard R. Cuffy, Orange Field Rd., Carapichaima; Augustus Roberts, Colonial Village, Carapichaima.
Caroni	Donald Cuffy; Clarence Harris.
Cedros	F. Greaves; C. N. Sullivan, Bonas Village.
Chaguanas	Joseph Frederick; John Sealy, Endeavour Village.
Couva	John Asson; Ashby K. Robinson, Dow Village
D'Abadie	Richard Brathwaite; J. R. Wilson

Enterprise	David Cyras; L. Sampson.
Gasparillo	Robert Gilkes; Julian Baptiste.
Guaico	Isaiah Phillip; Edward C. A. Phillip.
Iere Village	W. R. McIntosh; Charles Hall.
La Brea	Charles Alfred; Lionel Goncher, Cabeaux Town [sic].
Lily of the Nile	(28 Prince St., Port-of-Spain). E. J. Louis, 28 Prince St.; Miss Catherine S. Richards, 2 Marine Square.
Los Bajos	James S. Henson; Morgan Joseph.
Mucurapo (St. James)	William Beckles, 2 Clarence St., St. James; H. O. Carrington.
Marabella	no names given.
Matura	Herbert Absolam [sic]; Stephen Honow.
Morne Diablo	Isaac Martin, Penal Rock Junction; James E. Cooper, Penal Rock Junction.
Palmira	James Herbert; Livingston Small.
Penal	J. A. Sergeant, Rock Junction, Penal; Thomas Jeffers, Rock Junction.
Port-of-Spain	Joseph Charles; E. M. Joseph, 72 George and 63 Duke Streets.
Princes Town	C. Bowman; Mr. Carr.
Rio Claro	Lewis Charles; Isaac Jackson.
St. Mary (Moruga)	J. M. Jones; L. J. Leotaud.
Ste Madeleine	Henry Stewart; Vincent Arthur.
San Fernando	James Bobb; E. J. Sotere, 21 High St.
Siparia	no names given
Tableland	D. Alleyne; V. Lewis.
Victoria Village	no names given
Williamsville	no names given

Notes

1. For a full list of UNIA branches worldwide, see Tony Martin, *Race First: The Ideological and Organizational Struggles of Marcus Garvey and the Universal Negro Improvement Association* (Westport, Conn.: Greenwood Press, 1976), pp. 361–373.

2. Notes taken by author at a lecture by the late Basil Brentnol Blackman, Secretary-Treasurer, Caribbean Congress of Labour, at the St. Ann's Community Workshop,

Trinidad, in 1969; see also Martin, *Race First*, passim, for more on the Garveyite connections of West Indian labor leaders.

3. Denizens of Belmont will doubtless be familiar with Zampty Lane, named after Mr. Zampty's family. Material relating to Mr. Zampty comes mainly from a conversation between Mr. Zampty and the author recorded in Highland Park, Michigan, on April 17, 1973.

4. C. L. R. James, *The Life of Captain Cipriani* (Nelson, Lancs.: Coulton and Co., 1932), p. 40.

5. E.g., *Negro World*, August 23, 1924; November 29, 1924.

6. *Blackman*, February 15, 1930.

7. Governor J. R. Chancellor to Viscount Milner, Secretary of State for the Colonies, November 30, 1920, Public Record Office, London, Colonial Office records, C.O. 318/356.

8. W. M. Gordon, Acting Governor of Trinidad, to Governor of British Guiana, June 10, 1919, Gordon to Milner, June 18, 1919, C.O. 295/521.

9. *Ibid.*, minute by "G.G."

10. Henry D. Baker to Secretary of State, December 8, 1919, National Archives of the United States, General Records of the Department of State, Record Group (R.G.) 59, 844g, 5045/2.

11. Baker to Secretary of State, October 5, 1919, National Archives of the United States, Records of the Post Office Department, R.G. 28, Box 56, Unarranged #500. There were three wrappers, addressed to Herbert Thompson, St. Joseph; George Thomas, c/o Smith Bros. and Co., Chacon St., Port-of-Spain; and Charles Mariners, 65 Nelson St., Port-of-Spain; see also *ibid.*, Otto Praeger, Acting Postmaster General to Secretary of State, October 30, 1919. (Herbert Thompson appears elsewhere as Herman Thompson.).

12. C. L. R. James says he bought them every Saturday in St. Vincent St., Port-of-Spain, in 1919, despite the ban—"Document: C. L. R. James on the Origins," *Radical America*, II, 4, July–August 1968, p. 24.

13. *Messenger*, July 1919, p. 22.

14. Brinsley Samaroo, "The Trinidad Workingmen's Association and the Origins of Popular Protest in a Crown Colony," *Social and Economic Studies*, XXI, 2, June 1972, p. 219. Samaroo states that some TWA members wore red shirts in solidarity with the Russian revolutionaries of 1917.

15. On Garvey and communism see Martin, *Race First*, pp. 221–272.

16. Acting Governor, Trinidad to Milner, July 29, 1919, Secret, C.O. 295/521; *The Caribbee*, III, 3, March 1935, p. 12.

17. For three occasionally overlapping accounts of the 1919 riots and general upheaval see Tony Martin, "Revolutionary Upheaval in Trinidad, 1919: Views from British and American Sources," *Journal of Negro History*, LVIII, 3, July 1973, pp. 313–326; Samaroo, *op. cit.*; and W. F. Elkins, "Black Power in the British West Indies: The Trinidad Longshoremen's Strike of 1919," *Science and Society*, XXXIII, 1, Winter 1969, pp. 71–75.

18. R.G. 59, 844g.5045/2, *op cit.*

19. Augustus Duncan to Governor of British Guiana, January 9, 1920, C.O. 111/630; Amy Jacques Garvey, ed. *Philosophy and Opinions of Marcus Garvey* (London: Cass, 1967, first pub. 1923 and 1925), Vol. II, pp. 359–362.

20. Chancellor to Baker, February 6, 1920, Baker to Secretary of State, February 7, 1920, R.G. 59, 811.108/929.
21. *Negro World*, September 17, 1921.
22. *Emancipator* (New York), March 13, 1920.
23. Rev. E. Urban Lewis to H. M. Consul, New York, September 24, 1924, Public Record Office, London, Foreign Office records, F.O. 371/9633. On the African Orthodox Church see Martin, *Race First*, pp. 71–73.
24. John Sydney de Bourg, "Relative to the Charges Against Master and Chief Engineer S. S. Kanawha—Black Star Line, Inc.," sworn before American Consul Charles Latham, Kingston, Jamaica, June 14, 1921, National Archives of the United States, Records of the Bureau of Navigation, R.G. 41,122539.
25. Samaroo, *op. cit.*, pp. 208, 210.
26. Baker to Secretary of State, April 2, 1919, A. A. Adee, State Department, to Baker, May 1, 1919, R.G. 59, 844g. 111/-; Baker to Secretary of State, December 8, 1919, R.G. 59, 844g. 5045/2.
27. Garvey, *Philosophy and Opinions*, II, pp. 142, 143, 279.
28. C.O. 318/356, minute of December 9, 1920. Garvey, *Philosophy and Opinions*, II, p. 143, contains among the signatories an I. Braithwaite. The Colonial Office official may have taken this for James Braithwaite. It was in fact more probably I. Newton Braithwaite, co-principal with Trinidad-born Cyril Crichlow of a business school in Harlem. Crichlow is also among the signatories. Similarly a Prince Alfred McConney appears among the signatories. Samaroo *(op. cit.)* mentions a Bruce McConney of the Workingmen's Association deported to Barbados.
29. *Negro World*, February 12, 1921; October 29, 1921; July 2, 1921; July 29, 1922.
30. *Negro World*, June 10, 1922; July 1, 1922. Many of the UNIA members here, as in Cuba, were British West Indian workers.
31. *African World*, June 23, 1923, clipping in C.O. 525/104; *Negro World*, March 5, 1921.
32. *New York Amsterdam News*, October 17, 1923.
33. *Negro World*, August 23, 1924.
34. Garvey, *Philosophy and Opinions*, II, p. 278.
35. Chancellor to Milner, November 30, 1920, C.O. 318/358.
36. *The Argos*, Friday, February 13, 1920, clipping in National Archives of the United States, Records of the American Consulate, Port-of-Spain, 1920 correspondence; Baker to Inspector Costello, February 16, 1920, R.G. 84,840.1/2052; Costello to Baker, February 18, 1920, enclosing report by Sgt. Sylvester, R.G. 84, 840.1/2053; Sylvester to Detective Inspector, February 18, 1920, R.G. 84, 840.1/2054.
37. *Negro World*, August 14, 1920.
38. C.O. 295/521, minute of September 5, 1919.
39. *Emancipator*, April 17, 1920.
40. Chancellor to Milner, November 30, 1920, C.O. 318/356.
41. "Trinidad News Letter," *Crusader*, III, 5, January 1921, p. 23. This report mentions detectives seizing a copy of the *Promoter* from a house in Chaguanas; *Beacon*, August 1931, p. 3.
42. Baker to Secretary of State, March 5, 1920, R.G. 59, 844g. 04417; Baker to Secretary of State, March 5, 1920, R.G. 28, Box 53, Unarranged #398.
43. Quoted in *Negro World*, May 8, 1920.

44. *Report of the Twentieth Annual Conference of the Labour Party, Scarborough, 1920* (London: the Labour Party, 1920?), p. 146.
45. "Calypso Lore and Legend, An Afternoon with Patrick Jones; Stories and Chants from the Lips of the Greatest Oldtime Calypsonian," Cook (1956?), Long Playing record.
46. *Negro World*, May 8, 1920.
47. W. F. Elkins "Hercules and the Society of Peoples of African Origin," *Caribbean Studies*, XI, 4, January 1972, pp. 47–59.
48. *Emancipator*, March 20, 1920.
49. *Negro World*, March 12, 1921.
50. Quoted in James R. Hooker, *Black Revolutionary: George Padmore's Path from Communism to Pan-Africanism* (London: Pall Mall, 1967), p. 8.
51. Col. Hubert F. Julian, *Black Eagle* (London: Jarrolds, 1964), p. 41.
52. *Negro World*, June 4, 1921. It never did get to Africa.
53. Statement by Parris to U.S. Vice-Consul, Kingston, Jamaica, June 17, 1921, R.G. 41, 122539.
54. *Negro World*, May 8, 1920; February 19, 1921; February 4, 1922; *Philosophy and Opinions*, II, p. 365.
55. *Negro World*, May 19, 1925.
56. *Port-of-Spain Gazette*, June 5, 1921, reprinted in the *Negro World*, July 2, 1921.
57. "The Universal Negro Improvement Association . . .," March 7, 1924, C.O. 554/64.
58. *Negro World*, July 2, 1921.
59. On the South African UNIA see Martin, *Race First*, pp. 117–121.
60. *Gold Coast Leader*, August 10, 1922.
61. Gov./18053, destroyed file of March 26, 1923 in the Colonial Office records, Public Record Office. As in the case of many destroyed files, a brief synopsis of its contents survived: "UNIA," March 7, 1924, C.O. 554/64.
62. *Negro World*, July 28, 1923.
63. Governor Wilfred Collet to Rt. Hon. Winston Churchill, July 6, 1922, C.O. 318/371.
64. Churchill to officer administering the government, August 22, 1922, C.O. 318/371; Gov./51931, secret destroyed file, September 22, 1922; Governor Wilson of Trinidad to Churchill, January 20, 1923, F.O. 371/8450.
65. See Tony Martin, "Revolutionary Upheaval in Trinidad," *op. cit*.
66. *Negro World*, August 26, 1922.
67. *Ibid.*, August 15, 1923.
68. Martin, *Race First*, pp. 370, 371. Professor Francis Mark of the State University of New York has suggested to the author that some UNIA branches may possibly have co-incided with branches of the Workingmen's Association. Professor Maureen Warner Lewis of the University of the West Indies (Jamaica) has informed the author that many of the areas named are pockets of relatively strong remembrances of, and identification with Africa.
69. Melville and Frances Herskovits, *Trinidad Village* (New York: Octagon, 1964), p. 263.
70. *Negro World*, December 30, 1922; one report speaks of Black Cross Nurses in the village (presumably) of Choorcoo—*ibid.*, September 30, 1922.
71. *Ibid.*, March 7, 1931.

72. *Ibid.*, September 30, 1922, May 13, 1922.

73. E.g., on April 7, 1929 a Rev. Benjamin of the A.M.E. Church dedicated the new Liberty Hall at Rio Claro—*Blackman*, May 20, 1929; again, in 1924 we have A.M.E. clergyman Rev. Taylor officiating at a UNIA meeting in Penal—*Negro World*, October 4, 1924.

74. *Negro World*, June 14, 1924, February 2, 1924, December 30, 1922.

75. *Ibid.*, December 30, 1922.

76. *Ibid.*, September 20, 1924. There is no indication whether these were U.S. or British West Indian dollars.

77. *Ibid.*, August 19, 1922, September 30, 1922.

78. E.g., *ibid.*, August 30, 1924.

79. *Blackman*, August 12, 1929; *Negro World*, August 2, 1930.

80. *Negro World*, September 17, 1921.

81. *Ibid.*, October 21, 1922.

82. *Ibid.*, December 15, 1923; September 6, 1930; May 9, 1931; November 15, 1930.

83. *Ibid.*, May 13, 1922.

84. Martin, *Race First*, pp. 235, 267 n. 48.

85. *Negro World*, May 13, 1922.

86. For the meeting see *ibid.*, August 23, 1924. *The New Jamaican*, September 1, 1932, contains a reference to Cipriani presiding over the monthly meeting of the Trinidad Workingmen's Association at Liberty Hall.

87. After elections in 1931, the Lily of the Nile executive comprised the following— President, E. J. Louis; lady president, Miss Edith Devonshire; vice-president, James Gollop; general secretary, Miss Mable Clarke; treasurer, Thomas Murdurch; chaplain, James Reid; Board of Trustees, H. J. J. Chortes [sic], Samuel Lord, P. Thompson, James Gollop, E. P. Dair, James Reid, Thomas Murdurch, Edith Devonshire, Mable Clarke, Josephine Baptiste, Floretha Louis, Laura Fox and W. Phipps. See *Negro World*, March 7, 1931.

88. *Negro World*, February 24, 1923. Some reports spell his name "Burrowes," but most omit the "e".

89. *Negro World*, November 18, 1922.

90. Garvey and P. L. Burrows, Secretary-General to J. H. Thomas, H. M. Colonial Secretary, January 25, 1924, C.O. 554/60; *Negro World*, August 16, 1923.

91. *Negro World*, March 28, 1925.

92. *Ibid.*, December 7, 1929.

93. *Black Revolutionary*, *op. cit.*, p. 7; *Negro World*, December 22, 1928; interview with Dr. Cyril Ollivierre, Harlem, New York, 1974; Martin, *Race First*, pp. 261–265. Ollivierre said that the account in *Black Revolutionary* is not entirely accurate.

94. Governor of Trinidad to Lt. Col. L. S. Amery, Secretary of State, Colonial Office, December 20, 1927, C.O. 318/391.

95. Alfredo L. Demorest, Vice Consul in Charge, Trinidad, to Secretary of State, strictly confidential, April 10, 1928, R.G. 59, 844g. 044/3.

96. *Negro World*, October 27, 1928.

97. *Ibid.*, March 3, 1928.

98. George Padmore, *Negro Workers and the Imperialist War—Intervention in the Soviet Union* (Hamburg: I.T.U.C.N.W., n.d.), p. 16.

99. *Liberator* (New York), May 10, 1930, p. 1; the *Liberator*, organ of the Communist-backed A.N.L.C., also attacked Cipriani on December 7, 1929, p. 2. It regularly attacked Garvey.

100. Minutes of July 15 and July 16, 1937, C.O. 323/1518.

101. *Ibid.*, Murchison Fletcher to Sir Mark Young, Governor of Barbados, August 3, 1937.

102. *Ibid.*, two minutes of July 21, 1937; W. Ormsby-Gore, draft letter to governors in the West Indies, July 26, 1937.

103. Martin, *Race First*, passim.

104. This news agency was run by Garvey's long time Communist foe, Cyril Briggs. Mitchell's statement was quoted from *The People*, a weekly paper.

105. *The Caribbee* (Trinidad), Xmas Number, 1936, p. 8. Cipriani himself served on the City Council for close on two decades up to 1941 and was mayor eight times.

106. Governor Fletcher to W. G. A. Ormsby-Gore, November 10, 1937, C.O. 323/1518.

107. *Daily Gleaner* (Jamaica), October 20, 1937.

108. *Black Man*, II, 3, September-October 1936, p. 13; III, 10, July 1938, p. 19.

109. Adolph Edwards, *Marcus Garvey* (London: New Beacon, 1967), p. 33. Edwards says James told him this; also, lecture by James at the University of Michigan, April 2, 1972, notes taken by author. Apart from ideological differences, James was at this time running an organization in support of Ethiopia and Garvey, though as hostile as anybody else to the Italian invasion of Ethiopia, was highly critical of Haile Selassie.

110. Michigan lecture, *op. cit.*

111. C. L. R. James, "Document: C. L. R. On the Origins," *Radical America*, II, 4, July–August 1968, p. 24.

112. Confidential memorandum, "To London," February 12, 1931, R.G. 59,800.00 B—International Negro Improvement Association of the World/7. This organization was said to have been founded in 1929. Some officials investigating Paez identified Garvey as a Trinidadian, so the possibility of a similar error in placing Paez' nationality cannot be discounted.

113. *Blackman*, August 23, 1930.

114. *New Jamaican*, January 18, 1933.

115. *Black Man*, IV, 1, June 1939, pp. 5, 15.

116. *The African*, IV, 5, September 1946, p. 10; V, 6, June–July 1947, p. 5; V, 8, September 1947, p. 9.

117. Told to the author by Professor Maureen Warner Lewis of the University of the West Indies.

118. *The African*, V, 9–10, October–November 1947, p. 16.

119. Secret document "Unrest Among the Negroes," Special Report No. 10, Directorate of Intelligence (Home Office), October 7, 1919, R.G. 59, 811.4016/27.

6

Attempts to Bring Garvey Back to the United States*

Marcus Garvey came to the United States from Jamaica in 1916. He made his first attempts to set up a Harlem branch of his Universal Negro Improvement Association and African Communities League in 1917, and by 1919 had established himself as a leading figure in Black radical circles, not only in Harlem, but in the world. For by 1919 his *Negro World* newspaper was being widely circulated in the United States, Latin America, the West Indies and elsewhere and he had established his Black Star Line, still the most ambitious shipping enterprise ever launched by New World Africans. By 1919, too, he had come to the attention of the United States and British governments, both of which viewed with alarm his activities among their Black subjects.[1]

In the years after 1919 he went on to consolidate his power in the United States and elsewhere, and his following, variously estimated at between one and eleven million worldwide, is generally conceded to be the largest of any Black nationalist organization in Afro-American history.

Garvey's success led to problems with all types of rival organizations and with several governments, not least among them being that of the United States. In 1921 Garvey only narrowly escaped virtual deportation when for several months the State Department and its consular agents in the Caribbean would not give him a visa to re-enter the country after a short trip to the West Indies. The attempt to get him out of the country was resumed with more success in 1922 when Garvey was arrested on a charge of using the mails to defraud. The case was tried in 1923. The prosecution alleged that Garvey mailed, or

*Originally published in 1974

caused to be mailed, a circular containing a misleading prospectus for the Black Star Line. The prosecution could do no better than produce, in evidence, an empty envelope bearing the Black Star Line imprint. The contents of the envelope were not produced. Garvey was nevertheless given the maximum jail term and fine, ordered to pay the costs of the trial, and initially imprisoned without bail pending his appeal. He was later released on very high bail. In 1925 he lost the appeal and entered the federal penetentiary at Atlanta. The government was now able to do what it had long desired, namely ensure that he would leave the United States for good, for aliens convicted of a crime involving "moral turpitude" were under certain conditions liable to deportation. There is some doubt as to whether all these conditions were met in Garvey's case, but the authorities let it be known that he would be deported after the expiry of his sentence.

With Garvey in jail, a massive campaign was launched to obtain his freedom without deportation. The campaign was spearheaded by the *Negro World* and the UNIA hierarchy, but some of his former rivals and enemies joined their voices to the chorus for his release. Many of these now argued that Garvey was not really a crook, as some of them had suggested, but merely a misguided visionary.

As a result of this clamor, President Coolidge commuted Garvey's sentence late in November 1927, but Garvey was nevertheless deported to Jamaica, where he arrived to a hero's welcome in December. Garvey's followers in the United States now turned their attention to trying to effect his re-entry. The attempts were unsuccessful but the doggedness with which they were pursued, practically up to his death in 1940, are an eloquent testimony to the loyalty and devotion of some Garveyites.

The first stratagem employed to circumvent the prohibition on re-entry involved sending Garvey's wife, Amy Jacques Garvey, on a speaking and fund raising tour of the United States while Garvey himself sounded off from nearby Canada. This took place in October 1928, less than a year after the deportation by Coolidge. On their way back from Europe to Jamaica, the Garveys stopped in Canada. Mrs. Garvey proceeded on her speaking tour, Garvey's secretary went to Buffalo to visit relatives, and Garvey proceeded to speak in favor of Al Smith, Democratic candidate in the imminent presidential elections.[2] The Canadian immigration authorities promptly arrested him as he was about to address a Montreal audience and brought him before a board of enquiry of the local immigration office. The result was an order for his deportation under regulations prohibiting political agitators. On Garvey's explanation that he was merely an intransit passenger anyway, he was placed on a $100.00 bond, given until November 7 to leave, and ordered not to indulge in any further public statements.[3] Subsequent trips to Canada in the 1930s proved less eventful.

The *Negro World* presumed that all this must be the handiwork of the Republican Party,[4] and they were correct. For the United States consul general in Montreal unknown, of course, to the public, claimed credit for the action of the Canadian authorities. Writing to the State Department in Washington on the day after the deadline for Garvey's departure, he informed his superiors that Garvey had arrived in Canada two weeks previously and had delivered speeches in support of the Democratic Party. Garvey then, for some strange reason, called at the consul general's office but left before he could be interviewed. Whereupon the consul general's office lost no time in contacting the Canadian immigration authorities and informing them that Garvey was an ex-convict and inadmissable into Canada. The Canadians, in this American official's words, acted "quietly and promptly" against Garvey.[5]

This Canadian episode did not in any way diminish the desire for Garvey's return on the part of his more ardent disciples. A report of 1929, for example, stated that Black Chicago congressman Oscar de Priest and Robert Ephriam, president of the Chicago UNIA, had met together with others to discuss the possibility of getting Garvey back. Garvey at about this time though, said that he would not want to return to the United States except as a private citizen, since rotten U.S. politics had been a source of great trouble to him.[6] This statement notwithstanding, the *Negro World* in 1931 started a campaign for 100,000 signatures to support a petition for Garvey's return.[7] The move was opposed by veteran anti-Garveyist George S. Schuyler and the conservative *New York Age* which thought that Garvey's return would be a calamity.[8]

By 1935 Garvey seems to have changed his mind again for in January of that year he himself wrote the secretary of state and the attorney-general informing them that he wished to spend thirty-five days in transit in New York on his way to England. He wished to obtain medical treatment for diabetes and see friends while there.[9]

For several months in 1934 and 1935 the secretary of the Philadelphia UNIA sent a steady stream of letters to President Roosevelt, the Department of Justice and the Department of Labor's Immigration and

Naturalization Service asking for Garvey's return in spite of his conviction, or failing that then that his conviction be set aside to facilitate his return. He was met by stony official assurances that Garvey's conviction for a crime involving "moral turpitude" made him mandatorily excludable. He therefore found it necessary to remind the assistant attorney-general who was answering his correspondence that "Regardless of whether Mr. Garvey be allowed to return, the program will still go on, for Africa will be redeemed even if the Divine Creator has to raise up supermen in our stead; or use the elements in our behalf as in the days of Pharoah . . ." However, neither his assurances that Garvey had been framed nor the reminder that Black people had voted Democrat nor anything else could make any impression on official stoniness.[10]

Other elements within the UNIA kept up the effort, however, and in 1937 consideration was given to having a special bill introduced if all else failed.[11] Out of these attempts in 1937 and 1938 arose the Second Regional Conference Committee on Mr. Marcus Garvey's Visit to America, chaired by Thomas W. Harvey. This committee wanted a temporary permit which would allow Garvey to remain in the United States from June 1 to August 31 in order to hold an International Convention from August 1 to 17. These efforts also failed, despite the assistance of Senator Theodore G. Bilbo and some of his segregationist cronies who found in Garvey the Black separatist an unlikely but not unwelcome bedfellow of convenience, and despite the blessings of Garvey himself.[12] Representations were still being made to government officials in the latter part of 1939, but by this time Garvey was less than a year away from his grave. Only death could extinguish the hopes of his faithful followers that he might yet one day return to help them battle the monster of oppression.

Notes

1. See, e.g., Tony Martin, "Revolutionary Upheaval in Trinidad, 1919," *Journal of Negro History*, July 1973.
2. Amy Jacques Garvey, *Garvey and Garveyism* (New York: Collier, 1970), p. 195.
3. Public Record Office, London, records of the Colonial Office, C.O. 318/399/76634, Memorandum, [1930]; *New York Times*, Nov. 1, 1928, p. 31, Nov. 8, 1928, p. 26; *Negro Champion*, I, 19, Nov. 3, 1928, p. 8; *Negro World*, Nov. 10, 1928, p. 2.
4. *Negro World*, Nov. 17, 1928, editorial.

5. National Archives of the United States, records of the Department of State, R.G.59, 811.108 G 191/50, Wesley Frost, American Consul General, Montreal, to Secretary of State, Nov. 8, 1928.
6. *Blackman* (Jamaica), June 22, 1929, p. 12; August 16, 1929, p. 7.
7. *Negro World*, August 1, 1931, p. 3.
8. Ibid., pp. 1, 4.
9. Records of the Department of Justice, R.G.60, 198940, Garvey to Secretary of State, Jan. 7, 1935.
10. R.G.60, 39-51-821, Benjamin W. Jones, Secretary, UNIA, Philadelphia, to President F. D. Roosevelt, Sept. 17, 1934; Edward J. Shaughnessy, Deputy Commissioner, Department of Labor, Immigration and Naturalization Service to Attorney-General, Oct. 17, 1934; Keenan to Jones, Oct. 22, 1934; Jones to Keenan, Oct. 27, 1934; Jones to Roosevelt, Oct. 27, 1934; Jones to Roosevelt, Jan. 4, 1935; Keenan to Jones, Jan. 28, 1935; Jones to Keenan, June 3, 1935, and other letters in this correspondence.
11. UNIA Central Division (New York) files, Schomburg Collection, New York Public Library, Box 16, h. 10, A. L. King to Thomas Harvey, Nov. 9, 1937.
12. Ibid., Garvey to Harvey, Jan. 5, 1938; Earnest Sevier Cox to Garvey, Feb. 17, 1938; Cox to King, Feb. 18, 1938; Bilbo to King, Feb. 23, 1938; Harvey to King, March 31, 1938; Harvey to King, May 11, 1938; Ethel Waddell to King, Dec. 1, 1938. R.G.60, 198940, Harvey to Senator George McGill, April 8, 1938.

7

Carter G. Woodson and Marcus Garvey*

Whatever may be said about Garvey's mistakes, he cannot be recorded in history as a fanatic or a fool . . . His claim to be recorded in history lies in the fact that he attracted a larger following than any Negro who has been developed in modern times. Negroes here and there in America have been hailed as leaders, the press has given them great praise, and their friends have sung of their virtues in high tones; but a thorough analysis of these famous Negro leaders will disclose the fact that they owed their prominence mainly to white men who considered such spokesmen as those persons through whom they could work to keep the Negro in his place.
—Carter G. Woodson[1]

. . . men like DuBois, Pickens, Dr. Woodson and a host of lesser men have been stealing from the program and ideas of Marcus Garvey but have not the honesty and courage to give credit to the MASTER.
—Hucheshwar G. Mudgal, editor, *Negro World*[2]

Carter G. Woodson (1875–1950) is generally acknowledged as being one of the most important Black historians. Prolific author though he was, he was no armchair historian but popularized Black history among the mass of people. He also indulged in extensive social commentary and polemicized against all those, exalted or humble, in whom he discerned shortcomings.

Woodson was also, among other things, a contemporary of Marcus Garvey. The *Journal of Negro History*, founded by Woodson, first appeared in 1916, the year of Garvey's arrival in the United States. The celebration of Black History Week, pioneered by Woodson, was begun in 1926, the year before Garvey's deportation to Jamaica. And just as Woodson the historian also indulged in politically activist causes, so too Garvey, leader of the largest mass movement in Afro-America, was also keenly interested in Black history.[3] It stands to reason that the paths of

*Originally published in 1977

101

these two giants of the 1920s should have crossed. Garvey's publications commented regularly on Woodson and his work; the two men had mutual friends and acquaintances; Woodson's political activity brought him perilously close to being drawn into the "Marcus Garvey Must Go" campaign aimed at Garvey's imprisonment and deportation; and Woodson eventually became a regular columnist for Garvey's weekly *Negro World*.

Some of Woodson's earliest contacts with Garveyite circles came through his friendship with John Edward Bruce, Garvey's staunchest supporter among the Afro-American intelligentsia. Bruce, a journalist, historian and political activist, had founded the Negro Society for Historical Research in 1911. In this endeavor he was assisted by Arthur A. Schomburg, historian and bibliophile. Schomburg seemed a little peeved at the appearance of Woodson's *Journal of Negro History* in 1916. It was "a very creditable" effort, he wrote to Bruce, but one which was "stealing our thunder . . ."[4] This did not prevent him from unselfishly promoting Woodson's journal. He sent a copy to the prominent Nigerian churchman Mojola Agbebi,[5] one of whose relatives, Akinbami Agbebi, was soon to become a Nigerian agent for Garvey's Black Star Line.[6]

During a visit to Washington, D.C., Bruce tried but was unable to locate Woodson in order to introduce him to Duse Mohamed Ali, the Egyptian-Sudanese journalist, Pan-African activist and historian who was at that time associated with Garvey's Universal Negro Improvement Association, (UNIA).[7]

But not all of Woodson's early Garveyite contacts came through Bruce. An early contributor to the *Journal of Negro History* was Jamaican historian E. Ethelred Brown,[8] whose articles later appeared regularly in the *Negro World*.

The historical interests of Garvey, Bruce, Ali and Brown are symptomatic of a very widespread interest in Black history among Garvey's lieutenants. Among the editors of the *Negro World* were such professional and amateur historians as Hubert H. Harrison, William H. Ferris and Bruce himself. Other Black historians, such as Schomburg, Ali and J. A. Rogers, could be found among the paper's regular contributors. It comes as no surprise, then, to find that the *Negro World* was a frequent and favorable commentator on the work of Woodson and his Association for the Study of Negro Life and History.

A spate of such commentary took place in 1922 when Woodson accepted a grant of $50,000 from the Carnegie and Rockefeller foundations. Robert Lincoln Poston, sometime UNIA secretary general, acknowledged the predicament that Woodson found himself in. Woodson's cause was worthy and his funds were inadequate. Who was he to counsel Woodson against taking the money in those circumstances? He implored Woodson, though, to be careful, "For nothing could have a more harmful effect on the Negro than a Negro history dictated by white capitalists." William Ferris expressed the same concern, and a *Negro World* editorial commended Woodson on the gift while harboring the same reservations.[9]

The reservations expressed over this gift were rooted in the doctrine of Black self-reliance, one of the ideological rocks upon which the UNIA was built.[10] It was consistent with this position when, in 1927, *Negro World* columnist S. A. Haynes rushed to the support of Woodson in his effort to independently raise $20,000 "for the perpetuation of Negro History." "We are now informed by Dr. Carter Woodson, brilliant historian," Haynes wrote, that only $6,294.27 had been raised. He continued,

> This is an astounding revelation. Millions of useless churches, millions for white-controlled theatres, dance halls, cabarets, and industries, millions to the Jews for fine clothes, millions to the white insurance companies and banks in whose corporate body no Negro presides; millions for the frivolities of life, but not twenty thousand dollars to perpetuate the glory and splendor of our past and present achievements. Where is our pride, our love of self, our conception of vision and intelligence?
> . . . The Negro rightly demands life, liberty, and the pursuit of happiness—but a race that doesn't know where it came from doesn't know where it is going; and it is dangerous for such a race to possess these virtues minus this important compass.[11]

Woodson in the meantime had in 1923 approached Garvey with a request to publish in the *Negro World*. His letter was answered by editor T. Thomas Fortune, who wrote, "Your letter of the 15th instant, addressed to Mr. Garvey, was referred to me. I have deemed it good to publish the synopsis of Miss Sanborn's book, as sent us by you, in the magazine section of the *Negro World* of January 5."[12]

The general work and annual meetings of the Association for the Study of Negro Life and History continued over the years to receive favorable mention in the pages of the *Negro World* and later in Garvey's Jamaican newspapers.[13] But perhaps of greater interest is the fact that works published by Woodson and his Associated Publishers found in Garvey's publications, forums where they could be promptly reviewed by some of Afro-America's most distinguished historians and essayists.

These reviews, though certainly far from hostile, were nevertheless intellectually rigorous, and their authors were forthright alike in their praise and in their criticisms. The *Negro World* of January 14, 1922 announced that a copy of Woodson's *The History of the Negro Church* had been received and would be reviewed. The review, by William H. Ferris, appeared a mere two weeks later, on January 29. Ferris thought that the book was useful but sketchy. A few months later, on November 4, 1922, the *Negro World* carried a review, this time by Arthur A. Schomburg, of Woodson's *The Negro in Our History*. Schomburg lamented the lack of primary sources, found the material on Africa sketchy and questioned Woodson's suggestion that the continent had originally been peopled by mulattoes. He found some factual inaccuracies too, among them the assertion that Denmark Vesey was born in San Domingo (as opposed to St. Thomas). He considered Woodson to have erred in alleging that slavery in the West Indies had been milder than in the United States. He concluded that the book was not suitable for high school use.

Schomburg's review was followed a week later (on November 11) by a complaint from Bruce, who charged that the Negro Society for Historical Research (of which he and Schomburg were the major organizers) had supplied Woodson with photographs of his latest work on the understanding that there would be an acknowledgment. Woodson had not kept his promise, but, Bruce was quick to add, it was not too late. He would be looking for an acknowledgment in the *Journal of Negro History*. This matter seems to have been amicably settled, for on January 17, 1923, Bruce informed Woodson that he would be reviewing *The Negro in Our History* in Garvey's *Daily Negro Times*.[14] A few days later he inquired of Woodson whether he had received a copy of the *Daily Negro Times* containing references by Bruce to the *Journal of Negro History*.[15]

Ten years after the reviews by Ferris and Schomburg, the *Negro World* carried a review by historian Rayford W. Logan of an unnamed Associated Publishers book. The work, authored by Miss Sadie I. Daniel, contained biographical sketches of seven prominent Black women, including Mary McLeod Bethune and Nannie H. Burroughs.[16]

Woodson's most sustained contact with Garvey's organization came in 1931 and 1932, when he wrote a regular weekly column for the

Negro World. The first few articles in this lengthy series were in fact reports of speeches he had delivered (at Fisk University and Morgan State College, among other places). But most of them were original essays. Many of them were later published, with minor revisions, in book form in Woodson's seminal work, *The Mis-Education of the Negro*.[17] In the foreward to that work Woodson revealed that "The thoughts brought together in this volume have been expressed in recent addresses and articles written by the author," but he did not indicate where these articles and addresses had been published. The very first few pages of *Mis-Education* consist of an article which appeared in the *Negro World* under the title, "Negro History Week! He Fails to Learn His Past Altogether."[18]

The first original essay in Woodson's *Negro World* series was a piece entitled "Bicentennial and the Negro." It was not reproduced in *Mis-Education* and is worth quoting from, since it represents a fine example of Woodson's capacity for righteous anger at the antics of those whom he referred to as "genuflecting Negroes," "Negroes of the obsequious type," and "racial toadies," to quote but a few of the choice phrases directed at the unnamed Uncle Toms who formed the subjects of this article. He wrote,

> It was an easy matter to eliminate the Negro from the preparation for the George Washington Bicentennial. The traducers of the Negro race interested in so doing called in a Negro politician who is now being paid off by a job, and had him associate with him as advisors one or two others of the same character.
>
> The compromising mediators between the Negroes and their traducers actually bartered away the claims of the Negro in return for such cheap recognition as service upon a committee to provide for a jim-crow celebration.

Woodson was upset because "Negroes served in practically all of the engagements [of the American revolution] of consequence except those in the extreme South," and therefore "the celebration cannot ring true to history by injecting segregation into it." He was especially infuriated because the martyrdom of Crispus Attucks was being ignored by the bicentennial's organizers. "To pass over this important event," he wrote, "merely because the Negro was the star on that occasion is a most lamentable comment on the bias which permeates historical writing in this country and poisons the minds of the large majority of our self-styled patriots." He listed several other Black accomplishments of the revolutionary period which were being ignored and counselled Black people to remain aloof from the celebration if these deficiencies were not remedied. The proposed jim-crow bicentennial (which would relegate Black folk to one day of the nine months' long celebration) was, Woodson argued, no different from riding in a jim-crow streetcar. Acquiescence would strengthen the hands of those oppressing the race and would "ultimately mean the extermination of the Negro in America."[19]

Though it would be stretching a point to argue that there was a complete identity of ideological positions between Woodson and Garvey, Woodson's articles nevertheless revealed a substantial area of ideological similarity. His ideas were similar to Garvey's on the questions of history, self-reliance, race pride, the fear of reenslavement and extermination, a possible amalgamation of Black churches and frustration with the antics of the "highly educated" element.

Woodson also took a position similar to Garvey on the Booker T. Washington vs. W. E. B. DuBois debate. Garvey was an avowed disciple of Washington.[20] Woodson praised Washington in a *Negro World* article of July 16, 1932 for his observation that "The Negro is segregated from his white neighbor, but white business men are not prevented from doing business in Negro neighborhoods." In 1923 both Woodson and Garvey had guest lectured at Tuskegee during the same week.[21] The index to Woodson's *The Mis-Education of the Negro* contains two favorable references to Washington and nothing at all on DuBois.

In his *Negro World* article of April 9, 1932 Woodson attacked DuBois for having predicted failure for the *Journal of Negro History* when it first appeared. This failure, Woodson noted acidly, "has not yet come to pass." Eleven years earlier William Ferris, from the pages of the same paper, similarly attacked DuBois for predicting failure at the appearance of Duse Mohamed Ali's *Africa Times and Orient Review*.[22] So Woodson, by attacking DuBois in the pages of Garvey's paper, was placing himself in the midst of a long Garveyite tradition. Indeed, even Arthur A. Schomburg had utilized the paper in 1920 to take issue with DuBois. On that occasion several persons had objected to DuBois' receipt of a Spingarn Medal for allegedly starting the Pan-African idea. The objectors all felt that this was a slap in the face to the memory of Henry Sylvester Williams, whose pioneering Pan-African Conference had convened in 1900 in London. Schomburg agreed with the objectors (indeed he himself had collaborated with Sylvester Williams when the latter visited New York), but added, apparently tongue in cheek, that they should not worry about the Spingarn Medal. DuBois, he wrote, was the best recipient so far, "and when it comes to painting sky poetry you got to hand it to the learned professor. Why not leave him alone?"[23]

Woodson's problems with DuBois went back quite a few years. Even though they communicated and on occasion attempted to collaborate, they seem to have had little affection for each other.[24] And in 1935 Woodson even came close to supporting Garvey in his conflict with DuBois. He wrote, "To most practically minded people the Garvey movement made a more successful appeal than the Pan-African idea advanced by Dr. W. E. B. DuBois . . . DuBois' only known program was that of holding biennial meetings which proved so ineffective that the loosely connected association of protesting elements has ceased to function altogether."[25]

Never one to shy away from a controversial subject, Woodson also utilized the pages of the *Negro World* to add his contribution to the continuing debate over West Indian-Afro-American relations which swirled about the UNIA. His comments were contained in an article released to the press by the Association for the Study of Negro Life and History. The West Indian question became, for Woodson, a convenient stick with which to beat the mis-educated but "highly educated" element whom he despised so much.

A *Negro World* headline summarized Woodson's article—"American Negro Still Has Slave Psychology But No Race Pride: West Indian Negro Is Free." Woodson argued that West Indians had achieved a headstart by being (for the most part) emancipated two generations before Afro-Americans. This had enabled them to rise "to higher positions in the industrial and economic life of those parts than we occupy here. They have, therefore," he added, "less of the slave psychology than we have in this country. It requires time and realistic education to emancipate people. We have not had sufficient of either."

After reviewing with approval some West Indian efforts to inject Black materials into school curricula, Woodson concluded in predictable enough fashion—"It would hardly seem out of place to remark that while the 'highly educated Negroes' of this country oppose the teaching of Negro culture these leaders of the West Indies are boldly demanding it. . . ." And then the punchline—"Some of the 'highly educated Negroes' tell me that I am doing wrong to invite attention especially to the race. They say that we are not Negroes. We are American. . . ."[26]

Woodson's *Negro World* articles evoked considerable interest in

UNIA circles. Several of the paper's regular columnists (some of them high-ranking UNIA officials) commented on them. William L. Sherrill, in his column, "As I See It," quoted Woodson on the healthy scrutiny being directed at the Black church. Davis Lee in his "Opinions" column mentioned Woodson's articles. Leslie Bishop in his "Know Thyself" column praised Woodson's ideas on mis-education.[27] And in its section of editorial extracts from the Black press, the *Negro World* quoted the *St. Louis American's* agreement with Woodson's theories on mis-education.[28] Garvey's widow, Amy Jacques Garvey, also quoted extensively from a Woodson *Negro World* article in her biography of her husband.[29]

One of the most interesting responses came from Edward A. Johnson, described as an ex-dean of Shaw University's Law School and a "one time Congressional candidate from New York." He agreed with Woodson that Black graduates received a brainwashing that left them "saturated" with an inferiority complex. This reduced them to mere parasites living off the Black masses. Johnson claimed to have said the same things as Woodson as far back as 1891 when a Black history text written by him was adopted by the State Board of Education of North Carolina. The article continued,

> Regardless of what Dr. Woodson says concerning the lack of interest in the background of the black race by the group today, the fact remains, said the ex-Dean, that these copies of Negro history were eagerly sought for at this early age by thousands. This proves that these people were interested in their own welfare, progress and background.

Johnson was said to be the author of "'Light Ahead for the Negro', 'The Negro History,' and many other treatises."[30]

Not all the reactions to Woodson's articles consisted of unstinting praise, however. *Negro World* editor Hucheshwar G. Mudgal took the similarity of Woodson's ideas to Garvey's to mean that Woodson was plagiarizing Garvey. In an editorial on the same page as a Woodson article he wrote,

> Dr. Carter G. Woodson, the director of the Association for the Study of Negro Life and History, Inc., tells us that he is "not sufficiently informed about his [Garvey's] views" although he as one greatly interested in studying Negro Life and History, should have been the first to study this modern and most dynamic and practical Negro leader and his program which has impressed and alarmed the great imperialist nations of Europe; but even so he has been preaching Garveyism for the last three

months. . . . But we welcome all these men to preach Garveyism under any name they please so long as they are on the right road to racial emancipation.[31]

Mudgal's position is explicable by the fact that several of Garvey's erstwhile adversaries, including DuBois, communist George Padmore and Harlem politician George Harris, had indeed begun to co-opt bits and pieces of Garvey's philosophy and program after his deportation.[32]

Woodson's claim to be insufficiently cognizant of Garvey's views, noted by Mudgal, was on old ploy. Ten years earlier, in 1922, he had used the same excuse to avoid becoming identified with the "Marcus Garvey Must Go" campaign led by A. Philip Randolph, Chandler Owen, and a few others. Despite his participation, together with Randolph and the other anti-Garveyites, in the so-called Friends of Negro Freedom, he refused to be drawn actively into the campaign to discredit Garvey.[33]

Garvey's death in 1940, however, induced Woodson to make a public assessment of the man and his career. His obituary, published in the *Journal of Negro History*, still holds its own as one of the few sensible assessments of Garvey to come from a member of the "highly educated" element, the element to which Woodson belonged by training, if not by sentiment. Woodson paid homage to Garvey as a real leader of masses of Black people and ended, as Garvey might well have done had he been able to write his own obituary, with a scathing attack on those (no doubt "highly educated") "famous Negro leaders" who "owed their prominence mainly to white men" desirous of using them against the best interests of their own race.[34]

Notes

1. "Marcus Garvey," *Journal of Negro History*, XXV, 4, October 1940, p. 592.
2. *Negro World*, May 7, 1932.
3. On Garvey's historical interests see Tony Martin, *Race First: The Ideological and Organizational Struggles of Marcus Garvey and the Universal Negro Improvement Association* (Westport, Conn.: Greenwood Press, 1976), pp. 81–88.
4. Schomburg to Bruce, June [?] 13, 1916 [?], John E. Bruce Papers, Schomburg Collection, New York Public Library, quoted in Martin, *Race First*, p. 83.
5. Mojola Agbebi, director, Niger Delta Baptist Mission, Lagos, to Woodson, July 5, 1916. Agbebi promised to publicize the journal in his own magazine, *Imole Owuro*—Carter G. Woodson Papers, A69, box 5, Manuscript Division, Library of Congress.

6. Martin, *Race First,* p. 164.

7. Bruce to Woodson, January 25, February 8, 1922, Woodson Papers, folder 77, box 5.

8. E. Ethelred Brown of Church Street, Kingston to Woodson, enclosing article on "The Problem of Labour in Jamaica," Woodson Papers, B71, box 5. Brown's article was published as "Labor Conditions in Jamaica Prior to 1917," *Journal of Negro History,* IV, 4, October 1919, pp. 349–360.

9. *Negro World,* June 24, 1922, July 1, 1922.

10. See Martin, *Race First,* pp. 22–40.

11. *Negro World,* June 18, 1927.

12. T. Thomas Fortune to Woodson, December 21, 1923, Woodson Papers, folder 85, box 5.

13. E. g., *Negro World,* September 27, 1924, November 21, 1931, November 28, 1931; *Blackman,* July 13, 1929; *New Jamaican,* February 21, 1933.

14. Bruce to Woodson, January 17, 1923, Woodson Papers, folder 77, box 5.

15. Bruce to Woodson, January 20, 1923, Woodson Papers, folder 77, box 5.

16. *Negro World,* January 23, 1932.

17. (Washington, D.C.: Associated Publishers, 1933, 1969).

18. *Negro World,* February 7, 1931.

19. Ibid., December 26, 1931.

20. Martin, *Race First,* pp. 280–283 and passim.

21. Kenneth J. King, "The American Background of the Phelps-Stokes Commissions and Their Influences in Education in East Africa, especially in Kenya," Ph.D. dissertation, Edinburgh University, 1968, p. 327.

22. Martin, *Race First,* p. 292.

23. *Negro World,* June 26, 1920. Garvey wrote a favorable obituary on Schomburg's death. He had met Schomburg once or twice, he said, and they "shared the mutual friendship of others." He contrasted Schomburg with the "race blunderer" DuBois—*Black Man,* III, 10, July 1938, pp. 1, 2.

24. E. g., Herbert Aptheker, ed., *The Correspondence of W. E. B. DuBois: Volume I* (Amherst: University of Massachusetts Press, 1973), pp. 311–312, 448–449. Here, as elsewhere, Aptheker manages to cast DuBois in the glow of sweet innocence, while suggesting that the fault lay with the other party, in this case Woodson.

25. Carter G. Woodson, *The Story of the Negro Retold* (Washington, D.C.: Associated Publishers, 1935), p. 228.

26. *Negro World,* April 18, 1931.

27. Ibid., November 21, 1931, March 26, 1932, June 18, 1932.

28. Ibid., October 10, 1931.

29. Amy Jacques Garvey, *Garvey and Garveyism* (Kingston: A. J. Garvey, 1963), p. 68.

30. *Negro World,* February 14, 1931.

31. Ibid., May 7, 1932.

32. E. g., Martin, *Race First,* pp. 261–263, 309–310, 332.

33. Ibid., pp. 320, 324.

34. *Journal of Negro History,* XXV, 4, October 1940, pp. 590–592. There were a few minor factual errors here—e.g., Garvey's date of arrival in the United States was given as 1906 (instead of 1916), and the *Negro World* was called *The Voice of The Negro.*

8

Garvey and the Beginnings of Mass-based Party Politics in Jamaica*

Strike out the name of the white man on the ballot paper on election day in January, so that we can have a full body of men after election to speak for us and represent the thought of the people. . . . All I am asking you to do is to love yourselves.

—Marcus Garvey[1]

. . . we do not refuse to be governed by the Mother Country, and to remain a part of the great British Commonwealth, but we do object to be ruled and governed by ignorance, and therefore . . . as British subjects, we think it right for England to give us representations [sic] in the Mother Parliament, or give us Dominion Status as they have given to Canada. . . . The same is said of Australia and barbaric South Africa, and if [South] Africa can say that I do not see why we cannot say the same thing in cultured Jamaica.

—Marcus Garvey[2]

If Garvey's plans for Liberian colonization had been successful he may well have relocated there in the mid-1920s. If the United States authorities had not deported him he might well have remained in that country. As it was, Garvey returned home to Jamaica in December 1927 and promptly proceeded to dominate the nationalist political scene, building, in the process, one of the pioneer modern political parties in the Anglophone West Indies.[3]

By 1927 Garvey was, of course, no stranger to Jamaican politics. Through workers' struggles, through his participation in the National Club, and through his leadership of the UNIA in Jamaica from 1914, he had amassed a wealth of experience prior to emigrating to the United

*Delivered as a conference paper in 1976

111

States in 1916. And during his almost twelve years in the U.S. he maintained contact with Jamaica. In 1921 he suggested that Jamaican workers should unionize and elect their own representatives to the legislative council.[4] In 1923 the Kingston UNIA formed The Jamaica Political Reform Club which, though under UNIA auspices, was open to anyone wishing to take an active part in Jamaican politics. Fifty-four people were reported to have enrolled at its first meeting.[5]

The fear of a Garvey return to Jamaica had plagued some British colonialists, both in Jamaica and in London, for several years. In 1921, shortly after Garvey, on a visit home, had experienced difficulty in obtaining re-entry into the United States, a British Colonial Office official wrote, "Garvey is a very dangerous man. . . . Unfortunately he is a native of Jamaica and from that Colony we could not deport him."[6] In 1926, with Garvey's deportation from the United States seemingly imminent, the governor of Jamaica made an unsuccessful attempt to have London intercede with the U.S. officials against sending Garvey home.[7] Garvey sought to allay the fears of the colonialists on his return home by promptly disavowing any intention of seeking election to the legislative council.[8] He soon changed his mind though, and Governor R. E. Stubbs moved quickly to try and head him off. In February 1928, "after a long talk with Garvey," he set forth his position in a despatch to the Colonial Office. He compared Garvey with Sun Yat Sen of China. His observations are a singular mixture of sound insight and a colonialist mentality. He wrote:

> [Garvey] reminds me curiously of San Yat Sen. There is the same devotion to an idea—possibly spurious but, if so, wonderfully well counterfeited—; in Sun's case the unification and independence of China; in Garvey's the improvement of the status of the black races. They both have the same magnetic power over men, even quite intelligent men, and in each case there is the same childish vanity, incessant talk of 'my organization', 'my party', 'my ideals' etc. In both cases I got the same impression that while the man was genuinely zealous for the cause, he would rather see it fail under himself than succeed under anyone else. In both cases this vanity has led the man into absurdities; Garvey as Emperor of Africa; Sun as President of the Southern Republic. The main difference is that Sun was honest in money matters; . . ."

Stubbs thought that Garvey himself was not a particularly harmful character but his "followers, being mostly men by no means so well educated as himself or so skilled in the meaning of words," might misinterpret his pronouncements as a call to violence. The governor at this point was undoubtedly confused by Garvey's ability to uncompromisingly champion the cause of the disfranchised Jamaican masses while simultaneously employing the rhetoric of loyalty to the British empire. In any event he proposed amending existing laws specifically to remove any possibility of Garvey being elected to the legislative council. Under his proposals ex-convicts would be debarred from voting (and therefore, under existing legislation, from running for office) regardless of whether the sentence had been served or not. Alternatively, such persons would be ineligible to hold public office for ten years, regardless of where the imprisonment had taken place. (Garvey, of course, had been jailed in the United States on a trumped up charge of mail fraud). Such legislation was deemed necessary because Garvey on the legislative council would be "bound to take up the position that the negro is being kept out of his rights and a series of speeches to that effect will pre-dispose the lower classes to violent action if, as must be expected, there comes a bad year for crops and they feel the pinch of hard times."[9] By this time there were ample precedents in the West Indies and Africa for laws passed by British administrations specifically to deal with Garvey and Garvey-inspired activities. Among them were Seditious Publications ordinances passed in several West Indian territories in the early 1920s and laws such as the 1924 Undesirable Persons (Prevention of Immigration) Ordinance introduced into Sierra Leone to forestall Garvey's projected African tour.[10]

On this occasion, however, the Colonial Office officials were uniformly against the idea of special legislation. They agreed that such a stratagem would be tactically unwise and from their arguments it would appear that they were not entirely aware of the existing precedents. One official argued: "There is no precedent for a disqualification such as that proposed . . . it would be regarded as being, 'The Marcus Garvey (disqualification from election) Law'. . . . It is extraordinary that a man of Sir R. Stubbs' intelligence should not see this."[11] Another official, E. R. Darnley, argued that "Legislation ad hoc and obviously if not ostensibly in personam" would be an unpalatable admission of fear on the part of the British administration. He alluded to Garvey in terms unusually favorable for one in his position and reminiscent of Stubbs' own observations. Clearly Garvey was able to win the respect of at least some colonialist functionaries, even as they plotted to crush him. Darnley wrote,

I cannot follow the Governor in his indiscriminate condemnation of convicts. The list of them includes Jesus Christ, Bradlaugh, Parnall and innumerable others who will be remembered when Sir Edward Stubbs is forgotten, although, no doubt, they were highly inconvenient to the Government of the day. Imprisonment is the common penalty of the more drastic political and social reformers and other innovators, but if it were not for such innovators we should never have excelled the monkey.

Marcus Garvey specially excluded from the council and provided with a marketable grievance might well be more dangerous than Marcus Garvey on the Council, and if the electors of Jamaica emulated those of the United Kingdom in the case of John Wilkes, the Colonial Government would find itself involved in difficulties mainly attributable to its own unwisdom.

Darnley's condemnation of the Jamaican governor was a little too strong for the Secretary of State at the Colonial Office and he was forced to clarify his statement. "I am sorry that the Secretary of State should have believed that I meant to show contempt of Sir Edward Stubbs," he explained. "I have always reckoned him in the first rank of West Indian Governors. My remark was merely intended to indicate that he is not a conspicuous historical character like Parnell or Bradlaugh."[12]

The Colonial Office eventually turned down Stubbs' request, but with regrets. "I am sorry not to be more helpful," wrote whoever drafted the official reply. "I wish I could, as I know well what a d——d nuisance Garvey will be if he gets into the Council."[13] Yet the local ruling class did not give up the struggle. One year later Garvey reported an attempt, obviously aimed at him, by the legislative council to deprive of citizenship anyone who had ever applied for citizenship elsewhere, even if such foreign citizenship had not actually been obtained. Garvey commented, "Some people really think that they own the world and that by owning the world they may sell it to their friends."[14] As late as October 1929, shortly before Garvey's first electoral contest, local newspapers were spreading the rumor that he could not be elected due to his conviction in the United States.[15]

In April 1928 Garvey left Jamaica on a seven month trip which took him to Europe, Canada (where he was arrested), Bermuda (where he was not allowed to land) and the Bahamas. By this time the prevailing view at the Colonial Office seems to have been one of resignation to an inevitable Garvey victory at the next general elections.[16] But events were to show, again, that the local ruling class and its British allies on the spot were much less inclined to prematurely concede defeat.

Shortly after his return home Garvey announced the formation of a Peoples Political Party. Dismissing as nonsense the frequently expressed opinion that party politics could not work in Jamaica, he argued that the government and its non-elected minions acted like a de facto party in the legislative council, so it was time for elected members to organize in a similar fashion.[17]

Simultaneous with his active entry into Jamaican politics, Garvey advanced three major demands. The first was for Black majority rule. On this point his *Blackman* newspaper editorialized:

It is an Axiom that other things being equal
THE MAJORITY MUST RULE
and we shall see that other things are equal.[18]

The second demand flowed from the first and consisted of no less than a call for political independence for Jamaica. The expression used, "dominion status," was simply the terminology then utilized within the British empire to denote the de facto independence soon to be granted to the "white" colonies of Canada, Australia, New Zealand and South Africa. It implied, for the white "dominions," (and for most of the Black and brown British colonies which became independent many years later) a continued ceremonial allegiance to the British crown. Garvey had no problems with this. Hence his expressions of loyalty to the British empire were not necessarily inconsistent with his insistent anti-colonial thrust. Besides, it was good tactics. And this anti-colonialism went back at least two decades to his days in the National Club. In 1913, before the formation of the Universal Negro Improvement Association, he was already railing against "the red-tapists, who pull the strings of colonial conservatism from Downing Street, with a reckless disregard of the interests and wishes of the people."[19]

The difference between Garvey's pro-empire statements and his anti-colonial actions were well illustrated during the Empire Day celebrations of 1929. He greeted the occasion with a lot of God Save the King rhetoric, which did not prevent him from sharply attacking Governor Stubbs, who, during the Empire Day celebrations at the Ward theatre, had interrupted the speech of a Black Rev. J. T. Hudson. Stubbs ordered Hudson to shut up when he mildly criticized the British empire. Garvey reprintd the whole speech in the *Blackman*.[20] This paper, begun as a daily on March 30, 1929, greatly facilitated Garvey's entry into Jamaican politics.

Garvey's third basic demand was for a West Indian federation, a logical step for one who had long advocated the unity of African peoples and the linking of Third World struggles. In May 1929 the *Blackman* editorialized: "Federation of the West Indies with Dominion status is the consummation of Negro aspiration in this Archipelago."[21]

These three basic demands reflected the same tendency to long-range planning that had characterized Garvey's North American period. The first phase of this West Indian plan would involve a PPP foothold in the Jamaican legislative council. Phase two would call for the democratisation of the political system and majority rule, leading to phase three, dominion status for Jamaica. Phase four would see an independent Jamaica launching an initiative throughout the islands to stimulate their own drives towards majority rule and incorporation within the West Indian federation. This West Indian plan was similar to that which Garvey had earlier intended to put into effect in Africa, using Liberia as a base. It is similar to the Pan-African plan that Kwame Nkrumah, an admirer of Garvey, used with partial success operating out of Ghana nearly three decades later. Garvey's West Indian federation would reach out to embrace the non-English speaking islands. In the UNIA, which had branches throughout the Caribbean area (English, French, Spanish and Dutch speaking), Garvey had a ready made vehicle to push for federation, and he intended to use it for this purpose when the time was ripe.[22]

The PPP received its first opportunity to engage in electoral activity several months before the 1930 general election, its major target. In April 1929 the Rev. Dr. F. G. Veitch, described by the *Blackman* as a PPP candidate, won a legislative council bye-election for the Hanover seat by forty-six votes. His opponent campaigned under the slogan of saving Hanover from Garveyism.[23] A mere two months later the PPP won its second victory, this time at a bye-election for the Kingston and St. Andrew Corporation council's No. 2 Urban Ward. The PPP's John Coleman Beecher led with 238 votes, followed by a Mr. Sheerwood, 107, Cyril B. Wilks, 87, T. A. Gayle, 37, and A. Bain Alves, 37.[24] Beecher's association with Garvey dated back to the National Club, and he, like Garvey, had been influenced by the pioneer Black nationalist, Dr. J. Robert Love. He had run for election before but had been badly beaten at the polls.[25] Following his victory Garvey had cause to score his perennial adversaries at the *Gleaner* for commenting that "Voters of the Class Higher Up Kept Away from the Polling Stations."[26]

Fresh from these two victories, the Garvey machine rolled on, two months later, to the spectacular Sixth International Convention of the Negro Peoples of the World, held in Kingston throughout the month of August. Of Garvey's status as a world leader there could by this time have been no doubt. However, this convention could not help but bring it home, in a most pertinent way, to all and sundry. Twenty-five thousand people representing "nearly every Negro organization on earth" were said to have participated in the five mile long parade marking the opening of the convention. Ninety thousand were estimated to have lined the parade route.[27] With this kind of momentum going, and with the general elections less than half a year away, Garvey now loomed as a massive threat to the stability of British colonialism on the island. The British administration therefore reacted swiftly and ruthlessly. In the United States the courts had been a major device for harassing, and finally jailing and deporting Garvey. There he had been arrested and/or harassed for one thing or another during practically all of his international conventions.[28] The British colonialists now set out to emulate their North American co-thinkers, and within six months Garvey would be fined twice and imprisoned once for contempt, sentenced to six months for seditious libel (this conviction was overturned on appeal) and the courts would wrongfully sell the Kingston Liberty Hall.

As a preliminary to judicial harassment the authorities mounted a show of force. At the beginning of the convention extra police were placed in readiness with an extra ten rounds of ammunition each. They were augmented by British troops, the Argyle and Sutherland Highlanders, armed for the occasion with machine guns.[29] The convention had barely begun before the chief justice, Sir Fiennes Barrett Lennard, threatened to jail Garvey forthwith for contempt if he did not produce the books of his organization within half an hour.[30] This was in the case of *G. O. Marke vs UNIA* where Marke, a former UNIA deputy potentate, was suing to satisfy a judgement against the UNIA awarded in New York. Despite the fact that the books of the local UNIA were not technically in Garvey's possession he was summarily fined 25 pounds for contempt. The fine was paid by delegates to the convention.[31] The case itself dragged on for the whole of the convention month. To coincide with the end of the convention the chief justice ordered the Kingston Liberty Hall sold. Many foreign convention delegates were present when it was auctioned for 1,055 pounds.[32] This action was eventually overturned by the supreme court but it was over two years before the UNIA regained its Liberty Hall.[33]

Less than a week after the confiscation of Liberty Hall, the *Black-*

man announced that the first PPP meeting for the upcoming general election (now less than five months away) would be held shortly. "It is to arouse the peasant to the consciousness of his power," the paper editorialized, "that the Peoples Political Party has come into being."[34] The meeting took place on September 9, 1929 at Cross Roads in St. Andrews parish, and Garvey delivered a major speech. He recalled his days in the National Club, when "Men like the late Mr. S. A. G. Cox, Alexander Dixon, Mr. H. A. L. Simpson, Mr. DeLeon and myself fought . . . to break down the power of the plantocracy, and we succeeded, but another class took control of the Council . . . ." He announced that the PPP would soon be holding a national convention at Edelweis Park (his headquarters) to let the people nominate fourteen candidates to contest the elections. The convention would also formulate a platform which would have to be endorsed by all fourteen candidates. In the meantime, he presented an interim fourteen point platform which he hoped would be endorsed at the convention. Much of the speech was taken up with presentation of the fourteen points together with his explanations of each point. The points and his explanations can be summarized as follows:

1. A "larger modicum of self-government for Jamaica." This could be either through direct Jamaican representation in Parliament at London (as in the French colonies) or dominion status.
2. Protection of native labor.
3. Minimum wage legislation.
4. "The expansion and improvement of . . . urban areas, without the encumbrances or restraint of private proprietorship." This was aimed at big landowners who held idle lands adjacent to towns.
5. Land reform. The bulk of the land, he said, was owned by one percent of the population. He would tax huge landowners and force them to make unused land available to small holders. His uncle, a sharecropper, had been chased off his land on a trumped up charge before harvesting his crops. This kind of thing was still happening. He planned to change all that.
6. The United Fruit Company and other large corporations would be forced to contribute (e.g. hospitals, universities, docks) to the areas where they were extracting their billions.
7. The "promotion of Native industries," to end unemployment and its resultant emigration, leading to suffering in such places as Cuba.

8. A university and polytechnic with night courses.
9. "A National Theatre in Jamaica, where we can encourage Negro arts."
10. The impeachment of judges who abuse their authority.
11. Legal aid.
12. A law against procuring votes by duress, especially where this involved an abuse of the employer/employee relationship.
13. Granting Montego Bay and Port Antonio "the Corporate rights of Cities."
14. Upgrading the Kingston Race Course into a National Park.[35]

The next step on Garvey's well-organized campaign was to be a ten day tour of all of the country's fourteen parishes. He would take his program directly to the people and lay the groundwork for the national convention which would select candidates and endorse a platform. Before these plans could be put into effect, however, the colonialists struck again. Just over a month after being fined for contempt, and less than two weeks after the loss of Liberty Hall, Garvey was summoned to court to face new contempt charges. This was on the very first day of his country wide tour. This time the judges claimed to be peeved over "scurrilous abuse of the Court" and remarks capable of "inciting disaffection in the minds of the King's Subjects," arising out of Garvey's explanation of point 10 on his draft manifesto. The judges were armed with affidavits by police inspector John Courtenay Knollys and reporter Oscar Joseph Durant, both present at the PPP's first election meeting.[37] Garvey's alleged contempt was contained in the following remarks:

A law to impeach and imprison such judges who enter into agreements and arrangements with lawyers and other persons of influence to deprive other subjects in the realm of their rights in such Courts of Law over which they may preside; forcing the innocent parties to incur the additional costs of appeals and other legal expenses which would not have been but for the injustice occasioned by the illicit arrangements of such judges with their friends.

Now, this is an evil that Jamaica has suffered from for a long time, and we have not been able to tackle it. The time has come now for us to bring changes, and if we cannot settle it in Jamaica, we are going to settle it in England. We are not going to have judges here who can meet their friends and others in their club houses and connive and conspire to take away an innocent man's property or his rights simply because they want to satisfy their friends. . . . There is no man who is above the law, and if a judge breaks the law he can be dealt with as any other man who violates the law.

. . . the rich man sits beside the judge and the poor man cannot get his rights.[38]

At the contempt trial the supreme court asked for and received a written apology from Garvey, even though he insisted that his statement was not aimed specifically at this court. The three judge panel, with one dissenting, then imposed a sentence of three months in jail and a hundred pound fine, and admonished him for being a "hot headed and foolish man." The dissenting judge favored a heavier fine and no jail.[39] The wrath of the judges was so great that they transgressed one of the rules of colonial etiquette and fined Garvey's white lawyer, Lewis Ashenheim, 300 pounds on two charges of contempt. He was ordered to pay the costs of a third charge. His offence had been to caution against meddling with UNIA property.[40] Representatives of the legal profession approached the chief justice at the exclusive white club where he was wont to hang out, in a vain attempt to stay his action against Ashenheim. He threatened to cite the delegation for contempt too.[41]

Garvey's trial and imprisonment took care of three and a half of the four and a half months remaining to the election campaign. The fine meant a further depletion of campaign funds. But these types of trials and tribulations were nothing new to Garvey, who had been subjected to all manner of harassments and who had been jailed twice during his stay in the United States, not to mention jailed (it is thought) in Costa Rica, arrested in Canada and barred from entering several areas. Once again he manifested that indomitable spirit that had kept him steadfast on his program of racial emancipation through all vicissitudes. On the same day that he was sentenced to jail for contempt, he announced that he would run for the vacant seat in the No. 3 urban ward of the Kingston and St. Andrew Corporation council. The campaign would be handled by the PPP's Councillor John Coleman Beecher.[42] He would thus be running for both municipal and national office at the same time, and from jail.

A few days after entering jail Garvey was officially nominated for the KSAC seat at a PPP conclave attended by 5,000.[43] A month later he was elected. *Blackman* headlines summed up the situation thus: "Marcus Garvey, Negro Leader, Now Prisoner, Is Elected To Represent No. 3 Urban Ward In Corporation Council—An Event Without Precedent In The Political History of The World!" The voting was Garvey, 321 votes and W. F. Bailey, 102 votes.[44]

Almost two months still remained before Garvey's release from jail, however. And as the day drew near, the exact date of his release became a matter for new maneuvering on the part of the British admin- istration. No matter was too small to escape attention if it involved the possibility of harassing Garvey. An unsigned secret memo from the governor's residence to the Colonial Office tells his story:

> [Garvey] was due to come out of prison on the 24th December but we learnt that his release on Christmas Eve would mean that he would be hailed as a 'Black Messiah' and a monster procession from the goal at Spanish Town to Kingston a distance of 12 miles, with bands and all the rest of it, was being organized. That, of course, would not have done at all, so with a secrecy which was highly applauded throughout the Island, Mr. Garvey was released about three or four days before the proper time. He was shown the door of the prison at a moment's notice and found his own way back to Kingston. I think he came back in a Police car which we sent out to assist him![45]

Upon his release Garvey took his oath of office on the KSAC council and was able to attend a few meetings before the powers that be (this time with the local ruling class taking the initiative) struck again. His seat was declared vacant since he had missed three consecutive meet- ings while in jail, and this though his application from jail for leave of absence had been refused. The council was dominated by the class that Garvey opposed and, buttressed by the opinion of their counsel, Nor- man Washington Manley, they had their way.[46] At this point the legis- lative council elections were less than three weeks away.

Simultaneous with these problems on the KSAC council, Garvey was trying his best to pick up the pieces of his election campaign. Within days of his release he resumed his tour of the parishes, cut short by the judges three months earlier. He also opened election headquarters at 107 Water Lane.[47] Then came a revised twenty-six point manifesto, consisting of the earlier fourteen points plus an addi- tional twelve. The new points can be summarized as follows:

1. Workmen's compensation.
2. At least sixty per cent of local labor to be employed on "all indus- trial, agricultural and commercial activities. . . ."
3. An eight-hour working day.
4. Free secondary and night school education in each parish.

5. A public library in each parish.
6. The appointment of official court stenographers.
7. A government loan of at least three million pounds to develop Crown lands and thereby create "employment for our surplus unemployed population, and to find employment for stranded Jamaicans abroad;" also to purchase ships to facilitate the marketing of local produce.
8. The expansion of electrification "to such growing and prospering centers as are necessary."
9. Prison reform.
10. Health outreach programs for rural areas.
11. Decent low priced housing for the peasantry.
12. An end to profiteering "by heartless land sharks" "in urban and suburban areas to the detriment of expansion of healthy home life for citizens of moderate means."

Garvey's manifesto was progressive by any standard. At least twelve of the twenty-six planks spoke directly to the immediate needs of workers and peasants. Another eight planks spoke to areas of broad social concern (free education, libraries, etc.), designed to raise the educational and cultural levels of the broad mass of Jamaicans. The oppressed classes obviously stood to benefit most from these. At least four planks directly sought to curb the power of multi-national corporations, landowners and the local capitalist class. In addition most of the twenty-six provisions could only succeed at their expense. The provisions for self-government and the impeachment of judges were of course direct challenges to British colonialism.

The crowd which was on hand to hear Garvey present his twenty-six points cheered repeatedly. Cheering was reportedly loud and long for the planks dealing with the minimum wage, eight-hour day, free secondary education, legal aid, an end to procuring votes by duress, the government loan to increase employment, the National Park for Kingston, cheap housing for the peasantry, and a move against the land sharks. Cheering was "almost deafening" for the planks calling for workmen's compensation and a minimum of sixty per cent local labor in all areas of employment.[48]

The coincidence of class and color in Jamaica became a focal point of Garvey's campaign, since his main opponent for the St. Andrew seat which he contested was both white and mayor of Kingston up to two weeks before the election, making him an important member of the class that had harassed Garvey, both in and out of the KSAC council.

In his campaign speeches Garvey therefore harped on the principle of race first, as a means of countering the historic injustices heaped upon Black people by the white race."When you look at [Seymour's] face and lanky, overbearing personality," Garvey declared, "you see there the brutal slave master. . . ." He could not understand why, in 1930, "such men have the audacity to come to you and ask you—you the sons of the slaves whom they treated like brutes . . . to allow them . . . to exploit you." The question of white rulers over Black people naturally struck at the heart of Garvey's demand for Black majority rule. He noted that "The Legislative council for several terms past [was] made up chiefly of men of Seymour's race. The Council, during the term before the one that has just come to an end, was made up of men purely of his race. . . ."[49] The task facing voters was clear: "There must not be one white man on the elected side of the House in January. We have white men on the official and nominated side. But the side which the people elects must be represented by themselves."[50]

A few days before the election Garvey came up with a slate of twelve candidates whom he supported. Among them, perhaps surprisingly, was a Mr. R. Ehrenstein, a white man contesting the St. Thomas seat. This was not the first time that Garvey supported a white person he considered a renegade from his own race.[51]

To add to his imprisonment, the loss of his KSAC council seat, and all his other myriad problems during the campaign, Garvey also had to deal with sundry other election malpractices engineered by his opponents. He complained that people were telling taxpayers in Mavis Bank and Guava Ridge in St. Andrew that taxes were going up because of him. At a mass meeting a few days before the election he protested that Herbert George DeLisser, editor of the *Gleaner*, and D. T. Wint, a Black political opponent, were suggesting that he now had Black Jamaicans in a state of disorder similar to the 1865 Morant Bay uprising. For some days prior to the elections rumors were circulating that Garvey had been arrested and jailed again.[52] And to crown this incredibly relentless campaign of pressure, the judges struck again in the last days of the campaign, this time charging him with seditious libel.[53]

The elections were held on January 29, 1930, and Garvey lost. The results in St. Andrew were Seymour—1,677, Garvey—915 and Dillon (Black)—269.[54] One of the governor's aides wrote, in a secret memo:

> Garvey lives in the parish of St. Andrew a select residential area, where is also King's House, and he appeared as a candidate for the parish against a very well-known land-owner, the sitting member who had recently been

Mayor of Kingston. . . . Garvey's people . . . were responsible for rowdy-ism and attempts to break up meetings. But the result was that all the decent people in St. Andrew rallied to the support of the sitting member—many bed-ridden old ladies going down to record their votes for him—and Garvey was very heavily defeated.[55]

Garvey's initial response to the loss was to angrily blame the voters for having sold themselves for a mess of pottage. He could not afford to spend on rum and transportation to the polls like the other candidates, he said. He had based his campaign solely on his programme.[56] There were factors militating against Garvey, however, which were beyond his control. A *Blackman* editorial addressed itself to these:

In Jamaica there is no universal suffrage. The bulk of the population is Negroes, with a very small proportion of them enjoying the franchise. According to the last census, there are 900,000 people in the island, of which 700,000 are Negroes. We will be very near correct in saying that of the 900,000 population only about 112,000 are registered. . . . The supporters of the Universal Negro Improvement Association, we are told, are the voteless unit, and that being so, a paltry eighty or ninety thousand Negroes voting at a general election (although they did not all vote for the successful candidates), is no evidence whatsoever that [Garveyism] is on the wane.[57]

As for Garvey himself, his disappointment at his election reverse did not last very long. He bounced back with his accustomed resiliency and was soon explaining that this was only a retreat, not a defeat. The PPP had fared better, despite everything, than the British Labor Party on its first election bid. And his paper noted, correctly, that reform is, in general, in advance of its time ". . . yet, such movements eventually succeed. Not today, not tomorrow, perhaps, but eventually. And the leaders of such movements are acclaimed, their country prospers and their names go down in succeeding generations."[58]

In this post-election period Garvey also defended two of the major charges brought against him by the Jamaican ruling class. The first was the charge of racism. On this the *Blackman* editorialized: "It is unfortunate that in this country the proletariat or common people belong to a group that is ethnologically described as Negroes, and when one stands up for their economical, social or industrial advancement, the cry goes up that racial antagonism and colour prejudice are being disseminated among the people."[59] The other charge was that his manifesto was socialistic. On this Garvey retorted: "The United Fruit Company makes millions of dollars every year through the banana industry. Why could not your Government do the same? You would say that would be socialistic. Is it not socialistic for the Government to run the Railway?" He continued, "If the Government can plant bananas on the Prison Farm and sell to the United Fruit Company, the Government can plant bananas on a larger scale throughout the country and thus find employment for the people of the country."[60] Governor Stubbs thought Garvey's proposals to be so "grotesque" that they "could not bear even looking into, still less encouraging."[61]

Such election post mortems did not have Garvey's undivided attention, however, for the seditious libel case, initiated before the election, was tried shortly thereafter, from February 12 to 21, 1930. The judges based their case on a *Blackman* editorial entitled "The Vagabonds Again," which took the KSAC council to task for refusing to hear a lawyer whom the burgesses of Garvey's No. 3 ward had retained, at their own expense, to fight the council's determination to unseat Garvey. The editorial further suggested that the council, a "group of vagabonds," was campaigning for Mayor Seymour, and that as a result of their actions confidence in government was being "sorely tried."[62]

Charged along with Garvey were the PPP's John Coleman Beecher, business editor of the *Blackman*, and Theophilus Augustus Aikman, literary editor of the paper and national secretary of the PPP. (Garvey's official position in the PPP was chairman). The presiding judge was A. K. Agar, Kingston resident magistrate. He refused the defendants a jury trial.[63] Although the editorial had actually been written by Aikman, Garvey received the longest sentence. Indeed so carried away was the judge by his hatred for Garvey that he sentenced him to six months' hard labor. He had to be reminded by the crown solicitor that hard labor could not legally be imposed for such an offense. Aikman was sentenced to three months and Beecher, who had nothing to do with editorial matters, was acquitted. Garvey and Aikman appealed successfully.

Garvey wrote both Governor Stubbs and Phillip Snowdon, the British chancellor of the exchequer with whom he had corresponded while in England, setting forth his objections to these libel proceedings and other harassments. His imprisonment for contempt, he wrote, was a "political dodge." He had learned in advance of the chief justice's intention to convict him from the chief justice's chauffeur, a UNIA member. (The chief justice, according to Garvey, ordered the chauffeur to stop attending UNIA meetings). As for the libel case, Garvey argued that the judge used the courtroom to direct propaganda against UNIA members. The whole thing he saw as a "conspiracy" to prevent him from representing "the interest of the poor working and labouring classes and give them a voice that may probably help them to improve and better their condition."[64]

The libel charge was designed to do several things—first it was a "dirty trick" timed to do maximum harm to Garvey's campaign for the legislative council; second, it was part of the general campaign to tie up as much of Garvey's time and money as possible in court cases; third, if successfully prosecuted it would have put Garvey behind bars again for six months; and fourthly, if Garvey went to jail he would once more have lost his seat on the KSAC council.

On the same day that the libel case began the *Blackman* announced that Garvey had decided to enter the bye-election for his former KSAC council seat. The two other candidates, Cyril B. Wilks and E. A. Walters, therefore withdrew and Garvey was returned unopposed.[65] This was a mere two weeks after the legislative council elections. The swearing in ceremony took place a few days after the end of the trial and was marked by anti-Garvey filibustering and much general harassment. Garvey was warned that he was not qualified to sit on the council and much was made of the libel conviction.[66] He nevertheless could not be stopped this time, so in September 1930 the colonialists dissolved the whole council for a year using as a pretext an investigation into corruption on the part of some other councillors. Garvey and the PPP held protest meetings and the *Blackman*, none daunted by the recent libel proceedings, decided that the time for self-government had come, since the forcible dissolution of the council was "a most despotic act."[67]

Garvey was re-elected to a reconstituted council in 1931 while away in Europe and served until late 1934 when he declined to seek further re-election due to his impending relocation to England.[68] During this period he welcomed the formation of the Kingston Civic Voters League,[69] gave some qualified support to former members of the British West Indies Regiment who were demanding the vote,[70] and continued to make favorable utterances on the subject of socialism.[71]

Garvey's last few years in England (where he died in 1940) coincided with the workers' struggles in Jamaica which ushered into existence the Peoples National Party (PNP) and the Jamaican Labor Party (JLP), the two parties that have dominated Jamaican political life ever since. The strikes and riots met with his approval, as did the appointment of a

British royal commission into the matter. He disapproved, however, of the appointment of his old adversary, Sir Reginald E. Stubbs, as chairman, while welcoming the inclusion of the Labor Party's Sir Walter Citrine.[72] Eight years earlier, during Stubbs' administration, Garvey had called for a royal commission to investigate his persecution.[73] He submitted a memorandum to the 1938 commission.[74]

With Norman Washington Manley, who later emerged as head of the PNP, Garvey had had some unusual contact. For Manley, a prominent lawyer during the life of Garvey's PPP, became something of a fixture in legal proceedings against Garvey and the UNIA. In 1929 he appeared for the applicants in the case of *Bourne vs. UNIA*.[75] When Garvey was unseated by the KSAC council in 1930 it was partly on the opinion of Manley, who was retained by the council in that matter.[76] Later that year Manley represented the plaintiff, Mrs. Barnes Haylett, in a libel suit against Garvey and the *Blackman*. She was awarded thirty pounds on a claim for a thousand pounds. Garvey defended himself.[77] Yet Garvey approvingly called him "our popular barrister" and " a first rate man" when Manley became a king's council in 1932.[78] Garvey's Edelweis Park headquarters in 1939 became PNP headquarters.[79] In August 1941 a PNP meeting chaired by N. N. Nethersole stood in silence for a few minutes as a mark of respect for the fallen hero.[80] In 1938 Garvey welcomed the entry of the JLP's Alexander Bustamante into politics.[81]

As in the case of his activities in North America Garvey's political struggles in Jamaica were both a failure and a success. He can be said to have failed in so far as he was thwarted in his bid to consolidate his party and move towards Black majority rule, self-government and West Indian federation. But this is to take a very narrow view. He successfully demonstrated that political parties could work in Jamaica and in the process indoctrinated and politicized the workers and peasants on a scale probably more massive than they had experienced before. The hundreds and thousands who followed Garvey and attended his meetings were well-represented among the rioters and strikers of the late 1930s. In a way the leaders who emerged from these later struggles were more fortunate than Garvey. For one thing, they could build on foundations already laid by him. And people like Bustamante and Manley were able to reap the benefits of widespread and violent challenges to British colonialism. Garvey often cautioned his followers, at least in public, to be "constitutional," but there is no telling what may have happened if he had been fortunate enough to walk into a ready made situation of mass unrest, such as was the case in 1938. The fact that the post-Garvey violence was Pan-Caribbean in nature and came at a time when British imperialism was about to be severely weakened as a result of World War II, are also objective advantages that Garvey could certainly have used.

S. J. Garrick, a JLP organizer, was correct when he observed in 1941 that "if there wasn't a U.N.I.A. there could be no PNP or JLP. . . ."[82]

Notes

1. *Blackman*, December 27, 1929, p. 1.
2. Ibid., September 11, 1929, p. 7.
3. On Garvey's Liberian schemes see Tony Martin, *Race First: The Ideological and Organizational Struggles of Marcus Garvey and The Universal Negro Improvement Association* (Westport, Conn.: Greenwood Press, 1976), Chapter 7, "Africa." On his deportation see, ibid., pp. 196–205. For other treatment of the same general period covered in this article see Amy Jacques Garvey, *Garvey and Garveyism* (Kingston: A. J. Garvey, 1963), Chaps 31–37; Amy Jacques Garvey, "Political Activities of Marcus Garvey in Jamaica," *Jamaica Journal*, June 1972, pp 2–4, reprinted in John H. Clarke, ed., *Marcus Garvey and the Vision of Africa* (New York: Random House, 1974), pp 276–83; Rupert Lewis, "Garveyism in Jamaica" in E. David Cronon, ed., *Marcus Garvey (Englewood Cliffs, N.J.: Prentice-Hall, 1973), pp. 154–60*.
4. *Daily Gleaner*, June 2, 1921, p. 6, quoted in Adolph Edwards, *Marcus Garvey* (London: New Beacon, 1967), p. 15.
5. *Negro World*, September 1, 1923, p. 4.
6. Minute, July 28, 1921, CO 318/364, Colonial Office records, Public Record Office, London. On Garvey's 1921 efforts to re-enter the U.S. see Martin, *Race First*, pp. 184–187.
7. Destroyed file, March 31, 1926, register of correspondence for the West Indies, 1926, OAG/8674, Colonial Office records; ibid., destroyed file May 6, 1926, FO/8674.
8. Lenford Sylvester Nembhard, *Trials and Triumphs of Marcus Garvey* (Kingston: The Gleaner Co., Ltd., 1940), pp. 116–117
9. Governor R. E. Stubbs to [Sir S.] Wilson, Colonial Office, February 24, 1928, CO 318/391/56634.
10. Martin, *Race First*, pp. 94–96, 115.
11. Minute by R. R. Sedgwick[?], March 12, 1928, CO 318/391/56634. Of course he could have been correct if he meant that despite general precedents of special laws against Garvey, there was no precedent for the specific facts of this case, namely denying a person the right to run for office. See also, ibid., minutes by S. H. [E?], March 15, 1928, J. S. R., March 15, 1928, and G. G, March 16, 1928.
12. Minutes by E. R. Darnley, March 13, 30, 1928, CO 318/391/56634.
13. Draft of reply from Colonial Office to Sir. R. E. Stubbs, March 27, 1928, ibid.
14. *Blackman*, April 18, 1929, p. 7. Garvey had taken out his first citizenship papers in the United States.

15. *Blackman,* October 14, 1929, p. 7. quoting the *Jamaican Mail* of October 8 and the *Gleaner* of October 9, 1929.
16. Draft of Colonial Office to Lord Snowdon, June 14, 1928, CO 318/391/56634.
17. *Blackman,* April 12, 1929, p. 3.
18. Ibid., April 16, 1929, p. 2.
19. Marcus Garvey, "The British West Indies In the Mirror of Truth," *Africa Times and Orient Review,* October 1913, p. 159.
20. *Blackman,* May 28, 1929, p. 2, May 28, 1929, p. 1.
21. Ibid., May 2, 1929, p. 2. See also ibid., May 16, 1929, p. 2; *New Jamaican,* September 9, 1932, pp. 1, 5.
22. Amy Jacques Garvey, *Garvey and Garveyism* (Kingston: A. J. Garvey, 1963), p. 204; Nembhard, *Trials and Triumphs,* p. 92. For Garvey's Liberian plan see Martin, *Race First,* pp. 122–137; for a list of UNIA branches in the West Indies (and the world) see ibid., pp. 15, 16, 359–73.
23. *Blackman,* April 25, 1929, p. 1, April 26, 1929, p. 7.
24. Ibid., June 27, 1929, p. 1.
25. Ibid., June 4, 1929, pp. 1, 7, November 6, 1929, p. 2.
26. Ibid., June 28, 1929, p. 1. He called the *Gleaner* "the unofficial Government of Jamaica"—Ibid., July 8, 1929, p. 1.
27. *Negro World,* August 10, 1929, p. 1; *Blackman,* August 2, 1929, p. 1.
28. Martin, *Race First,* p. 187.
29. *Blackman,* August 5, 1929, p. 1.
30. Ibid., p. 4.
31. Ibid., August 8, 1929, p. 1, August 13, 1929, p. 5. For more on this case see Garvey, *Garvey and Garveyism,* pp. 193–94.
32. *Blackman,* September 4, 1929, p. 7.
33. Ibid., August 30, 1930, p. 2; December 13, 1930, p. 5; October 24, 1931, p. 8.
34. Ibid., September 7, 1929, p. 4.
35. Garvey, *Garvey and Garveyism,* p. 196, lists the fourteen points. The embellishments can be found in *Blackman,* September 11, 1929, p. 7, September 12, 1929, pp. 1, 7.
36. *Blackman,* September 13, 1929. p. 1.
37. Ibid., September 14, 1929, p. 3.
38. Ibid., September 12, 1929, p. 7.
39. Ibid., September 26, 1929, p. 7, September 27, 1929, p. 1. The judges were Chief Justice Sir Fiennes Barrett Lennard, Mr. Justice C. E. Law, and Mr. Justice Adrian Clark, dissenting.
40. Ibid., October 1, 1929, p. 1, September 14, 1929, p. 4.
41. Interview with Mrs. Amy Jacques Garvey, Kingston, March 6, 1972.
42. *Blackman,* September 27, 1929, p. 1.
43. Ibid., October 1, 1929.
44. Ibid., October 31, 1929, p. 1.
45. Secret unsigned memo from King's House, Kingston, June 30, 1930, CO 318/399/76634. See also *Blackman,* December 20, 1929, p. 1.
46. *Blackman,* December 31, 1929, p. 1, January 6, 1930, pp. 1, 7, January 14, 1930, pp. 1, 7, January 13, 1930, pp. 1, 2; Garvey to Rt. Hon. Phillip Snowdon, Chancellor of the Exchequer, February 27, 1930, CO 318/399/76634.

47. *Blackman*, December 20, 1929, p. 1, December 24, 1929, p. 7.

48. Ibid., January 2, 1930, p. 8. The twenty-six points are at ibid., p. 2. They are reproduced in Amy Jacques Garvey, "Political Activities of Marcus Garvey in Jamaica," op. cit.

49. *Blackman*, January 8, 1930, p. 1.

50. Ibid., December 28, 1929, p. 14.

51. Ibid., January 25, 1930, p. 1, January 23, 1930, p. 1. Ehrenstein's platform was similar to Garvey's and his manifesto appeared several times in the *Blackman*. It is not clear whether all twelve persons on Garvey's slate were actually PPP members. For other examples of Garvey's occasional support of renegade whites see Martin, *Race First*, pp. 31, 233.

52. *Blackman*, September 10, 1929, p. 1; ibid., January 25, 1930, p. 13, Garvey to Sir Reginald E. Stubbs, February 7, 1930, CO 318/399/76634; *Blackman*, January 28, 1930, p. 1.

53. Garvey to Rt. Hon. Phillip Snowdon, February 27, 1930, CO 318/399/76634.

54. *Blackman*, January 31, 1930, p. 1.

55. Unsigned secret memo from King's House, Kingston, June 30, 1930, CO 318/399/76634.

56. *Blackman*, February 1, 1930, p. 1.

57. Ibid., February 4, 1920, p. 2.

58. Ibid., February 15, 1930, p. 12, February 2, 1930, p. 2.

59. Ibid., February 12, 1930, p. 2.

60. Ibid., March 29, 1930, p. 13.

61. Unsigned secret memo from King's House, Kingston, June 30, 1930, CO 318/399/76634. According to the memo, Garvey "saw Sir Edward Stubbs two or three months ago" to put forward his proposals.

62. *Blackman*, January 14, 1930, p. 2.

63. Ibid., February 13, 1930, p. 1.

64. Garvey to H. E. Sir Reginald Edward Stubbs, governor of Jamaica, February 21, February 22, 1930, CO 318/399/76634; ibid., Garvey to Rt. Hon. Phillip Snowdon, Chancellor of the Exchequer, February 27, 1930. In this correspondence Garvey expressed a desire to appeal the libel case all the way to the privy council, if necessary. Somebody at the Colonial Office commented (on the libel case) that though Garvey was "a danger to good order" he should not be subjected to such blatant persecution—minute, June 30, 1930, CO 318/399/76634.

65. *Blackman*, February 12, 1930, p. 1.

66. Ibid., February 24, 1930, p. 1, February 26, 1930, p. 7.

67. Ibid., August 30, 1930, p. 4, September 13, 1930, p. 1. September 27, 1930, p. 1, September 27, 1930, p. 1, November 29, 1930, p. 4.

68. *Ethiopian World*, May 26, 1934. According to this report Garvey would not be contesting the November elections because he would be departing for England where he planned to become a Labor Party member of parliament for West Kensington.

69. *New Jamaican*, January 16, 1933, p. 1. The League was formed by a Mr. Vivian Durham and others.

70. Ibid., January 13, 1933, p. 1.

71. Ibid., October 12, 1932, p. 1, November 1, 1932, p. 2, November 23, 1932, p. 2. Included here are statements by Garvey as well as editorials in his newspaper. For a

discussion of the complete relationship between Garvey, communists and communism, and working class struggles in Jamaica and elsewhere, see Martin, *Race First*, pp. 221–272.

72. *Black Man* (magazine, not to be confused with the *Blackman* newspaper), III, 10, July 1938, pp. 5–7, III, 11 November 1938, p. 19.

73. Garvey to Rt. Hon. Phillip Snowdon, February 27, 1930, CO 318/399/76634. Garvey thanked the Colonial Office for acceding to his request, but they expressed puzzlement since no royal commission was being contemplated at that time— *Blackman*, August 23, 1930, p. 1; Garvey to Secretary of State, Colonial Office, via the Officer Administering the Government, Jamaica, September 4, 1930, CO 318/399/76634; ibid., Secretary of State, Lord Passfield to OAG, Jamaica, September 18, 1930. In January 1930 Garvey and nine others had presented a petition "On behalf of the labourers of Jamaica," to a visiting West Indian Sugar Commission, led by Lord Olivier—*Blackman*, January 11, 1930, p. 2.

74. Garvey, Memorandum to West India Royal Commission, September 24, 1938, CO 950/44. The memorandum traced the history of Black West Indians after emancipation—the importation of foreign labor to depress wages, the consequent migrations to Panama, Cuba, etc. in search of work, the usurpation of commercial activity by Chinese, Syrians, etc. It also dealt with the race/class question in the islands and the persecution of popular Black leaders.

75. *Blackman*, October 25, 1929, p. 1. Manley was instructed here by J. H. Cargill. Mr. N. N. Ashenheim appeared for the respondents.

76. Ibid., January 14, 1930, pp. 1 and 7.

77. Ibid., November 1, 1930, p. 10.

78. *New Jamaican*, September 19, 1932, p. 5.

79. R. N. Murray, ed., *J. J. Mills—His Own Account of His Life and Times* (Kingston: Collins and Sangster, 1969), pp. 110–111.

80. *National Negro Voice*, August 23, 1941, p. 8.

81. *Black Man*, July 1938, p. 6.

82. *National Negro Voice*, August 30, 1941, p. 5.

9
Marcus Garvey and Southern Africa*

One of the many absurd stories that are being circulated among the natives is that the notorious Marcus Garvey of Black Star Line fame will soon arrive in South Africa with a large force of black soldiers to drive the white man out of the country.

—*Cape Argus* (1923)[1]

It can be readily seen that the propaganda of the Universal Negro Improvement Association is bearing fruit in Africa. If we have accomplished nothing else but the bringing to the natives of Africa a consciousness of themselves and a desire on their part to free themselves from the thraldom of alien races and nations, we would have justified the existence of this great organization, because the primary object of this movement is to redeem Africa; to make Africa the land of the black peoples of the world, even as Europe has become the land of the whites and Asia the land of the brown and yellow peoples.

. . . it will mean not so much fighting from without as the rising of the people from within with a new consciousness of their power which is gradually being realized, even by the admission of General Smuts and his white compatriots. Let us, therefore, redouble our energies in putting over the program for the liberation of Africa.

—Marcus Garvey[2]

SOUTH AFRICA (AZANIA)

Marcus Mosiah Garvey (1887–1940) founded the Universal Negro Improvement Association (UNIA) in Jamaica in 1914, after having observed first hand the plight of African peoples in many countries around the world. Garvey relocated to the United States in 1916, reestablished the UNIA there about a year later, and by 1919 was well on his way to the building up of the largest Pan-African movement of its

*Originially published in 1979

133

kind in history. By the mid 1920s the UNIA had over 1,100 branches in more than forty countries, with a membership quite possibly in the millions.[3]

Southern Africa played a critical role in the very formation of the UNIA. Garvey himself later commented on this—

> Where did the name of the organization come from? It was while speaking to a West Indian Negro who was a passenger on the ship with me from Southampton [in 1914] who was returning home to the West Indies from Basutoland with his Basuto wife, that I further learned of the horrors of native life in Africa. He related to me such horrible and pitiable tales that my heart bled within me. Retiring to my cabin, all day and the following night I pondered over the subject matter of that conversation, and at midnight, lying flat on my back, the vision and thought came to me that I should name the organization the Universal Negro Improvement Association and African Communities (Imperial) League. Such a name I thought would embrace the purpose of all black humanity.[4]

The UNIA spread rapidly to Africa in general and South Africa in particular. Cape Town especially, as a major seaport, became an important focus for the spread of Garveyite activity to surrounding areas. The 1921 Report of the South African Department of Native Affairs noted the presence of Garveyite propaganda in Cape Town and Johannesburg and reported four UNIA branches operating in the Cape Peninsula.[5]

Early in 1922 Garvey's Harlem-based organ, the *Negro World*, reported the organization of a UNIA division in Claremont, Cape Town, by T. L. Robertson of New York.[6] The Woodstock, Cape Town, division was founded in the same year.[7] In July 1923 five new South African divisions were reported, followed by the formation of divisions in East London and Pretoria in 1924.[8] The Pretoria branch in 1929 had about one hundred members and was under the leadership of Mr. P. A. Mokharia, president and Mr. L. B. Sabata, acting executive secretary. Meetings took place in the Marabastad location.[9]

Surviving UNIA files list seven branches for South Africa (more than for any other African country) ca. 1926. Their locations, together with their chief officers, where this information is listed in the files, were as follows—

Cape Town—William Osborne Jackson, president; Julius Caesar Allen, secretary.

Claremont, Cape Town—J. Herbert, president; David Mullins, secretary.

Woodstock—M. E. G. Johnson, president; John Oliphant, secretary.

Goodwood—H. S. Davids, president; J. P. Peters, secretary.

New Clare (Evaton)—G. Carman Kalinda, president; Benjamin Majafi, secretary.

Pretoria

East London—J. J. Samuels, president; Mrs. W. J. Samuels, secretary.[10]

Benjamin Majafi, secretary of the New Clare (Evaton) division, in a letter of 1927 also mentioned UNIA branches at Sophiatown, Waterpan and Johannesburg. The Evaton branch, he wrote, was holding their meetings in the open, since local Uncle Tom ministers were denying Garveyites the use of church or school halls for UNIA meetings.[11]

Several factors explain the rapid spread of the Garvey movement in South Africa. For one thing, the South African situation was perhaps closer to that of Afro-America than that of any other African country. South Africans faced a more highly industrialized country than was true for most of Europe's tropical dependencies, the white population, though still a minority, was larger than elsewhere in Africa and the local brand of racism was not very different from jim-crow in the United States.

Afro-American-South African relations also predated the Garvey movement by several years. The African Methodist Episcopal (AME) Church, Afro-America's first national Christian denomination, had established branches in South Africa in the late nineteenth century. Several South Africans had by Garvey's time also studied in and/or undertaken lecture tours in Afro-America. One of the more important of these was Solomon T. Plaatje, who toured the United States in 1921 and 1922, raising funds for his mission among miners in Kimberley.

Plaatje was one of the founders of the African National Congress (then known as the South African Native National Congress) in 1912. He was the ANC's first secretary-general. Prior to journeying to the United States, he was part of an ANC delegation to the post-World War I Peace Conference at Versailles, France, in 1919. In France he attended the Pan-African Congress organized by Afro-American scholar and activist, Dr. W. E. B. DuBois. From France the delegation journeyed to London for fruitless discussions with Prime Minister

David Lloyd George and other deaf-eared British officials. While in London, delegation member and then ANC secretary-general R. V. Selope-Thema, published a defence of Garvey in the English press. An English journalist had in November, 1919 attacked Garvey's statement that "we have been used to fight in every war, but the time has come when we will fight for ourselves, we will fight to make the Negro free." Selope-Thema wrote,

> It is because the white man relies on his military superiority which modern scientific progress has conferred on him that he has refused or neglected to pay attention to the black man's cry for justice and liberty, and consequently some of the educated black men have been forced much against their will, to come to the conclusion that what the white man respects, is not constitutional and peaceful appeal, but brute force.
>
> Hence Mr. Marcus Garvey's threatening appeal to the 400,000,000 Africans to prepare themselves to fight. This 'wild and threatening language' comes from a broken heart that can no longer tolerate the exploitation of Africa and her peoples.

From London, Selope-Thema and the rest of the delegation returned to South Africa, while Plaatje toured Canada and the United States.[12]

Though Plaatje's United States tour was not confined to the UNIA, his interactions with Garvey and his movement were extensive. Plaatje met Garvey in Toronto, where the local UNIA division entertained him.[13] On his arrival in the United States he therefore found Garvey's nationwide network of UNIA branches at his disposal. By July 1921 he had spoken six times at Liberty Hall, the UNIA's headquarters meeting place in Harlem, New York.[14] He had also been entertained at a private reception attended by UNIA leaders and had addressed the first annual convention and banquet of the St. Andrews Brotherhood and Auxiliary of the Church of the Good Shepherd at 224 W. 135th St. in Harlem, the first church of what was soon to become the African Orthodox Church.[15]Plaatje also addressed UNIA branches in Brooklyn, N.Y., New Bedford, Mass. and Boston, among other places. UNIA branches all over the country provided him with free board and lodging.[16]

In his lectures to UNIA audiences Plaatje described conditions in South Africa, pointed out their similarities to the racial situation in the United States and on one occasion sang an African song. He also sold many copies of his publications, *Native Life in South Africa*, *The Mote and The Beam* (a pamphlet on Black-white sexual relations in South

Africa) and a collection of Bechuana proverbs. *Negro World* editor, Hubert H. Harrison, complained in April 1921 that he had sent several hundred copies of *Native Life in South Africa* to W. E. B. Du Bois, editor of the *Crisis* (organ of the National Association for the Advancement of Colored People), but that DuBois had failed to publicize them.[17]

Plaatje was himself among those South Africans whose contacts with Afro-America went back many years. He had entertained Bishop and Mrs. Levi J. Coppin of the AME Church at his home in Mafeking many years previously.[18] He had also corresponded with John Edward Bruce, literary editor of the UNIA's *Negro World*, for some thirty years before his tour of the United States.[19]

On his return home in 1922, Plaatje helped spread the word of Garveyism, so much so that the British authorities in Basutoland (Lesotho) and South Africa expressed concern.[20] In the United States by this time Plaatje's *Native Life in South Africa* was being offered free with a one year subscription to the *Negro World*. [21]

West Indian interest in South Africa also ran deep and helped facilitate the spread of the Garvey movement there. Some West Indians had come to South Africa during the Boer War and by the early years of the century there were already several West Indians living in Cape Town, where racism, though severe, was not yet as outrageous as in the Boer states. At the pioneer Pan-African Conference organized by Henry Sylvester Williams of Trinidad in London in 1900, South Africa was the major item on the agenda. Williams himself shortly thereafter (1903–1905) became part of Cape Town's West Indian community.[22] South Africa's West Indian immigrants were closely tied to an Afro-American immigrant population, some of whose members were West Indians who had previously lived in the United States. Afro-Americans, it is of interest to note, were also stirred up by the Boer War, and some had volunteered to fight against the Dutch. Benito Sylvain, the Haitian Pan-Africanist and colleague of Henry Sylvester Williams, recalled that Williams' Pan-African Association counselled these Afro-Americans against participating at that point, since the adversaries (British and Boers) deserved each other.[23]

The story of one of these West Indian immigrants, Garveyite Arthur Cecil Grainger, is typical of the tens of thousands of West Indians over the years, whose families have been scattered in the wake of emigration to here, there and everywhere. Grainger was a native of Kingstown, St. Vincent, and went to South Africa during the Boer War.

After the war he settled in Cape Town, where he practised his trade as a motor mechanic. At his death in 1925 at age 42, he had resided in Cape Town for twenty-five years. By this time his mother, his sisters and an older brother were living in Boston, Massachusetts. His older brother was a veteran of the United States Navy.[24] Several of South Africa's West Indians were active in the UNIA.[25]

In South Africa, as everywhere else, Garveyites preached a doctrine of "race first" (meaning that Black people should put their racial self-interest first and foremost), self-reliance and nationhood. Nationhood was of especial importance, for Garvey's slogan of "Africa for the Africans" was a warning to the colonialist and imperialist nations that they had no business in Africa. The freedom of Africa was a major cause behind which Garvey sought to unite his followers in over forty countries, from Canada to Brazil, from Australia to Panama, in practically every place that people of African origin lived. Garvey's great goal was to see African countries free from alien rule, and an eventual United States of Africa. On this latter point he expressed himself poetically—

> Hail! United States of Africa—free!
> Hail! Motherhood most bright, divinely fair!
> State in perfect sisterhood united,
> Born of truth; mighty thou shalt ever be.[26]

"Africa for the Africans" was especially worrisome to South Africa's white overlords. The white *Cape Argus* of January 29, 1923 reported that whites were particularly upset by the following clauses from the UNIA's Declaration of Rights of the Negro Peoples of the World, which was circulating in South Africa—

> We believe in the freedom of Africa for the Negro people of the world, and by the principle of Europe for the Europeans and Asia for the Asiatics, we also demand Africa for the Africans at home and abroad.
>
> We believe in the inherent right of the Negro to possess himself of Africa, and that his possession of same shall not be regarded as an infringement on any claim or purchase made by any race or nation.

The *Cape Argus* article was but a small part of a widespread counter-propaganda effort directed by white South Africa against the UNIA. An African Garveyite writing from Liddesdaale, Evaton, in 1927 explained that

> In Transvaal we are working very heavy. The white race taught the black race that a black man will not achieve his destiny, telling these so-called educated natives that if the Universal Negro Improvement Associa-

tion pass through with their propaganda to redeem Africa Garveyism will treat them worse than a white man. But most of our people who read the *Negro World* are awakened, because your speeches are encouraging us a great deal. . . .[27]

Among those encouraged by Garveyite propaganda were several of the important leaders of the African National Congress (ANC) and the Industrial and Commercial Workers Union (ICU), two of the most powerful African organizations within South Africa at the time.

Garvey's influence on ANC leaders, as has been seen, went back at least as far as the 1919 article by R. V. Selope-Thema and Plaatje's tour of the United States. Another of the main vehicles for Garveyite influence within the African National Congress was Professor James Thaele, an alumnus of Wilberforce University, an AME Church-owned institution in Ohio in the United States. After fifteen years in the United States, "Marcus Garvey inspired him to return to South Africa," as one commentator put it.[28] Thaele's admiration for Garvey's ideas was expressed clearly in his article, "Garvey and Garveyism," which appeared in *Africa Voice* (Cape Town) on September 22, 1923. He wrote,

> Among the combinations and permutations that go to make up the kaleidoscope of human history, Marcus Garvey, the potentate of the Universal Negro Improvement Association, will indeed remain a shining constellation.

A staunch Pan-Africanist, Thaele argued that the New Negro of the twentieth century "should solve this race problem by developing a greater Africa." He continued, "The Garvey program must be studied by the Bantu politicals in season and out of season. His adamant stand in championing the sacred cause of freedom for the Negro peoples of the world must be nurtured in our mind as leaders. . . ."

Earlier that year, on April 14, 1923, the *Negro World* had published an article by Thaele in which he supported the spread of Garveyism in South Africa. The article was a rebuttal to an item from the *Cape Argus*. In 1924 Thaele was elected president of the ANC's Western Cape Congress.[29] Not long afterwards, the *African World*, an organ of the ANC, appeared under his editorship. The *Negro World* was very pleased with its South African counterpart and editorialized to the effect that the *African World* and the ANC were the nearest thing on the African continent to the *Negro World* and the UNIA.[30] The UNIA organ also reprinted an editorial from the very first issue of Thaele's paper. It read in part,

> I believe that it is essential to the early success of our cause that the Africans here at home should seek co-operation with the Africans abroad. The Universal Negro Improvement Association and African Communities League is the biggest thing today in Negro modern organizations. Its program must be scrutinized, imbibed and assimilated by us.

The article "commended to all" the "brilliant editorials" of the *Negro World*, which, it argued, "must be a Bible to us. . . ."[31]

The motto of the *African World* was as Garveyite as it could be— "Europe for Europeans and Africa for Africans."[32] In 1925 it published a translation of Garvey's famous essay on "African Fundamentalism" into an African language. Translations into many more African languages were promised.[33]

The appearance of the *African World* was very upsetting to white South African publications. Garvey reported a request from the white *Sunday Times* for the government to ban the ANC paper. "A more treacherous, inflammatory, deluded and deluding publication it is difficult to imagine," the *Sunday Times* raved.[34] White South Africa, in its continuing effort to usurp the designation "African," not surprisingly also possessed an *African World* of its own. The white *African World* did not take too kindly to a Black namesake and accordingly issued to "the 'Negro World' and its latest offspring in South Africa, which has quite illegally assumed our name, a grave warning, in their best interest, to abstain from any interference in native affairs south of the Equator."[35]

The *Negro World* on October 10, 1925 carried a photograph of the new Cape ANC headquarters building and Garvey (at that time incarcerated in Atlanta penitentiary), shortly afterwards sent Thaele a cable of support.[36] And the ANC's support for Garvey during his imprisonment was unswerving. The organization, like UNIA branches and other organizations around the world, kept up a constant pressure on the United States government for the release of Marcus Garvey. The ANC celebrated "Marcus Garvey Day" and passed resolutions condemning Garvey's imprisonment by the United States authorities. One such resolution was passed in plenary session in Johannesburg in April 1925, at a Congress session which decided to boycott the visit of the Prince of Wales, as a mark of protest at a recent massacre of Africans. This resolution reaffirmed that nothing could extinguish the seed planted by Garvey in the hearts of African people.[37] At its annual convention in Bloemfontein in July 1927 the ANC again passed a resolution, this time calling upon the Union government to convey the

ANC's sentiments to the government of the United States. The resolution read,

> The convention humbly requests the Union government to communicate its petition to the United States Government to have clemency in the prolonged incarceration of Marcus Garvey, President of the U.N.I.A., who is now reported to be suffering from asthma in Atlanta Penitentiary.[38]

ANC support for Garveyism was manifested in other ways. Thaele was a frequent speaker at UNIA functions.[39] Another ANC admirer of Garvey, T. D. Mweli Skota, was largely responsible for introducing, in 1925, the ANC's flag of gold, black and green, modelled after Garvey's red, black and green.[40] An article by ex-ANC president, the Rev. Z. R. Mahabane, on the Native Franchise Bill of 1929, appeared in the *Negro World* on August 10, 1929. *Abantu Batho*, an ANC organ published in Johannesburg, also played a role similar to the *African World* in Cape Town, as a major disseminator of Garvey's ideas. *Abantu Batho* was owned by James Gumede, who was elected president-general of the ANC in 1927.[41]

Among other publications with UNIA connections were the *Black Man*, edited by the president of the Cape Town UNIA[42] and the *African Leader* of Johannesburg, whose appearance was welcomed editorially by the *Negro World* in 1932.[43]

Like the ANC, the Industrial and Commercial Workers Union of Clements Kadalie also maintained ties with the UNIA. Kadalie himself seems to have been no more than lukewarm to Garveyism, and indeed seems to have been close to A. Philip Randolph, one of Garvey's major adversaries in Afro-America.[44] Some of the ICU leadership (among whom there were several West Indians), however were staunch Garveyites,[45] as were, apparently, some of the rank and file.[46] ICU officers also published in the *Negro World*. H. D. Tyamzashe, the ICU complaints and research secretary and sub-editor of the *Workers' Herald*, wrote a special article for Garvey's paper in 1927.[47] A letter of 1932 from J. J. Magade, provincial secretary of the Cape Province Independent ICU, stated that "The Africans take much interest in the UNIA movement with hopes that a day shall come when we shall join hands together as brothers and sisters of AFRICA."[48]

Garveyism also appealed to some churchmen in South Africa. The Rev. Daniel William Alexander of Griqualand West was by 1925 vicar apostolic of the African Orthodox Church. He was later consecrated to the episcopate by Archbishop George McGuire, primate of the church and former chaplain-general of the UNIA. Alexander was born in Africa of Martiniquan parents.[49] In the Transkei in the 1920s the preacher Wellington Butelezi preached Garveyism.[50] One nationalist ("Ethiopian") church, the Afro-Athlican Constructive Church, is said to have incorporated Garvey into its credo—"We believe in one God, Maker of all things, Father of Ethiopia . . . who did Athlyi, Marcus Garvey and colleagues come to save? The down-trodden children of Ethiopia that they might rise to be a great power among the nations."[51]

One indication of the great impact of Garveyism on the South African consciousness was the large number of letters from South Africans appearing in the pages of the *Negro World* right up to its demise in 1933. More letters appeared from South Africa than from any other African country. A sampling of these letters is instructive. Peter O. Daniels, an ex-company sergeant major, 1st Cape Corps, wrote from Cape Town in 1922 to report that the UNIA was doing well in and around Cape Town.[52] J. C. Diraath of Kimberley wrote in praise of the *Negro World* in 1924.[53] In 1925·J. Barnard Belman of Johannesburg informed fellow readers that the people in Transvaal swore by Marcus Garvey. The *Negro World,* he said, had a large circulation there.[54] In 1928 and 1929 Professor D. P. S. Adams, M.A., Ph.D., described as a professor of languages and education from Port Elizabeth, wrote in praise of Marcus Garvey. Adams had previously published articles in the *Negro World* in 1926 and 1928, on conditions in South Africa.[55] Letters appeared in late 1928 and January 1929 from Moses Mphahlete of 134 Anderson St., Johannesburg and F. J. Smith of Transvaal, respectively.[56] Enock Mazilinko of Johannesburg in February 1929 affirmed the African "determination to attain the noble ideals of Garveyism," despite "the Draconian laws of Hertzog and Roos. . . ."[57]

Benjamin J. Majafi of Liddesdaale, Evaton, a Garveyite of long standing, in January 1931 suggested an African name for Marcus Garvey, Jr., who was born on September 27, 1930. He wrote, "Let the child be called Musi, a Ruler, Tsepo, Hope to be Free in our Motherland, Africa. Name: Tsepo-Musi."[58] Another reader, one Alfred J. David, agreed with this suggestion.[59] And back in 1924 the *Negro World* had reported a South African having named his child Garvey.[60] A letter of December 1931 from "Yours Africanly," E. Solo-Oengwa of P.O. Emfundisweni, Eastern Pondoland, called Garvey a Moses and a saint. J. L. Whlapo in 1932 expressed an interest in establishing contacts with Afro-Americans and inquired about Black colleges in the

United States.[61] From Cape Town that year, "Yours Africanly," James Stehazu, called the UNIA the only hope for Africans and attacked W. E. B. Du Bois, William Pickens (both of the NAACP) and other foes of Garvey.[62] The sentiment of so many of these letters was poignantly summarized by Samuel Matsalula in 1932. "Oh that I should live," he wrote, "until that seemingly fallacious and impossible time came to pass, when the Afro-Americans, together with the African Negroes shall be as free as air, in their God given Africa."[63]

These letters, as has been seen, were reinforced by frequent *Negro World* reprints of articles from both the Black and white South African press. Such articles usually appeared within two months of their original publication in South Africa. Some articles written by South Africans especially for the *Negro World* have already been mentioned.

In addition to their work in South Africa itself, members (and non-members too) of the South African UNIA participated actively in international UNIA functions. There were South African representatives at Garvey's epochal First International Convention of the Negro Peoples of the World held in New York in 1920.[64] At the 1921 convention there were South Africans among the thirty delegates who came from Africa.[65] A delegate from Natal attended the 1924 convention.[66] In 1928 the Pretoria branch reported meeting in Marabastad location, Pretoria, to elect delegates to the 1929 convention held in Kingston, Jamaica (the first after Garvey's deportation from the United States in 1927).[67] A South African, Mr. H. Illitintro, of Entweni College, P.O. Port St. Johns, Cape Province, was one of seven students successfully completing the second sitting of Garvey's School of African Philosophy in London in 1938. A Ugandan and a Nigerian were also among the graduates. "The School of African Philosophy," Garvey announced, "is a University through which those aspiring to become leaders in the U.N.I.A. and in world affairs must graduate."[68]

In the United States, one of the founders of the Buffalo, New York UNIA division, ca. 1920, was Dr. Theodore Kakaza, a South African physician practising in the area.[69] This Buffalo branch in 1925 hosted a guest speaker, Mr. K. L. Demo of South Africa.[70] Around the same time a Wilberforce University student from South Africa, Mr. Joseph Rankwe, addressed the Columbus, Ohio division.[71]

Like the parent body, the South African UNIA was not averse to expressions of solidarity with other oppressed peoples. When, in 1924, Indian poetess Mrs. Sarojina Naidu addressed a meeting organized by the Indian community at City Hall, Cape Town, an address was presented to her by four combined UNIA divisions. It was signed by presidents W. O. Jackson of the Cape Town division, H. S. Davids of the Goodwood division, J. Herbert of the Claremont division and M. E. G. Johnson of the Woodstock division. On March 31, 1924 Mrs. Naidu was the principal speaker at a meeting at the National Theatre organized by the Cape Town divisions. Members of the Cape Indian Council were on the platform. Among the items on the agenda was a gramophone recording of Marcus Garvey's speech on his return to the United States from the West Indies in 1921. Mrs. Naidu in her address said that Garvey's program was the only one for the solution of Africa's problems.[72]

A June 15, 1930 protest meeting in the Orange Free State against the Riotous Assemblies Act was reportedly held under the auspices of the UNIA. Twelve hundred Africans attended.[73] The UNIA was also among the thirty organizations and two hundred delegates which attempted to establish a nationwide united front at the Non-European Conference held in Kimberly in June 1927. The ANC, ICU and Indian Congress were also present. One of the conference organizers was Cape Malay political activist Dr. A. Abdurahman, who over two decades earlier had been a political colleague of Trinidad lawyer, Henry Sylvester Williams, during the latter's sojourn in South Africa.[74]

Garvey was of course very aware of the effect of his propaganda in South Africa, and it gave him great satisfaction. In 1921 he read to his followers a London *Times* report which credited his propaganda with causing "problems" in South Africa.[75] In another speech that year he opined that the UNIA had the whites on the defensive in South Africa.[76] In 1923 the white *Cape Argus* reported that Garvey's propaganda "is having an unsettling effect, and is beginning to cause anxiety among the white people, who have worked for the good of the natives, and among the educated natives, who foresee danger in the present situation." Garvey retorted, "The only good work that they have done in South Africa . . . was that of keeping the native in his place; when the native was not even allowed to walk on the sidewalks in some of the cities of the Union, when he was forced to live in compounds and segregated and denied the privileges of ordinary human beings."[77]

The fulminations of the *Cape Argus* were symptomatic of the widespread official and semi-official white concern over the Garvey movement in South Africa. The major imperialist powers of the day swapped information and otherwise cooperated among themselves in their efforts against the UNIA. As early as 1919 the United States Post Office

Department objected to a *Negro World* article of June 14, 1919 attacking British racism in South Africa.[78]

The British Foreign Office records contain references to files, now officially destroyed, which contained information on the UNIA that the Foreign Office passed on to the South African government.[79] UNIA leader Rev. J. W. H. Eason in 1921 referred to British parliamentary proceedings in which a member of parliament complained that a Black West Indian (Garvey) was making the Black South Africans smart.[80] "His Royal Highness, the Prince of Wales" also lent his aristocratic prestige to the struggle against Garveyism during a South African tour. In the words of the white *Sunday Times*, the prince "warned the Bantu races . . . to beware of 'tendencies to mistrust those in authority or to turn to those whose smooth promises have yet to be translated into performance.'" The cause of all this upset was the ANC's *African World* ("this seditious native organ") which, fumed the *Sunday Times*, had "the barefaced impudence to refer to 'the imperishable message of His Highness Marcus Garvey. . . .'" As far as the white paper was concerned, "Every well-informed native knows Marcus Garvey to be an unprincipled rogue and swindler. . . ."[81]

Prime Minister J. C. Smuts of South Africa in 1923 admitted that the UNIA was being "carefully watched," though he seemed confident of his ability to contain it.[82] Garvey, at his 1924 international convention in Harlem reported, however, that Smuts had petitioned the British government to keep the *Negro World* out of certain parts of Africa. By 1927 the paper was reported banned in the diamond fields of Kimberly and in the Rand area.[83] The government was by then also tampering with UNIA mail.[84]

The mayor of Harrismith, Orange Free State, provided another perspective on official South African concern over Garveyism. He admitted that the UNIA was being watched and suggested that "The movement is carried on quietly among the natives. They realize that the time for action is not yet ripe but there are many evidences of their organizing activities."[85]

The Belgian consul-general in Johannesburg was also part of the official information swapping network of UNIA watchers. Among the recipients of his information was the British acting governor of Nyasaland (Malawi) in 1925.[86]

The imperialist surveillance and harassment of the UNIA were so well known that some of Garvey's Black enemies took it upon themselves to write the South African (and other) governments with unsolicited information on the UNIA's secret South African plans.[87] One of these tellers of tales was M. Mokete Manoedi of Leribe, Basutoland, who fell in among Garvey's enemies in the United States. In 1922 he wrote Winston Churchill, then secretary of state for the colonies,

> . . . I am conducting a vigorous, systematic, organized campaign of educational propaganda against the Garvey Movement, the work of which doubtless you have heard something. Its purpose is to arouse the native Africans to insurrection against the rule of the white men of all nations. Garvey poses as the Provisional President of Africa. It has taken some effect on the unthinking masses of Negroes in America, the West Indies, South and Central America, and, also, in Africa. Garvey preaches the most dangerous and vicious kind of doctrines. Unquestionably we can not afford to allow him to proceed uncurbed with his destructive work—that of impressing the American people with the idea that the British African is dissatisfied with British rule.[88]

After much deliberation between the British Colonial Office, the British resident commissioner in Maseru and the Smuts government, it was decided not to give Manoedi the money he requested to promote his anti-Garvey effort. The British authorities were uniformly impressed by his activities, however.[89]

Similar to Manoedi was the case of J. E. Kwegyir Aggrey, the well-known Gold Coast (Ghana) educator, who was used in South Africa (and elsewhere on the continent) to attack Garvey. His efforts called forth much African opposition.[90]

In South Africa, as in the United States and elsewhere, the colonialists and imperialists were not the only elements in white society that the UNIA had to contend with. Communists everywhere also proved stubborn opponents. Garveyites and Communists engaged in struggle within the ICU, resulting in the defeat of the latter.[91]

In 1928 the Sixth Congress of the Communist International meeting in Moscow decreed for the Communist Party of South Africa the new slogan of an "independent native South African republic based on the organization of the laborers and peasants, guaranteeing (at the same time) the rights of the national minorities." Similar slogans were imposed upon the United States ("self-determination in the Black Belt") and Cuba. This new slogan was too much for many of the majority white party to take, for it reminded them uncomfortably of Garveyism. *Pravda* reported S. P. Bunting, a white South African delegate to the Moscow deliberations, as saying that the majority of the South African party rejected the new slogan, since "class war has a more pronounced revolutionary character, and is likely to lead more easily to liberation from foreign supremacy, than national or racial struggle. . . ." Bunting claimed that South Africa had no appreciable national movement, since the ANC was but a "semi-corpse." The Communist Party, for which he claimed a membership of 1,750 was, in his opinion, the only real leader of the national movement in South Africa.[92] Like the Workers (Communist) Party of the United States, Bunting thought that "principal attention should be given to the labor movement pure and simple. . . ."[93]

A white member of the South African party, Manuel Lopes, was explicit in his belief that the Comintern's "Native Republicanism" was but "Marcus Garveyism" under a different guise.[94]

And yet, in an age when radicals and Communists were often equated in the minds of imperialist officialdom, Garvey was sometimes erroneously described as communist. The *Cape Argus* so described Garvey in 1923, and furthermore called Tom Mann, a white radical, the "white Garvey" of South Africa. Garvey's comment shows the role he thought white radicals could best play, namely that of combating the racism of their own community. He wrote,

> Everybody knows that the Universal Negro Improvement Association is not made up of Bolshevists, and we are not well acquainted personally with Tom Mann, who is referred to as the 'white Garvey,' nevertheless, Tom Mann seems to be doing good work, very helpful to the program of the Universal Negro Improvement Association in Africa. We hope he will continue until he has helped to save our white friends of the Union of South Africa from themselves.[95]

SOUTH WEST AFRICA (NAMIBIA)

The UNIA was active all over Africa and naturally its South African activities spilled over into neighboring territories. The surviving UNIA records show South West African UNIA divisions in the mid-1920s in Luderitz (president, Fitzherbert Headley; secretary, Arthur B. Wille) and in Windhoek (secretary, Paul D. Ayehoavi).[96] The Luderitz division (No. 294) was begun early in 1921 and within a few months had already instituted sickness and death benefits. President Headley, a frequent writer to the *Negro World*, proudly boasted that the UNIA was a pioneer among the African population in the payment of such benefits.[97]

By 1922 the South African administration had sought to curtail UNIA activity in the protectorate, under pretext of a law against amusements on Sundays.[98] In 1923 the *Luderitz Zeitung,* a German language newspaper, attacked Garvey in an article entitled, "Der Neger-Kaiser ein Spitzbube." Headley sent the paper the following response—

> You seem to be more concerned about the Negro movement than you are about the French occupation of your fatherland, Germany, and the fact that Negroes send money from Africa to help the parent body [of the UNIA] troubles you a great deal more than the gold marks which the French are squeezing from your militaristic people for the atrocities committed during the regime of your lord-god 'Der Kaiser.'

Headley further warned that the UNIA knew full well that Germany had designs on reoccupying South West Africa. Such a thing would never happen. "We shall not turn back or grow weary in the fight for a free and redeemed Africa," he promised, "until the Teuton and Slav, Anglo-Saxon and Latin restore to the sons of Ham that which they have stolen from them."[99]

In 1922 Garvey sent a delegation to the League of Nations. Among other things, they lobbied for the ex-German African territories, including South West Africa, to be turned over to Black administrators.[100] Nineteen twenty-two was also the year of the Bondelzwarts massacre, when the Smuts government sent in aeroplanes against a section of the local population. James Thaele stated later that the UNIA, acting through the Haitian representative, had the Bondelzwarts matter placed before the League after the British government refused.[101] It is certain, however, that the Persian delegation did place before the League the UNIA petition for Black rule in the ex-German colonies.[102] The *Gold Coast Leader,* published by Pan-Africanist J. E. Casely Hayford, supported the UNIA's petition to the League. The *Leader* thought that the lynching and discrimination faced by Afro-Americans left them no alternative but bloody revolution or exodus, and South West Africa seemed a good potential haven for repatriated African-Americans, for blood was thicker than water.[103]

Most, if not all of the areas around South Africa and South West Africa also felt UNIA influence. The Basutoland division (No. 849) in 1926 reported 500 to 600 financial members a month, making it perhaps the largest in the area.[104] In 1924 a UNIA organizer, Joseph Masagha (formerly Joseph Lechwenyo), reported taking UNIA propaganda (including books and photos), to Bechuanaland (Botswana) to his relatives, Chiefs Botlhasitse and Mothibi, children of the great Chief Mankuroane.[105]

In Southern Africa, as in so many other places, the contribution of the UNIA in the two decades of so after World War I was immense. To appreciate the UNIA's contribution one has to reflect on the sad plight of African peoples in the period. With the invasion of Haiti by the United States military in 1915 the world was left with a mere two African countries (Liberia and Ethiopia), that maintained some semblance of independence. The African race was universally bent beneath the burden of jim-crow, apartheid, lynching, disfranchisement, racism, colonialism, imperialism and (as in the Belgian Congo), genocide. It was into this picture of universal gloom that Marcus Garvey was able to bring hope. He instilled a determination to struggle. He gave his people backbones, as Mrs. Amy Jacques Garvey aptly expressed it, where they had wishbones. Everywhere he sowed or nurtured the seeds of self-reliance and nationalism, whether in Ethiopian churches, the ANC or in the UNIA itself. The UNIA was a nursery for organizational skills. It provided a powerful international African propaganda machine the like of which had not existed on such a scale before, and perhaps has not existed since. For a season Garvey took the propaganda initiative away from the imperialist media and had them on the defensive. Above all, Garvey demonstrated the possibilities of Pan-African cooperation on a global scale. He showed that there was a common denominator through which African peoples throughout the world could be reached. He exposed the potential wrapped up in his slogan of "One God, One Aim, One Destiny."

Notes

1. *Cape Argus*, January 29, 1923, quoted in the *Negro World*, March 17, 1923.
2. *Negro World*, March 17, 1923.
3. See Tony Martin, *Race First: The Ideological and Organizational Struggles of Marcus Garvey and the Universal Negro Improvement Association* (Westport, Connecticut: Greenwood Press, 1976), especially Chapter 1.
4. Amy Jacques Garvey, ed., *The Philosophy and Opinions of Marcus Garvey, or, Africa for the Africans* (New York: 1923 and 1925. Reprint. London: Frank Cass, 1967), pp 126, 127.
5. A. P. Walshe, "Black American Thought and African Political Attitudes in South Africa," *Review of Politics*, XXXII, 1, January 1970, p. 62.

6. *Negro World,* March 18 and July 22, 1922. For the history of the *Negro World,* see Martin, *Race First,* pp. 90–100.

7. Its third anniversary was celebrated with a parade in Cape Town—*Negro World,* October 24, 1925.

8. Ibid, July 21, 1923, November 8, 1924, January 26, 1929.

9. Ibid, January 26, 1929.

10. From membership cards in the UNIA Central Division (New York) files, Schomburg Collection, New York Public Library. See also Martin, *Race First,* p. 373.

11. *Negro World,* April 30, 1927.

12. Mary Benson, *South Africa: The Struggle for a Birthright* (Middlesex: Penguin, 1966), pp. 25–27, 41–42; *Emancipator* (New York), March 20, 1920; for Selope-Thorpe's article see Amy Jacques Garvey, *Garvey and Garveyism* (Kingston: A. J. Garvey, 1963), pp. 39–40.

13. *Negro World,* February 12, 1921. Plaatje's non-UNIA speaking engagements included an address to an NAACP convention in Detroit on June 26, 1921—*Negro World,* August 20, 1921.

14. Ibid, July 16, 1921.

15. Ibid, February 26 and February 19, 1921. The African Orthodox Church was closely connected to (though not a part of) the UNIA—see Martin, *Race First,* pp. 71–73.

16. *Negro World,* March 19 and July 2, 1921, April 29, 1922, June 18, 1921.

17. Ibid, April 23, 1921, Harrison suggested that *The Mote and the Beam* was being sold too expensively, but Plaatje reminded him that the proceeds would go to his Native Brotherhood Building Fund—*Negro World,* June 18, 1921.

18. *Negro World,* February 12, 1921.

19. Ibid, July 16, 1921.

20. E. C. F. Garraway, Resident Commissioner, Maseru, Basutoland to H. C. Pretoria, December 12, 1922, Foreign Office files, FO 371/8513, Public Record Office, London.

21. *Negro World,* April 28, 1923.

22. See Owen C. Mathurin, *Henry Sylvester Williams and The Origins of the Pan-African Movement, 1869–1911* (Westport, Connecticut: Greenwood Press, 1976) and James R. Hooker, *Henry Sylvester Williams* (London: Rex Collings, 1975).

23. Tony Martin, "Benito Sylvain of Haiti on the Pan-African Conference of 1900," *Pan-African Journal,* VIII, 2, Summer 1975, p. 186.

24. *Negro World,* August 8, 1925.

25. For more on South Africa's West Indians, see Martin, *Race First,* pp. 118–120.

26. In Tony Martin, *Literary Garveyism,* forthcoming.

27. *Negro World,* April 30, 1927—letter from Benjamin Majafi.

28. Mary Benson, *South Africa: The Struggle for a Birthright* (Middlesex: Penguin, 1966), p. 57.

29. Walshe, "Black American Thought," pp. 63, 64.

30. *Negro World,* July 11, 1925.

31. Ibid, July 4, 1925.

32. Ibid, August 8, 1925.

33. Ibid, September 12, 1925.

34. Amy Jacques Garvey, ed., *Philosophy and Opinions,* II, p. 355.

35. Ibid, p. 356.
36. Ibid, October 31, 1925. On Garvey's trial and imprisonment see Martin, *Race First*, pp. 191–205 and passim.
37. *Abantu Batho*, March 17, 1927, *Negro World*, May 2, 1925. For other calls for Garvey's release, see Martin, *Race First*, pp. 195, 196.
38. *Negro World*, September 3, 1927.
39. On at least one occasion he sent a representative when he could not make it. In 1925 Mr. H. Saaldon of the Cape Town ANC represented Thaele at the parade marking the third anniversary of the Woodstock UNIA division—*Negro World*, October 24, 1925.
40. Benson, *South Africa*, pp. 46, 47. Skota was also responsible for adoption of the ANC anthem "Nkosi Sikelel' i-Africa" ("Lord Bless Africa"). The red, black and green flag was widely adopted in Africa and elsewhere—see Martin, *Race First*, pp. 43–45.
41. Walshe, "Black American Thought," p. 65.
42. *Negro World*, March 5, 1921.
43. Ibid, March 19, 1932.
44. See Clements Kadalie, *My Life and the ICU* (New York: Humanities Press, 1970), pp. 220, 221; Martin, *Race First*, pp. 119, 120. In 1927 Kadalie was a guest in the United States of Randolph's Brotherhood of Sleeping Car Porters—*Negro World*, September 3, 1927. For the Randolph-Garvey dispute, see Martin, *Race First*, pp. 319–333.
45. Kadalie, *My Life*, p. 220, Martin, *Race First*, p. 119.
46. Walshe, "Black American Thought," p. 63.
47. *Negro World*, November 12, 1927.
48. Ibid, January 9, 1932.
49. Ibid, February 7, 1925.
50. Walshe, "Black American Thought," p. 63.
51. Quoted in Bengt Sundkler, *Bantu Prophets in South Africa* (London: Oxford University Press, 1961), p. 58, and in Tony Martin, "Some Reflections on Evangelical Pan-Africanism, or, Black Missionaries, White Missionaries and the Struggle for African Souls, 1890–1930," *Ufahamu*, I, 3, Winter 1971, p. 84.
52. *Negro World*, January 14, 1922.
53. Ibid, October 18, 1924.
54. Ibid, October 24, 1925.
55. Ibid, July 28, 1928, February 2, 1929, September 4, 1926, January 14, 1928.
56. Ibid, September 15, 1928, January 26, 1929.
57. Ibid, February 9, 1929.
58. Ibid, January 31, 1931.
59. Ibid, February 14, 1931.
60. Ibid, November 29, 1924.
61. Ibid, March 5, 1932.
62. Ibid, July 16, 1932.
63. Ibid, May 21, 1932.
64. Ibid, July 2, 1921.
65. Ibid, August 3, 1921.
66. *Daily Worker*, August 13, 1924.

67. *Johannesburg Daily Star*, November 23, 1928, reprinted in *Negro World*, January 26, 1929.
68. *Black Man*, IV, 1, June 1939, p. 8.
69. Ralph Watkins, "The Marcus Garvey Movement in Buffalo, New York," *Afro-Americans in New York Life and History*, I, 1, January 1977, p. 40.
70. *Negro World*, August 22, 1925.
71. Ibid, July 4, 1925. Rankwe may possibly have been one of twelve students sent to the United States by James Thaele. At least one of them published a pro-Garvey article—Walshe, "Black American Thought," p. 65.
72. *Negro World*, May 17, 1924. On Garvey's gramophone record see Martin, *Race First*, p. 379.
73. *Blackman* (Jamaica), August 28, 1930.
74. George Padmore, *How Britain Rules Africa* (London: Wishart, 1936), p. 370; Benson, *South Africa*, p. 49. On Abdurahman and Sylvester Williams see Mathurin, *Henry Sylvester Williams. . .* , pp. 119–124 and Hooker, *Henry Sylvester Williams*, p. 70.
75. *Negro World*, October 8, 1921.
76. Ibid, November 5, 1921.
77. *Cape Argus*, January 29, 1923, p. 1, quoted in *Negro World*, March 17, 1923.
78. Memorandum by third assistant postmaster general, July 11, 1919, in Record Group 28, Unarranged, File 500, Records of the Post Office Department, National Archives of the United States, Washington, D.C.
79. Destroyed file, A 4758/4758/60, Foreign Office Index to General Correspondence, 1924, Foreign Office files, Public Record Office, London.
80. *Negro World*, August 27, 1921.
81. Garvey, *Philosophy and Opinions*, II, p. 350.
82. Martin, *Race First*, p. 121.
83. *Negro World*, August 23, 1924, July 16, 1927. For the banning of the paper in British African colonies and harassment of one of its South African agents, see Martin, *Race First*, p. 94.
84. *Negro World*, April 30, 1927.
85. *Negro World*, August 1, 1925.
86. Acting Governor, R. Rankine of Nyasaland to H. E., Governor-General and High Commissioner, Cape Town, May 15, 1925, Colonial Office files, CO 525/104, Public Record Office, London.
87. Augustus Duncan, Executive-Secretary, West Indian Protective Society of America to H. E., Governor General of the Union of South Africa, January 9, 1920, Colonial Office files, CO 551/124; Garvey, *Philosophy and Opinions*, II, p. 361; Rev. Edwin Urban Lewis to H. M. Consul, New York, November 1, 1924, Foreign Office files, FO 371/9633.
88. M. Mokete Manoedi to the Rt. Hon. Winston Spencer Churchill, Secretary of State of the Colonies, September 30, 1922, FO 371/8513.
89. Martin, *Race First*, pp. 139–140.
90. See ibid, pp. 138–139.
91. Ibid, p. 120.
92. "Humbert-Droz' Parallel Report on 'The Revolutionary Movement in the Colonies and Semi-Colonies" (summary from *Pravda*, August 24, 1928), Records of the

Department of State, Record Group (RG) 59, 861.00—Congress, Communist International VI/13, enclosure no. 37, National Archives, Washington, D.C.

93. Speech by Bunting, *Pravda*, July 26, 1928, RG 59, 861.00—Congress, Communist International VI/9.
94. *Negro World*, November 8, 1930. On Garvey and the Communists generally, see Martin, *Race First*, pp. 221–272.
95. *Negro World*, March 17, 1923.
96. UNIA Central Division (New York) files, Schomburg Collection.
97. *Negro World*, October 8, 1921.
98. Ibid, April 1, 1922.
99. Ibid, September 8, 1923.
100. Martin, *Race First*, pp. 45–47.
101. *Johannesburg Star*, July 14, 1926, reprinted in the *Negro World*, September 4, 1926.
102. See Martin, *Race First*, pp. 45, 46.
103. *Gold Coast Leader*, n.d., reprinted in the *Negro World*, February 9, 1924.
104. UNIA Central Division (New York) files, Schomburg Collection.
105. *Negro World*, September 27, 1924. See Martin, *Race First*, for references to UNIA activity in such other neighboring countries as Swaziland, Rhodesia, Nyasaland and Mozambique.

10

George Padmore as a Prototype of the Black Historian in the Age of Militancy*

The decade of the 1960s has witnessed the advance to a form of independence of most countries on the African continent. This process has been paralleled by the raising of the revolutionary slogan of Black Power among dispersed African communities in North America, the West Indies, Britain, Australia and elsewhere. In the wake of these developments has come the cry of Black History taught by Black Scholars from a Black Point of View.

This cry is not new. Like everything else on the contemporary Black scene, this phenomenon has historical antecedents of a respectable vintage. The names of early scholar-activists like Edward Wilmot Blyden, Marcus Garvey, W. E. B. DuBois, J. A. Rogers, and Carter G. Woodson immediately come to mind. There were many others. But it would not be rash to suggest that none came closer to the ideal currently enjoying vogue than George Padmore.

As in the case of any other historian, a discussion of Padmore's approach to history must be prefaced by at least a brief sketch of his biographical background.[1]

Padmore was born in Trinidad in 1902 and attended universities in the United States from 1924 to 1929. During this period he joined and enjoyed meteoric success in the Communist Party of the USA. In 1929 he was sent to Moscow, where his ascent to prominence was no less spectacular. Among other things, he was elected to the Moscow City Soviet (together with Stalin) and became head of the Negro Bureau of the Profintern (Red International of Labor Unions). He even sat on a

*Originally published in 1971

commission which investigated charges of ultra-left deviationism brought by Mao Tse-tung against a Chinese comrade. In 1933 he broke with Moscow, though not with Marxism, and devoted the rest of his life to the cause of Pan-Africanism. From 1957 to 1959 he served as advisor on African affairs to President Kwame Nkrumah of Ghana. He died in the latter year and, in the words of his biographer, "It only remained for the Ghanaians to institutionalize him, which they quickly did."

Even this brief outline reveals that there were two dominant ideological influences on Padmore's life. These were Marxism and his Pan-Africanist passion for the freedom of all Black people everywhere. It is these two influences which dictated the orientation of Padmore's historical (and other) writing.

When compared with his reputation as a revolutionary and a journalist, Padmore's reputation as a historian is insignificant, if indeed it exists at all. This fact alone is significant for an examination of Padmore as a historian, for it says something about the dominant definition of what constitutes history in "scholarly" circles. Most persons who have expended the best portions of their lives in the time-consuming pursuit of PhD's would probably refer to Padmore's historical endeavors as "journalistic" or "polemical" writings, but not history properly so-called. Yet, as will be argued in this paper, his accuracy could usually stand comparison with the most distinguished.

Certainly, he himself took his writing seriously. His biographer, noting the absence of human references in his books, explained that Padmore himself remarked that he "wanted nothing to get in the way of the main point—the indictment of colonialism on a sound academic basis."[2] And Padmore did not entirely lack experience of an academic environment, for though his revolutionary activities prevented him from graduating from university, he nevertheless lectured for a while on colonialism at the University of the Toilers of the East (Kutvu) in the Soviet Union as well as to university summer-schools in the United Kingdom.

And, whatever establishmentarian academics might think, his qualities as a historian were certainly appreciated by progressive Africans, as witness the following extract from an otherwise hostile review of one of his books, by a member of the West African Students' Union—

> There is no need for us to vindicate the claim of George Padmore to be one of the outstanding historians of the African nationalist

background. . . . In the past some of his books have shown some refresh-
ing respect for facts which most books written by British historians have
hopefully lacked.[3]

The truth of this statement will be demonstrated later.

Padmore's relevance for contemporary militant Black (and radical
white) historiography can be demonstrated, as well as in any other
respect, in his honesty. And being both honest and uncompromisingly
committed to certain points of view, he was led inevitably to a total
rejection of the cult of "impartiality" behind which so many historians
hid (and continue to hide) their biases.

Padmore's observations on this subject should be compulsory reading for every student of history, and must be quoted at length. In a
letter to a French Socialist who had criticized one of his books he had
this to say—

> I distrust people who talk to me about objectivity and despise people who
> run with the hares and hunt with the hounds. It makes me angry when I
> hear one author condemning the work of another on the spurious ground
> of 'objectivity.' Leave that to *The Times* and God! . . . No nationalist can
> be objective where the fate of his country's freedom is involved. The
> trouble with most British people is that they have not had any foreigners
> sitting on their necks since the Danes and the Normans. So they are the
> only people who make a fetish of 'objectivity' except when Napoleon and
> Hitler were threatening to 'visit' them and turn them into 'natives'—as
> conquered people are called. I presume Miss Lucy [generic for the white
> madam] should be 'objective' and take her kicks![4]

He launched into a similar discussion right at the beginning of his
Africa: Britain's Third Empire. This time, however, he sought to dis-
tinguish between "impartiality" and "objectivity." On this occasion he
seems to have used "impartiality" for the idea conveyed by "objectivity" in the passage quoted above, while assigning to "objectivity" a
more restricted meaning.

> It is hardly necessary for me to say that, as a life-long Anti-Imperialist, I
> make no pretense (as is the fashion among imperialist writers on Colonies)
> to impartiality. Nevertheless, I have tried to be as objective as possible in
> presenting the facts, yet critical in my interpretation and analysis of these
> facts. . . . In this respect the book constitutes an indictment of a social
> system—Imperialism—from the point of view of an African.[5]

Such honesty is hard to come by among historians. As an aside may be
noted his use of the term "African" to describe himself, a product of the

African dispersion. This, too, would make him a prototype of the contemporary Pan-African activist.

The passage above continued in the mockingly eloquent language at which he was an adept, and which caused many of his books, scholarly or otherwise, to be banned from colonial territories as unsavory propaganda. This anti-imperialism, he said,

> need arouse no alarm in official circles. For there never was a time when British Imperialism had so many apologists and defenders, even in the ranks of the Left, since the Labour government has assumed custodianship of the remains of what Mr. Herbert Morrison once proudly described as the 'jolly old Empire.'

Padmore's honesty and forthrightness were reinforced by a sufficient quantity of realism. He knew very well that his unashamedly Anti-Imperialist perspective would, where his works were not banned, often cause his efforts to be dismissed as frivolous or biased beyond acceptable limits. He therefore applied a tactic utilized by Karl Marx himself, as well as by other historians who have found themselves in a similar predicament. He studied assiduously the works of the imperialists themselves, and, whenever possible, he would prove his point by quoting the words of the very persons he was attacking.

Hence scattered throughout his historical and other writings one can find observations like the following—

> To avoid the charge of exaggeration we will quote evidence from the writings of bourgeois travellers who have visited Angola and investigated conditions [of slavery].[6]

This particular passage was followed by the testimony of "Mr. Joseph Burtt, a representative of the British chocolate manufacturers, the Cadbury Co. Ltd.," a British peer, and other unimpeachable representatives of the most exalted imperialist circles.

It is interesting to note here in passing that Eric Williams, the Trinidadian prime minister-historian who was at one time a personal friend and admirer of Padmore, expressly adopted the same tactic. Said he, in his much maligned *History of the People of Trinidad and Tobago*,

> The book is twice as long as originally planned but it has been thought better, . . . partly to forestall uninformed challenges, to let the documents speak for themselves and to quote them rather than to summarize or condense.[7]

This pre-emptive stroke did not quite pay off, however, for this particular work was attacked by reviewers of diverse persuasions. One British reviewer outdid most others in calling it "less history than a tract denouncing colonialism."[8]

Padmore's necessary reliance on imperialist sources did not in any way detract from his anti-imperialism. Where he could use his enemies' utterances to prove his point he obviously did so. But he was equally happy admitting the good deeds of imperialists only to expose the self-interest which often stalked behind the mask of altruism. This was a much better tactic than an alternative which he abhorred. As he himself put it in a letter to a critic,

> . . . after all, I cannot write history like the Stalinist—leave out the names of people because I disapprove of their policies.[9]

But having mentioned the person or institution he disliked he would proceed to demolish it in the exquisite invective that arises only out of strong emotional involvement in one's subject-matter. "However," he said on one such occasion, after having described an apparently fine gesture on the part of the Anglican Church, "we must not permit ourselves to be fooled by this ecclesiastical gesture . . . the religious dope peddlers are doing their best to direct the growing revolutionary spirit among the masses into safe channels. . . ."[10]

Padmore did not often mention other historians. But in so far as he did, it is feasible to surmise that the member of that profession he liked least was Margery Perham, the prolific British Africanist. This lady, after several decades of academic activity, mostly emanating from Oxford University, is still held in the highest esteem in British scholarly circles. She represents the "best traditions" of British historical scholarship, and Padmore's Marxist/Pan-Africanist interpretation of events can profitably be illustrated by comparing the accounts of these two historians of two episodes in West African history, namely Indirect Rule and the Aba Riots of 1929 in South-Eastern Nigeria.

Indirect rule was the system of governing through the existing governmental apparatus, which was utilized in several parts of the British Empire. The popularization of the idea was due chiefly to its relative success in Northern Nigeria, where it had been introduced by the British soldier Sir Frederick Lugard, following his conquest of the area, largely completed between 1900 and 1903.

Padmore's case was simply that because Lugard was faced with a conquered country several times the size of Britain, for the occupation of which he had a mere handful of white troops and their African levies, and because Britain was at the time too preoccupied with the South African Boer War to divert too much assistance,

> He had no alternative but to leave these feudal autocrats in office, . . . The experiment succeeded beyond expectation and was extended to Southern Nigeria, where there were no such large units existing;[11]

From this premise he proceeded to accuse Miss Perham of acting as an apologist for British imperialism—

> Indirect Rule is now universally acclaimed as the cheapest and easiest method of governing huge territories inhabited by primitive races. The experiences of the pioneers in Northern Nigeria were collected and later rationalized into a theory—a new philosophy of colonial government. Books have been written extolling the benefits which Indirect Rule has conferred upon the Africans. One of the most enthusiastic theoreticians and prolific apologists of the system is Miss Margery Perham, lecturer on Native Administration at Nuffield College, Oxford. Miss Perham's views have been expounded at some length in her book, *Native Administration in Nigeria*, which has become a sort of Bible for British Political Officers in Africa. . . .[12]

It might be noted in passing that the book in question (first published in 1937) is still something of a Bible in at least some British academic circles. The writer of this article discovered this to his cost, when, as an undergraduate in an English university in 1967, he was audacious enough to suggest to his Commonwealth History lecturer that, despite Miss Perham's undoubted excellence, etc., it might nevertheless be less than irresponsible to entertain the possibility, however slight, that the good lady's approach to Indirect Rule constituted something less than the ultimate distillation of wisdom on that subject.

Miss Perham's version admitted that "[Lugard] was not in a position to take over the direct administration of this immense area. He had neither the money, the staff, the communications. . . ." Yet, after all this, she could contradictorily conclude that "it is a superficial view that the decision to rule through the native authorities was dictated by no more than the necessity of the moment."[13] Her reason for this assertion was that Lugard had become endeared to the system by sojourns in Uganda and India. Yet she failed to point out that in both these areas British administrators faced the same fact of ancient well-developed political structures, and especially in the case of India, a huge population and immense land area, that she faced in Northern Nigeria. Padmore's version was therefore undoubtedly preferable. The distinction between the honest polemicist and the "objective" product of the "best British traditions" is even more clearly revealed by their respective treatments of the Aba Riots. In this case thousands of Eastern Nigerian women had risen up against their British oppressors when the latter attempted to enumerate the women and their possessions for tax purposes in the middle of the Great Depression, at a time when the women were already in the throes of economic distress.

Miss Perham opened her discussion of this subject with a general observation on the basic ignorance of Africans . . .

> People who do not know to communicate or even to formulate their sense of grievance in constitutional terms may resort to violence as the only effective way in which they can show their dissatisfaction. . . .[14]

This was immediately followed by a claim to objectivity: "The events will first be summarized as far as possible without comment, . . ." If there was no overt comment, however, there was much implied comment in her choice of words. She thus provided an excellent example of the basic dishonesty of the self-righteously "objective" school of historians. This implied comment is demonstrated in the following piece of apparently straight narration—

> Police and troops were sent, and as, on two occasions, the women ran towards them with frenzied shouts, fire was opened with a Lewis gun as well as with rifles, and eighteen women were killed and nineteen wounded.[15]

This "objective" scholarly narration leaves one with the feeling that "as" the women charged with frenzied shouts, "therefore" (not expressed, but logically implied) the troops were justified in killing and wounding a large number of them at point blank range. Miss Perham's lack of comment continued in similar vein:

> [The women] demanded, out of their half knowledge of legal forms, that [the District Officer] should sign the document; that the signature should be witnessed by the interpreter and the office clerk and stamped with the office stamp.[16]

But what is so suggestive of "half-knowledge" here? Her account seems rather to provide evidence of a distinct familiarity with legal forms.

When she did allow herself to comment, it was to attribute to the

womens' spirited defence of themselves at the subsequent inquiry
"second thoughts, as a measure of such abuse is generally taken for
granted by Africans."[17]

By the time Miss Perham's chapter drew to a close she had warmed
considerably to her task. "Here the Aba riots point a moral that is
applicable far beyond Nigeria," she pontificated learnedly, for

> beyond the peculiar local symptoms lies a pathological condition common
> to the whole of negro [sic] Africa. It is produced by the sudden strain
> thrown upon primitive communities by the strong, all-embracing pres-
> sure of European influence.[18]

It is conceivable that the dear lady may also have considered Irish
resistance to British rule a manifestation of primitiveness, but one
wonders how she would have explained French resistance to the German occupation during World War II. Nor was Padmore slow to spot
this basic contradiction. His biographer had paraphrased him elsewhere to the effect that "Even indirect rule was practised by the Nazis:
their chiefs and emirs were called Quislings. Curiously, Europeans
could not see that the epithet applied outside Norway."[19]

Padmore's treatment of the Aba episode was entirely different. As a
Marxist, he went, as he always did, straight to the economic roots of
the disturbance—

> The world economic crisis of capitalism has had a tremendous effect upon
> Nigeria. . . . So the Government, in order to find a way out of its financial
> dilemma, attempted to throw the whole burden upon the toiling masses,
> especially the peasants, by increasing direct taxation upon them. . . . In
> this way the Government hoped to force the women and children to leave
> the villages and seek work on the plantations and other industries owned
> by foreign capitalists in order to provide the money to pay the tax-
> gatherers.[20]

He mentioned many of the oppressive measures such as martial law
and censorship which accompanied the event, as well as the official
cynicism and reprisals which followed, all facts either completely
omitted or apologetically glossed over by Miss Perham. He also,
significantly, quoted the much larger figure of casualties believed by
Nigerians, rather than the conservative official British estimate preferred by Miss Perham.

These two illustrations show Padmore, the unashamed anti-
imperialist as honest to what he professes to be and generally immune,
for that reason, from becoming enmeshed in unresolvable contradic-

tions. Perham, on the other hand, could be at once true to her pro-imperialist bias and true to her self-professed "objectivity" only at the price of some distortion of the evidence. This is as clear an example as will ever be found of the dilemma of the "objective" historian.

The present resurgence of the tendency away from sterile "objectivity" can only be welcomed. It represents a trend towards honesty. It also represents a trend towards the humanization of history. For historians are people too, and it is the very quintessence of arrogance for ivory-towered stiff-upper-lipped apologists of oppression to define the mould within which an oppressed people and their progressive sympathizers should construct their history. As W. E. B. DuBois long ago discovered, "one could not be a calm, cool, and detached scientist while Negroes were lynched, murdered and starved. . . ."[21]

Notes

1. For a detailed treatment of Padmore's life, political thought and Pan-Africanist connections, see James R. Hooker, *Black Revolutionary: George Padmore's Path from Communism to Pan-Africanism* (London: Pall Mall, 1967), from which this resumé is taken.
2. *Ibid.*, p. 41.
3. *Ibid.*, pp. 116–117.
4. Quoted *ibid.*, pp. 125 and 126.
5. George Padmore, *Africa: Britain's Third Empire* (London: Dobson, 1949), p. 9.
6. George Padmore, *The Life and Struggles of Negro Toilers* (London: Published by the Red International of Labour Union's Magazine for the International Trade Union Committee of Negro Workers, 1931), p. 41.
7. Eric Williams, *History of the People of Trinidad and Tobago* (London: Deutsch, 1964), p. ix.
8. *Times Literary Supplement*, 1964, p. 324.
9. Quoted in Hooker, *op. cit.*, p. 129.
10. *Life and Struggles, op. cit.*, p. 58.
11. *Africa: Britain's Third Empire, op. cit.*, p. 127.
12. *Ibid.*
13. Margery Perham, *Native Administration in Nigeria* (London: OUP, 1937), p. 43.
14. *Ibid.*, p. 206.
15. *Ibid.*, p. 209.
16. *Ibid.*, p. 210.
17. *Ibid.*, p. 217.
18. *Ibid.*, p. 218.
19. Hooker, *op. cit.*, p. 63.
20. *Life and Struggles, op. cit.*, p. 88.
21. W. E. B. DuBois, *Dusk of Dawn*, (N.Y.: Schoken, 1968, first pub., 1940), P. 67.

11

C. L. R. James and the Race/Class Question*

The twentieth century has witnessed an intensification of the worldwide struggle of Black people for freedom from colonialism and race prejudice. This struggle has its roots in the nineteenth century and before. At various stages in this struggle the ranks of Black revolutionaries have been augmented by volunteers, as it were, from among the ranks of white liberals and radicals.

One of the most vexing problems, at both the theoretical and practical levels, with which persons involved in this struggle have had to deal, is the question of the relative weights which should be assigned to the rival factors of race and class. In other words, should the struggle be articulated essentially in terms of a racial conflict, or should it rather be viewed as a variant, albeit a special one, of the struggle of oppressed classes? On the one hand, people like Marcus Garvey, though by no means oblivious of the class distinctions affecting Black people, have nevertheless argued (in Garvey's case with phenomenal success) for the primacy of race, and have therefore emphasized the Black Nationalist aspects of the struggle. On the other hand, we have the example of a host of Black communists, Trotskyites, and other Marxists who reached political maturity in the 1920s and 1930s, and who were firm advocates of the primacy of the class struggle as a vehicle for Black liberation. These Black Marxists felt very keenly the racial injustices meted out to their people, but nevertheless frowned, in varying degrees, upon what they characterized as the "petit-bourgeois nationalism" of people like Garvey. This group did not necessarily minimize the race factor. Indeed, the Communist Party of the United States had by 1928 come to the conclusion (on the direction of Moscow) that Afro-Americans exhibited the attributes of an oppressed nation, while Leon

*Originally published in 1972

Trotsky, at least as early as 1933, seemed to be moving towards a similar position.[1]

BIOGRAPHICAL SKETCH

Among the more important Black Marxists engaged in the worldwide struggle of oppressed Black people from the 1930s onwards was C. L. R. James,[2] and his approach to this problem, though not necessarily identical with anybody else's, nevertheless provides an insightful case study of the way in which a Black Marxist could attempt to resolve the problem.

James was born in Trinidad in 1901, one year after the epochal Pan-African Conference held in London had bequeathed the term "Pan-Africanism" to the worldwide struggle of Black peoples.[3] This conference had been convened by another Trinidadian, Henry Sylvester Williams, and had been attended by, among other people, W. E. B. DuBois. In 1932, after some political and literary activity in Trinidad, James moved to England, where his predilection for left-wing politics brought him to the Trotskyite movement. By 1937, with the publication of his *World Revolution, 1917–1936*[4] he had already established himself as a leading theoretician of the movement. His interests were catholic, however, and his output prolific. For in this period he also produced works of fiction ranging from plays to novels, was a cricket correspondent for the *Manchester Guardian*, and wrote books on Black history, including his *magnum opus, The Black Jacobins*.[5]

1938 found him in the United States engaged in a lecture tour and studying the condition of Afro-American communities. In 1939 he engaged in discussions with Leon Trotsky at Coyoacan, Mexico, on the "Negro question", to use the terminology of the age.[6] This American period lasted until 1952, when James was expelled from the United States, a victim of the McCarthyite period of communist-hunting.[7] During this first American period (for he was to return later) James participated actively, among other things, in organizational work among sharecroppers in south-east Missouri and among workers in Detroit and elsewhere.

The year of James' arrival in the United States (1938) was the same in which the Trotskyite Socialist Workers Party (S.W.P.) was formed. James' reputation had apparently preceded him, for he seems to have assumed a position of pre-eminence in American Trotskyite circles right from the beginning. The following account of his role in the 1939 discussions between the S.W.P. and Trotsky gives some indication of his importance:

> The principal figure in the delegation that visited [Trotsky] was J. R. Johnson [James' political pseudonym], a revolutionary black intellectual from one of the British colonies and a member of the Fourth International. Johnson had been living in the United States for the previous six months, acquainting himself, among other things, with the state of the American Negro community.[8]

In 1940 James was one of a minority which split from the S.W.P. and formed the Workers Party. Shortly thereafter, James and a few of his disciples coalesced into a faction within the Workers Party. A publication of this faction in 1947 explained that "the Johnson-Forest tendency", as it became known, "became conscious of itself early in 1941 in the discussion of the Russian question".[9] In 1947 the Johnson-Forest tendency re-entered the S.W.P., where it remained until 1951.[10]

James' deportation from the United States induced a sojourn in England until 1958, when he returned to Trinidad, at the request of Eric Williams, the island's premier, to edit *The Nation*, organ of Williams' Peoples National Movement (P.N.M.). He also became secretary of the West Indian Federal Labour Party, ruling party of the short-lived Federation of the West Indies. Ideological and other differences between James and members of the P.N.M.'s hierarchy caused him to resign his editorship of *The Nation* in 1960 and to return to England a couple of years later.

In 1965 James returned to Trinidad in his role as a cricket reporter to cover an international series, whereupon he was placed under what amounted to house arrest by the Williams government.[11] James retaliated by helping organize a Workers and Farmers Party, which, however, did not fare well in the general election of 1966. Another brief sojourn in England followed.

For the last two or three years James has been a university professor at Black colleges in the United States. He was recently (1971) awarded an honorary doctorate by the University of the West Indies.

James' importance for the history of the Pan-African struggle of the last four decades proceeds largely from the fact that he has worked closely with, and often influenced, many of the persons who have led that struggle in various parts of the world. First among these was George Padmore, the Trinidadian who, in 1929, became head of the Negro bureau of the Red International of Labor Unions (Profintern), whose headquarters were in Moscow. They were co-founders in 1937 of the International African Service Bureau, of whose organ, *International African Opinion*, James was editor.[12] Previous to this they had collaborated in an organization formed by James known as The International African Friends of Ethiopia. In fact, their friendship dated back to their boyhood days in Trinidad.[13]

Padmore is one of the most important figures in the history of the Pan-African idea. Together with Kwame Nkrumah, first president of independent Ghana, he organized the Fifth Pan-African Congress held in Manchester in 1945. This conference is generally considered to be one of the most important events in the history of Pan-Africanism. Padmore's last contribution to the struggle was as Nkrumah's adviser on African affairs. He died in 1959.

James' role in the evolution of the Pan-African idea can be seen equally well in his association with Kwame Nkrumah himself. James first came in contact with Nkrumah during the latter's student days in the United States, and Nkrumah, in his autobiography, duly paid tribute to James for having initiated him into the intricacies of how an underground movement worked.[14]

It was James also who provided Nkrumah with the letter of introduction to George Padmore. According to James, Nkrumah at that point still suffered from certain ideological shortcomings—"he used to talk a lot about imperialism and Leninism and export of capital, and he used to talk a lot of nonsense".[15] The letter nevertheless stated, "George, this young man is coming to you. He is not very bright, but nevertheless do what you can for him because he's determined to throw the Europeans out of Africa."[16]

In 1967 James became very interested in the political development of Stokely Carmichael and was moved to proffer much unsolicited advice to this young Pan-Africanist.[17] It is interesting to note that Carmichael, like James and Padmore before him, was associated with Nkrumah prior to the latter's death. They both lived in Guinea.

James' influence, of course, has not been limited to persons who were outstanding advocates of Pan-Africanism. Thus Jomo Kenyatta was also a member of the International African Service Bureau, and Eric Williams regarded him as something of a mentor before their break in 1960.[18] In addition, generations of Black students have treated him with veneration and have enlisted his support and advice for all manner of revolutionary causes.[19]

THE RACE/CLASS QUESTION

More than most other Pan-African revolutionaries, James has been a Marxist first and foremost, and his ideas on issues relevant to the international Black struggle have been developed within the general framework of his Marxist theories. In fact, his whole Pan-Africanist involvement may justifiably be viewed as no more than one aspect (though a very important aspect) of his Marxist activities. And unlike most of the other leading Pan-African ideologists of the last few decades, his prolific writings contain a large proportion of material on Marxist theory, in which aspects of the Pan-African struggle do not appear or appear only peripherally.[20] This circumstance does not, of course, diminish his contribution to the worldwide political development of Black peoples.

James' independent interpretations of Marxist theory took organizational form, as has been seen, through the Johnson-Forest tendency. And among the theoretical principles which were central to the tendency were the rejection of the idea of Stalinist Russia as a workers' state, the rejection of Lenin's theory of the vanguard party as correct for the changed circumstances of the post-1917 world, and support for the control of industry and politics by workers (as manifested by the workers' councils which emerged during the Hungarian Revolution of 1956) as the basis of the future ideal state. The Johnson-Forest tendency, in a word, set out to update Marx and Lenin and correct Trotsky, while attempting nevertheless to remain true to the essentials of Marxism-Leninism.

As a Marxist, quite naturally, James had little difficulty making his mind up on the question of the ascendancy of class over race. Even when accepting the applicability of Lenin's ideas on national minorities to the movement for self-determination among Afro-Americans, for example, or when appearing to condone the rhetoric of Black Power, he has never deviated from his view that race is subordinate to class.

This is illustrated in practically everything he ever wrote on the race question. His *magnum opus, The Black Jacobins* (a history of the Haitian Revolution), was thus conceived not so much as the triumph of Black slaves over their white oppressors, as an "analysis of a revolution for self-determination in a colonial territory".[21] It constituted, in his opinion, "a book of general historical interest written especially with a view to the elucidation of the African revolution. The point about that book is that it kept an even balance between general history and Marxist policy."[22] His preparation for writing the book included a study of Lenin.[23] It is not surprising to find in this work, therefore, a clear summation of his theory of race, from which he has never seriously deviated: "The race question is subsidiary to the class question in politics, and to think of imperialism in terms of race is disastrous. But to neglect the racial factor as merely incidental [is] an error only less grave than to make it fundamental."[24] Indeed, James sometimes appears to be possessed of a certain detachment from any personal emotional involvement in the racial injustice he thunders against. His resolution on the "Negro Problem" to the Socialist Workers Party convention of 1948 gives an inkling of this tendency. This resolution contained an excellent historical analysis of the Black experience in America. The concluding sentence reads:

> Anyone who knows them, who knows their history, is able to talk to them intimately, watches them at their own theatres, watches them at their dances, watches them in their churches, reads their press with a discerning eye, must recognize that although their social force may not be able to compare with the social force of a corresponding number of organized workers, the hatred of bourgeois society and the readiness to destroy it when the opportunity should present itself, rests among them to a degree greater than in any other section of the population in the United States.[25]

It is difficult to find in this coldly incisive analysis the sense of personal hurt against personally experienced racial injustice that one finds in Fanon,[26] or that characterized Nkrumah's experience in the United States,[27] or, strange to say, that is sometimes expressed in the work of Eric Williams, or that is inherent in the invective of a Stokely Carmichael. And one just cannot conceive of James ever being affected to the extent of Garvey, who is said to have been moved to tears after viewing a parade of the decimated ranks of Black veterans returning to Harlem after World War One.[28] Garvey's empathy with the vain sacrifices of these Black soldiers was complete.

This unusual ability of James to suppress any sense of personal bitterness on the race question seems even to have antedated his conversion to Marxism. For in reminiscences of his adolescence he mentions a case of racial discrimination meted out to him personally, but which he seems to have dismissed with no hard feelings. He had attempted to enlist in the Merchants and Planters Contingent (white) rather than in the white-officered British West Indies Regiment which was set aside

for Black West Indian patriots during World War One. James explained:

> The rumour was, and the facts seemed to show, that the merchants
> selected only white or brown people. But though I was dark, I was widely
> known as a coming cricketer and I kept goal for the college teams in the
> first-class football league. I was tall and very fit . . . I went down to the
> office where one of the big merchants, perhaps the biggest of all, ex-
> amined the would-be warriors. . . . When my turn came I walked to his
> desk. He took one look at me, saw my dark skin, and shaking his head
> vigorously, motioned me violently away.
>   What matters is that I was not unduly disturbed . . . It didn't hurt for
> long because for so many years these crude intrusions from the world
> which surrounded us had been excluded. I had not even been wounded,
> for no scar was left.[29]

The "crude intrusions from the world" outside had been excluded by
the atmosphere at Queen's Royal College in Trinidad which he attended, and which he called "our little Eden".[30] At this time the
teaching staff was composed almost entirely of English graduates of
Oxford and Cambridge, and the college itself was still largely the
school for sons of white civil servants. James had entered it by winning
one of the few competitive scholarships awarded annually. His "little
Eden" contrasts markedly with the recorded experiences of a later
generation of Black students who passed through similar schools in the
West Indies at a time when race relations can be presumed to have
improved, but who described anything but a "little Eden."[31]

With this attitude towards race then, proceeding from his Marxism
and apparently reinforced by his adolescent experiences, James, like
most other Marxists involved in the race question, enthusiastically
welcomed the breakthrough in race relations which seemed to be
heralded by the appearance of the Congress of Industrial Organizations
in the mid-1930s. Here, for once, it seemed that his ideas on the
proletarian and the race questions, as well as his belief in the spon-
taneity of the masses as superior to the dictates of "vanguard parties",
were actually being demonstrated in practice. For the workers had,

> seized capitalist property by force. Secondly, they opened their gates to
> Negroes, since the Civil War the biggest action on this running sore of
> American society. Thirdly, in general they acted in a manner that showed
> the revolutionary fervour that was moving in them, . . . The specific
> American readiness for action without theory is here seen at its best.[32]

It may be for these reasons that he could ascribe the apparent slackening of Black nationalist activity in the late 1930s to the Black man's newly-found "opportunity to fight with the organized workers and to gain something".[33] The decay and bureaucratization of the C.I.O. only served to reinforce his animosity towards union leaders, to whom he is as opposed as to the leaders of the Soviet Union.

His enthusiasm for the C.I.O. seems to have led him to extreme lengths to demonstrate the affinity between white and Black workers. Thus in the early 1940s in a propaganda pamphlet published by a C.I.O. affiliate we find him making the dubious claim, in a section headed "To the White Workers Especially", that, "There was a lynching in Sikeston the other day and the Negroes are bitter about it, but that lynching was a landlord's trick to divide us. All our brothers in Sikeston are ready to join with you in the most important thing before you and us—the fight for 30c an hour."[34]

James' enthusiasm for the C.I.O. is further illuminated by reference to his very orthodox Marxist position on the dependence of the Black revolution on the success of the wider proletarian struggle. He stated this argument very clearly in 1960 to an audience in Trinidad:

> The great problem of the United States, with all due respect to the colour of the majority of my audience, is not the Negro Question. (If this question of the workers' independent political organization were solved the Negro Question would be solved. As long as this is not solved the Negro Question will never be solved).[35]

And two decades before this he had proposed a historical framework to substantiate his case during his discussions with Trotsky in Mexico:

1. The study of Negro history and historic propaganda should be:
   (a) Emancipation of Negroes in San Domingo linked with the French Revolution.
   (b) Emancipation of the slaves in the British Empire linked with the British Reform Bill of 1832.
   (c) Emancipation of the Negroes in the United States linked with the Civil War in America. This leads easily up to the conclusion that the emancipation of the Negro in the United States and abroad is linked with the emancipation of the white working class.
   (d) The economic roots of racial discrimination.
   (e) Fascism.
   (f) The necessity for self-determination for Negro peoples in Africa and a similar policy in China, India, etc.[36]

In presenting this argument James has sometimes shifted the emphasis in a manner which is barely perceptible but very significant. On these occasions he seems to view the white proletariat, not necessarily as ready and willing to join hands with the oppressed Black masses, but as the means of heightening the contradictions within white society, contradictions which Black people can use to their advantage. In this argument he seems to be hinting around the periphery of what Marcus Garvey characteristically asserted with a minimum of circumspection: "Negroes have no right with white peoples' fights or quarrels, except like the humble, hungry, meagre dog, to run off with the bone when both contestants drop it, being sure to separate himself from the big, well-fed dogs, by a good distance, otherwise to be overtaken, and then completely outdone."[37]

Both these lines of thought—that Black people should unite with white workers, and that Black people should capitalize on the contradictions within white society, are usually found together in James' writings and flow from the same analysis. He does not normally consider them opposed to each other but complementary. Both streams can easily be discerned, for example, in his 1939 conversations with Trotsky and in his 1948 resolution on the race question. They are seen even more clearly in a document written probably only a few months after that 1939 meeting. In this document James looks forward to the second civil war in America which will complete the emancipation of Black people:

> Sooner or later the workers and farmers of America, who are now fighting against the landlords and capitalists in unions, on the WPA, in struggles for better relief, will ultimately be driven to the same civil war that we have seen take place in country after country during the last 25 years. A Negro therefore who is looking at the political situation, not as it appears on the surface, but is seeing into the reality of the struggle between the classes, can have confidence in the future. He will realize that all white America is not solid. There is a tremendous division, a great split opening up. We can already see the signs of it very clearly. And as this struggle approaches and then actually flares out into the inevitable civil war, Negroes can be certain that many white workers and farmers who today are prejudiced will seek Negro assistance in the same way that Lincoln did when he fought the South. Negroes in the last civil war made one great step forward, and so, in this coming civil war, the worker's war, Negroes have a great chance to complete their long journey to full freedom.[38]

This statement leads on naturally to an examination of one of the most important aspects of James' position on the race/class question. For within the general framework of the unity of struggle between white workers and Black toilers, he recognized, and in fact stressed, the independent validity of the Black struggle. We have a unique opportunity to see him clarifying this position in the record of his conversations with Trotsky in 1939.

For this meeting James prepared a preliminary statement which served as a basis for the discussion. In it he postulated that "the Negro, fortunately for socialism, does not want self-determination", but nevertheless "*if he wanted self-determination*, then however reactionary it might be in every other respect, it would be the business of the revolutionary party to raise that slogan." (Emphasis in the original). He went on to develop this argument during the conversation:

> The white workers have centuries of prejudice to overcome, but at the present time many of them are working with the Negroes in the Southern sharecroppers' union and with the rise of the struggle there is every possibility that they will be able to overcome their agelong prejudices. But for us to propose that the Negro have this black state for himself is asking too much from the white workers, especially when the Negro himself is not making the same demand.[39]

He sealed his arguments against advocating self-determination by alleging that the Black population in the United States lacked the "tradition of language, literature and history to add to the economic and political oppression."[40]

To these arguments Trotsky and another participant objected. They could see nothing inherently reactionary in self-determination and they disagreed that the Afro-American lacked the necessary cultural and historical basis to form a separate nation. Trotsky also insisted (in opposition to James) that Garvey's movement represented a sublimated desire for self-determination. Accord was easily reached by the parties and James shortly afterwards drafted a resolution on "The SWP and Negro Work" which recognized the validity of "black chauvinism" in view of the betrayal of Black people by white Democrats, Republicans, communists, and others, and condemned "white American chauvinism, the expression of racial domination", as "reactionary".[41] The resolution went on to propose the organization of a "Negro mass organization" on the initiative of Black S.W.P. members. James' authorship of the resolution showed clearly in the proviso that such an organization would not "invalidate the necessary struggle for unity of both black and white workers. But that road is not likely to be a broad highway."[42]

This resolution of 1939 remains a true summation of James's main ideas on the position of race in the revolutionary struggle, and he has remained true to it even to the extent of terminating political alliances rather than compromise on it. In 1947, for example, we find included in the case of the Johnson-Forest tendency against the Workers Party, the latter's abandonment of the 1939 position:

> One of Trotsky's greatest contributions to the American party was his insistence for over ten years on the need to adapt the Leninist policy on the national question to the Negro problem in the United States. The American comrades resisted or gave an acquiescence which was worse than resistance. Finally, in 1939 under Trotsky's careful supervision a policy was adopted. As if by reflex action no sooner did the minority split than Coolidge attacked the position adopted almost unanimously in the SWP. Stage by stage the position was abandoned, accompanied by the most ignorant and unscrupulous attacks upon the whole past of the discussions in our movement and our political tradition. The Minority fought in vain to stem this tide. The result is that the party today is in a mass of unbelievable confusion on a question which in the United States stands second only to the basic conflict between the bourgeoisie and the proletariat itself, besides being of worldwide importance.[43]

And immediately he abandoned the Workers Party to rejoin the S.W.P. he presented his 1948 resolution which was an amplified restatement of the 1939 position.[44]

Whereas in 1947 he had attacked the Workers Party for ignoring the independent aspect of the race question, in 1961 his own small organization split over the opposite problem, namely that of giving too much weight to race *vis-à-vis* class. Some members of the organization, in the words of a member who adhered to James' view, had failed "to link up the revolutionary struggle of the Negroes with that of the working class". This comrade went on—"To stress only the race angle is to surrender the paper's treatment of the question either to the liberals, on the one hand, who see only the extension of Rights, or the Muslims, on the other hand, who see only the extension of Race."[45]

Round about 1967 James became very impressed by the intensification of the Black struggle for liberation as exemplified by the advocates of Black Power. And his enthusiasm for the young militants who appeared on the scene on occasion infused his sentiments with expressions which were almost unlike him. On one occasion, for example, he informed a youthful audience, in the midst of an approving analysis of H. "Rap" Brown, that "the singlemindedness, the determination to fight to the death if need be, which now permeates the Negro movement, will not be corrupted, modified, or in any way twisted from its all-embracing purpose by white do-gooders and well-wishers."[46]

He felt the need to qualify this statement, however, for he hastened to explain that this was not racism but politics. Furthermore, he assured his audience, racism was on the decline in the United States anyway. What was on the increase was Black people fighting the police, rather than white people fighting Black people. This tendency to consign racism to a premature demise was evident as early as 1939, and is a trait which crops up from time to time in the works of Marxists.

The case of James, then, though not necessarily identical with any other, nevertheless provides an interesting case study of one Black Marxist's quest for a reconciliation of the class and race struggles. The primacy of class in James is, of course, common to all Marxists. His impatience with those who emphasize the race aspect at the expense of a class analysis, is also typical. Yet several Black Marxists, including his friend George Padmore, have from time to time actually broken off their communist affiliations (though this has not always been followed by a rejection of Marxism) because as Black men they found themselves irresistibly attracted to the cause of Black solidarity, even at the expense of their Marxist training. Padmore was specifically charged with this offence (in his case deserting a class position to engage in "petit-bourgeois" pro-Liberia activities) upon his expulsion from among the ranks of communists. James has been less affected by this attraction than most, no doubt because he has always been a much more thorough-going Marxist than many, Black or white. Yet his record of participation in Black causes seems to suggest that for him, at least, there has been no insurmountable contradiction.

Notes

1. See George Breitman, ed., *Leon Trotsky on Black Nationalism and Self-Determination* (New York: Merit Publishers, 1967), passim.
2. Many of James' works contain biographical information. In addition, a biographical sketch can be found in Martin Glaberman's introduction to the *C. L. R. James Special Issue* of *Radical America* (Vol. IV, No. 4, May 1970). I am grateful to Mr. Glaberman for allowing me to obtain copies of publications by James which are out of print and difficult to come by, and for not appearing to be importuned by my many questions. Mr. Glaberman is a long-time political associate of Mr. James.
3. Since the famous Fifth Pan-African Congress held at Manchester in 1945, the term

"Pan-Africanism" has increasingly been applied to the question of political unity on the African continent. Its original meaning (which included both the above usage and the idea of a community of interest among African people all over the world) still enjoys wide currency. See, e.g., Stokely Carmichael, "We Are All Africans", *The Black Scholar* (Vol. I, No. 7, 1970), pp. 15–19. James himself reflected this resurgence of the original Pan-African outlook when he reprinted his *A History of Negro Protest* (London: 1936) as *A History of Pan-African Revolt* (Washington, D.C.: Drum and Spear Press, 1969).

4. C. L. R. James, *World Revolution, 1917–1936—The Rise and Fall of the Communist International* (London: Secker and Warburg, 1937).

5. C. L. R. James, *The Black Jacobins* (New York: Vintage, 1963; first published 1938).

6. *Leon Trotsky on Black Nationalism*, passim.

7. James' own account of the tribulations surrounding his deportation can be found in his *Mariners, Renegades and Castaways—The Story of Herman Melville and the World We Live In* (New York: published by C. L. R. James, 1953).

8. *Leon Trotsky on Black Nationalism*, p. 21.

9. Johnson-Forest Tendency, *Balance Sheet: The Workers Party and the Johnson–Forest Tendency* (n.p.; pub. by Johnson–Forest Tendency, August 1947), p. 8.

10. The date of re-entry into the S.W.P. is erroneously given as 1951 in Ivar Oxaal, *Black Intellectuals Come to Power*, q.v. for much biographical information on James (Cambridge, Mass.: Schenkman, 1968), p. 77. The 1951 date of final exit is given by James himself in J. R. Johnson, *Letter on Organization* (Detroit: Facing Reality Publishing Committee, n.d.), p. 3.

11. See C. L. R. James, "Dr. Williams's Trinidad: An Attack", *Venture* (January 1966).

12. C. L. R. James, "African Development", *Speak Out*, journal of the Facing Reality Publishing Committee (Vol. II, No. 4, April 1969), p. 4. The date given here for the formation of the Bureau is 1935. The date usually given is 1937. Also, the formation of the I.A.S.B. is usually credited solely to Padmore. For more on the relationship between Padmore and James, see C. L. R. James, "Document: C. L. R. James on the Origins", ɹRadical America (Vol. II, No. 4, July–August 1968), pp. 24–7, and J. R. Hooker, *Black Revolutionary: George Padmore's Path from Communism to Pan-Africanism* (London: Pall Mall, 1967), passim.

13. "Document: C. L. R. James on the Origins", op. cit., p. 24.

14. Kwame Nkrumah, *Ghana* (London: Nelson, 1959), p. 36.

15. "Document: C. L. R. James on the Origins", op. cit., p. 26.   16. Ibid.

17. See C. L. R. James, *Black Power: Its Past, Today, and the Way Ahead* (Detroit: Facing Reality, 1968), passim; and Facing Reality Publishing Committee, *The Gathering Forces* (Detroit: Facing Reality, 1967), pp. 65–7. This was a draft of a statement to celebrate the fiftieth anniversary of the October Socialist Revolution in the Soviet Union. It was a collective effort. Mr. Glaberman indicated to me the passages written by James.

18. Williams, in his autobiography, says he gave up an opportunity to visit Nigeria in order to confer with James in London in 1956 on his party's draft programme and Trinidad's draft constitution. Padmore and West Indian economist W. Arthur Lewis also participated in these discussions. See Eric Williams, *Inward Hunger* (London: Deutsch, 1969), p. 143.

19. Black students in London organized a "C. L. R. James School" recently—*Bumbo* (journal of the West Indian Students Union in London, n.p., n.d., c. April 1970); a recent case of James' participation in protest activities of Black students in London

can be found in the *Trinidad Guardian* (18 August 1967), p. 1. The occasion was the banning of Stokely Carmichael by the British and Trinidad governments.

20. James' major works on Marxist theory are *World Revolution; State Capitalism and World Revolution* (Detroit: Facing Reality, 1969, first pub. 1950); and *Facing Reality* (Detroit: Correspondence, 1958).

21. *Black Power*, p. 12.

22. J. R. Johnson, *Letters on Organization* (Detroit: Facing Reality, 1963), p. 14.

23. *Black Power*, p. 12.

24. *Black Jacobins*, p. 283.

25. C. L. R. James, 'The Revolutionary Solution to the Negro Problem in the United States', *Radical America* (Vol. IV, No. 4, May 1970), p. 18. The date given for the resolution here is 1947. James gives it as 1948 in C. L. R. James, *Perspectives and Proposals* (Detroit: Facing Reality, 1966), p. 31.

26. Especially in *Black Skin, White Masks* (New York: Grove Press, 1967).

27. E.g. in *Ghana*.

28. J. Saunders Redding, *The Lonesome Road* (New York: Doubleday, 1958), p. 227.

29. C. L. R. James, *Beyond A Boundary* (London: Hutchinson, 1963), p. 40.

30. Ibid., p. 39.

31. See, e.g., Elliott Bastien, "The Weary Road to Whiteness and the Hasty Retreat into Nationalism", in Henri Tajfel and John Dawson, eds., *Disappointed Guests* (London: Oxford University Press for the Institute of Race Relations, 1965), p. 44; Austin Clarke, "Harrison College and Me", *New World Quarterly* (Vol. III, Nos. 1 and 2, Barbados Independence Issue, Dead Season 1966 and Croptime 1967), pp. 31–5.

32. J. R. Johnson, *Marxism and the Intellectuals* (Detroit: Facing Reality, 1962), p. 14.

33. Conversation with Trotsky in *Leon Trotsky on Black Nationalism*, p. 26.

34. J. R. Johnson, *Down With Starvation Wages in South-East Missouri* (Local 313, UCAPAWA-CIO, n.d.), p. 5.

35. C. L. R. James, *Modern Politics* (Port-of-Spain: P. N. M. Publishing Company, 1960), p. 45.

36. *Leon Trotsky on Black Nationalism*, p. 38.

37. Marcus Garvey, "The Negro, Communism, Trade Unionism and His [?] Friend", in Amy Jacques Garvey, ed., *The Philosophy and Opinions of Marcus Garvey* (London: Frank Cass, 1967), Vol. II, p. 70.

38. J. R. Johnson, *Why Negroes Should Oppose the War* (New York: Pioneer Publishers, for the S.W.P. and the Young Peoples Socialist League, n.d.), p. 26.

39. *Leon Trotsky on Black Nationalism*, p. 26.

40. Ibid., pp. 24, 25.

41. Ibid., p. 51.

42. Ibid., p. 52.

43. *The Balance Sheet*, p. 12.

44. "The Revolutionary Solution to the Negro Problem . . .", op. cit.; for a later statement of James' group on the race question see "Negro Americans and American Politics", in C. L. R. James, *Every Cook Can Govern* (Detroit: Correspondence, 1956), p. 19 ff.

45. *Marxism and the Intellectuals*, p. 29.

46. *Black Power*, p. 9.

12
Rescuing Fanon from the Critics*

My real interest in Fanon dates from a night in August 1967 when, together with a couple hundred West Indian students in London, we converged on our Students' Center to listen to a lecture delivered by Stokely Carmichael. One or two of us in the audience had even been at primary school with him in Trinidad, though he probably did not suspect it. "Can't you remember him?" asked an old classmate of mine, trying to jolt my memory. "He was always fighting!"

My recollections from that night are several—the white *agent provocateur* who entered the building and tried unsuccessfully to incite us to violence against him; the contingent of policemen who, transported in an assortment of vehicles, swooped down on the building from all directions as we stood talking to Stokely after the lecture; the haste with which Stokely was spirited away from the scene by his friends wishing to avoid an "incident"; the anguish with which I watched some of my friends come to within an inch of blowing their cool in the face of the police provocations—yet a riot was avoided, and though the British government still banned Stokely from the country shortly afterwards, their arguments would have looked much more plausible if we had succumbed to the provocations of that night.

But my most vivid recollection from that night was the frequency and reverence with which Carmichael quoted another West Indian, Frantz Fanon. The deference accorded to Fanon by this outstanding revolutionary of our time was the deference which some men pay to the quotations of Jesus Christ, and others to Karl Marx or Mao Tse Tung. Wherein lies the appeal of Fanon? This paper will attempt to find out by analysing some of his ideas. In the course of this analysis, it is hoped that some of the slanderous interpretations of Fanon's life and works will be discredited.

*Originally published in 1970

179

The biographical details of Frantz Fanon are fairly well-known[1]—his early bourgeois upbringing in Martinique; his enlistment in the French army at the age of seventeen; his discovery of the realities of being a Black man in the metropolis; his psychiatric studies at Lyon; his left-wing student politics; his involvement in Algeria, first on the staff of a French hospital at Blida, then as a member of the revolutionary government operating from Tunisia, and as an editor of *El Moudjahid* (the Freedom Fighter), organ of the revolution; his involvement in Pan-African conferences as a representative of the Algerian Revolutionary Government and subsequent appointment as Algerian ambassador to Accra; the French attempts on his life; his death from leukemia in December 1961 at the age of thirty-seven, almost simultaneously with the publication of his masterpiece, *The Wretched of the Earth*—tragically cut off in his prime.

Even this brief outline of his life shows that Fanon fits into a type of character of which the last hundred years has thrown up a surprisingly large number of magnificent examples—the master theoretician who is also a man of action. Marx, Lenin, Mao, Che Guevara, Castro, and now Fanon—all these men (the list could be extended) have fused, in their own lives, thought and action. The calm of the scholar's study has become, in these men, but an appendage to the direct involvement of the political activist, even where this has meant, as in the case of Guevara, living and dying, gun in hand, in the jungle.

"The Philosophers have only *interpreted* the world in various ways," said Marx. "The point, however, is to *change* it."[2] And Fanon set out to change it. And the signs are already clear that, in spite of a thousand quibblings over minutiae by a thousand scholars betraying varying degrees of hostility, he will probably succeed.

The key to an appreciation lies in his personality. Fanon was no Draconian monster, as some have tried to paint him (see Isaacs 1965). On the contrary, he was an extremely sensitive individual, whose outstanding personality trait was probably his ability to empathize with the abject suffering which he observed being meted out to his Black brothers around the world. Nor did his abhorrence of suffering stop with the plight of Black people. His humanism, on which his ideas were founded, reached out to embrace all mankind, as I shall endeavor to show later in this paper. This aspect of Fanon's character is eloquently summed up in a line he quotes from Aimé Césaire's *Et les Chiens se Taisent:* "In the whole world no poor devil is lynched, no wretch is tortured, in whom I too am not degraded and murdered."

It would, of course, be surprising if this ability to empathize with the wretched in distant corners of the world were not to be matched by an equal earnestness to probe, to explain, and to prescribe a cure for the suffering which he himself had to endure at the hands of the inhabitants of the metropolis and that which he observed at close quarters.

Fanon's sensitivity to human suffering crops up in the most unexpected places. Despite the tendency of some critics to see him as a Sorel-type advocate of violence, allegedly for its own sake,[3] Fanon abhors violence even while recognizing it as a necessary evil in some circumstances. Simone de Beauvoir in her autobiography recalls the pain which he experiences at the contemplation of the results of violence, whether inflicted by the enemy or his own side (1963; quoted in Seigel 1968). For he is too closely attuned to the desire of humanity for justice to view violence in strictly macropolitical terms. He cannot ignore the suffering of *individuals*. For Fanon, the individual is never lost in a mass of statistics. Who can deny the sincerity of these words:

> No man's death is indispensable for the triumph of freedom. It happens that one must accept the risk of death in order to bring freedom to birth, but it is not lightly that one witnesses so many massacres and so many acts of ignominy (1967c, p. 95).

Indeed, perhaps the most eloquent testimony to the depravity of French colonialism is provided by the fact that it could have driven a man as desirous of justice and a true humanism as Fanon was to the inescapable conclusion that violence was the only answer. Fanon the humanist, the revolutionary who did not want to be a professional revolutionary (de Beauvoir 1963), who was willing to sacrifice the future he worked for so many years to secure to help his suffering brothers in Algeria, who in the midst of an entry in his diary concerning a hazardous mission in enemy territory (1967c, p. 185) could write, "This part of the Sahara is not monotonous. Even the sky up there is constantly changing. Some days ago we saw a sunset that turned the robe of heaven a bright violet"—yes, this was Fanon.

Not only was Fanon a sensitive humanist. He was also a West Indian. And out of these two apparently unrelated attributes his friend Aimé Césaire has come up with a thought-provoking synthesis:

> Fanon probably soared to such heights and was possessed of so wide a horizon because he was a West Indian, meaning that he started from so lowly and narrow a basis. Maybe it was necessary to be West Indian, that is, to be so destituted, so depersonalized, in order to go forth with such

ardour to the conquest of oneself and of plenitude; West Indian, this is to say, so mystified in the beginning as to finally be able to expose the most secret motives of mystification, and with such mastery; finally, West Indian to be capable of so forcefully escaping from impotency by action, and from solitude by fraternity ("Homage . . ." 1962).

When one considers the formidable list of West Indians who have over the years abandoned the stultifying atmosphere of the West Indies to make their influence felt on the international field of Pan-African involvement—Edward Blyden, George Padmore, Henry Sylvester Williams, Marcus Garvey, C. L. R. James, Césaire himself, Stokely Carmichael, Fanon—one wonders whether Césaire has not unwittingly stumbled upon a key to explaining this important phenomenon.

FANON AND MARX

Fanon's writings reveal the influence of several people—Hegel, Marx, Sartre and Césaire, to name but a few. But most commentators have evaluated his philosophy around the concept of Marxism. He has been described as a "Marxist ideologist," "not Marxist . . . [but] populist," "[not] a dogmatic Marxist," "a Marxist," and one whose "borrowings [were] heaviest from Mao" (Brace 1965, Denis 1967, Grohs 1968, Geismar 1969, Isaacs 1965).

Certainly, there are indications of his affinity to Marx which are evident even without a close look at his philosophy—the fact, for example, that two of his three books bore titles directly suggestive of a conscious identification with Marx: *Les Damnés de la Terre*, which is taken from the first line of the *Internationale*, and *L'An Cinq de la Révolution Algérienne*, which bears an obvious similarity to Marx's *The Eighteenth Brumaire of Louis Bonaparte*. These connections suffered with their translation into English. The translation of *L'An Cinq* into *Studies in a Dying Colonialism* was particularly unfortunate, however picturesque the English rendering. (Translators will have to learn that sometimes a literal rendering is best, whatever they might have been taught at school!).

The Eighteenth Brumaire seems to have had a special attraction for Fanon, for it provided him with the *leitmotiv* of his philosophy. Towards the end of his first book he includes a lengthy and famous quotation from it beginning, "The social revolution . . . cannot draw its poetry from the past; but only from the future . . ." (1967a, p. 223). This theme recurs throughout Fanon's works and forms the basis for his controversial rejection of the Senghorian version of Negritude.

There is another quotation from *The Eighteenth Brumaire* which does not appear in Fanon but which also sheds considerable light on his ideas, particularly his idea of history. It is this: "Men make their own history, but they do not make it just as they please; they do not make it under circumstances chosen by themselves, but under circumstances directly encountered, given and transmitted from the past." In this quotation, Marx effects a synthesis of the dialectical necessity inherent in historical development on the one hand, and human initiative, on the other. And here Fanon follows him very closely. For though he nowhere specifically discusses his theory of history, his works are scattered with numerous references to a deterministic conception of history which nevertheless requires human involvement to realize the goals to which historical necessity is pointing. "Each generation," he says, "must, out of relative obscurity, discover its mission, fulfill it, or betray it" (1967d, p. 166). In other words, the mission is there, preordained by history, but it is up to individual initiative to discover and fulfill history. Again,

> The colonialist . . . reaches the point of no longer being able to imagine a time occurring without him. His eruption into the history of the colonized people is deified, transformed into absolute necessity. Now a "historic look at history" requires, on the contrary, that the French colonialist retire, for it has become historically necessary for the national time in Algeria to exist (1967c, p. 159; see 1967c, pp. 170, 173).

There is another similarity between *L'An Cinq* and *The Eighteenth Brumaire*, and undoubtedly the main factor which led Fanon to base his title on Marx's work. This is the fact that both books are conceptually similar. For they both are analyses of a given stage in a revolutionary situation (see Grohs 1968).

It follows from the foregoing that it is wrong to argue, as one commentator does, that Fanon's position in *Black Skin, White Masks* was non-Marxist because he declared that he was not a prisoner of history (Seigel 1968). This conclusion is based on a faulty appraisal of Marx and a superficial understanding of Fanon's theory of history.

Fanon can be considered a Marxist. This is not to say that he adhered rigidly to every word that has come down to us from Marx's pen. He did not. But he was Marxist in the sense that Lenin or Castro or Mao are Marxist. That is, he accepted Marx's basic analysis of society as given and proceeded from there to elaborate on that analysis and modify it where necessary to suit his own historical and geographical context.

Furthermore, while on a *political* level he speaks very often of neutrality and the necessity to stand aloof from the cold war, at the level of *social organization* he is quite clear as to what type of society he wants:

> The concrete problem we find ourselves up against is not that of a choice, cost what it may, between socialism and capitalism as they have been defined by men of other continents and of other ages. Of course we know that the capitalist regime . . . cannot leave us free to perform our work at home, nor our duty in the world. Capitalist exploitation and cartels and monopolies are the enemies of underdeveloped countries. On the other hand the choice of a socialist regime, a regime which is completely oriented towards the people as a whole and based on the principle that man is the most precious of all possessions, will allow us to go forward more quickly and more harmoniously, and thus make impossible that caricature of society where all economic and political power is held in the hands of a few who regard the nation as a whole with scorn and contempt (1967d, p. 78).

Thus by 1960, with four years of high-level contacts with African leaders behind him, he could lament in his diary the fact that, based on these contacts, it seemed to him that the greatest danger threatening Africa was not colonialism and its derivatives but the absence of ideology (1967c, p. 186).

Like the Marxist that he is, Fanon postulates an economic basis for most things. This includes racism and colonialism. In his discussions of the economic basis of colonialism he is, in addition, very close to the Leninist stance, which he seems to have largely adopted.

His utterances on these matters reveal a Fanon torn in two directions. On the one hand, he is struggling to be true to the orthodox Marxist position of a community of interest between the metropolitan workers and the whole populations of the proletarianized Third World. On the other hand, he is faced with the clear evidence of French chauvinism which has transcended class lines. So that in two successive weeks in *El Moudjahid* he appears to make conflicting statements concerning the relationship of these two groups.

About one year later, however, he is able to make a dialectical reconciliation between these two conflicting positions by utilizing a Leninist-Hobsonian analysis (1967c, pp. 76, 82, 144; 1967b, p. 55).

According to his argument, it is both true that the solidarity between metropolitan workers and colonized peoples is a theoretical verity, and also true that experience has revealed many examples of the nonviability of this thesis. The apparent contradiction is explained by the fact that the retreat of imperialism in the face of national wars of liberation is accompanied by a deterioration in the economic position of workers in the metropolis. He continues in classic Leninist vein, "The 'metropolitan' capitalists allow social advantages and wage increases to be wrung from them by their workers to the exact extent to which the colonialist state allows them to exploit . . . the occupied territories." The struggle against this problem must therefore be intensified. So it is not entirely correct to say, as one critic does, that Fanon is contemptuous of international class solidarity (Worsley 1969).

His position *vis-à-vis* metropolitan intellectuals is not dissimilar. For while he recognizes the theoretical bonds linking progressive elements in the metropolis to the colonized masses, and appeals for the strengthening of these bonds, he has no time for those French left-wingers, who, when the chips are down, reveal themselves in all their "egocentric, sociocentric thinking which has become the characteristic of the French" (1967c, p. 71), and their paternalism which "feeds on the ambivalent sources of kindness to the oppressed, or a thirst to *do* something, to be useful, etc. . . ." (1967c, p. 100).

Fanon's elaborations on Marx begin to show themselves clearly in his discussions of the relative positions and constitutions of the main classes in society—bourgeoisie, proletariat, peasants and lumpenproletariat.

Fanon's argument here begins with the observation that the African proletariat is both numerically minuscule and relatively pampered. This is an argument which, strangely, is repeated by Senghor, on whom Fanon frequently vents his antireactionary spleen. But whereas Senghor, in his *On African Socialism,* comes to the conclusion that workers' wages must be kept down, Fanon concludes that the peasant masses are the most revolutionary in the colonial situation and must be mobilized.

This does not mean, as one commentator has grotesquely suggested, that Fanon is in favor of a peasant-led Mau-Mau type *jacquerie* (Dieng 1967). Though he castigates the Kenyan nationalist leaders for not supporting the Mau-Mau uprising, he seems to favor a peasant revolution led by revolutionary intellectuals and urban militants who have rediscovered the masses. And it goes without saying that any mass uprising in Africa is likely to be a peasant uprising, since wage laborers constitute as little as 4 per cent of the population in many countries (Davies 1966, p. 24).

Fanon is aware that the role of the peasantry has proved a thorny theoretical question for Marxists for a number of years. Marx himself, in his *Critique of the Gotha Programme*, published posthumously by Engels, showed some awareness of the problem. There he suggested that peasant discontent could be channeled into support for proletarian-led parties. Fanon has taken this much further—"the peasants alone are revolutionary, for they have nothing to lose and everything to gain" (1967d, p. 47).

Indeed, if the word "peasantry" could be substituted for "proletariat," then Fanon's position is, surprisingly, identical to Marx's early position as articulated in the *Communist Manifesto:*

> All previous historical movements were movements of minorities, or in the interests of minorities. The proletarian movement is the self-conscious, independent movement of the immense majority, in the interests of the immense majority.

Fanon's position is logically (if not theoretically) very near to this. For all he is saying is that the peasants in the colonies are the ones who comprise the vast underprivileged majority that the proletarians presented in mid-nineteenth century England. This argument, however, probably will not appeal to too many Marxists. At least one has attacked Fanon for this position (Ghe 1963). This critic argues that the Vietnamese revolution, though overwhelmingly peasant in composition, has been proletarian-led.

On the other hand, an Algerian communist who has attacked Fanon in more than one journal admits in one place that the big mistake which caused the Algerian communist party to remain aloof from the war of independence for most of the duration of the struggle "sprang from a persistent tendency to underestimate the national factor and the peasantry and to overestimate the role of the European workers" (Ali 1965; see Dieng 1967, Gordon 1966). This critic mentions in the same article that Algeria was 80 per cent peasant on the eve of the revolution. His statistics further include about one million rural unemployed, 500,000 urban unemployed, a "middle bourgeoisie" of 11,000 families, a small, weak national bourgeoisie, and about 300,000 permanent and seasonal workers of whom the majority "had one foot in the village." He does not break down the figures into settlers and others, or give the total population, but even with these crude figures, if they are correct, it can be seen that among the proletarian minority, the majority were in fact only partly proletarianized. Indeed, the migrant and semipeasant nature of much of the African labor force has been noticed elsewhere (Davies 1966). Still, though these considerations highlight the problem of the narrowness of the proletarian base, they do not solve the problem of which class is the repository of the true revolutionary potential. The problem is intensified when it is remembered that the Soviet Union itself in the pre-1917 period manifested many of the same problems—semipeasant labor force, overwhelming preponderance of peasants in the population, migrant labor, even foreign ownership of many of the industrial establishments. Moreover, the same debates over the possibility of proletarian revolution and the feasibility of skipping the bourgeois stage were conducted, possibly with even greater vehemence than they are debated today.

Yet to return to Fanon, it is significant that even where he appears to make his greatest apparent deviation from classical Marxism, he characteristically grounds his theory in a solid base of the orthodox Marx. For, as pointed out above, he accepts Marx's analysis of the peasantry for the time and place that Marx was describing. His elaboration here, he emphasizes, is based on his analysis of the colonial situation, which has revealed a peasantry of a fundamentally different character from the nineteenth century European peasants that Marx described. The main difference, for Fanon, is the fact that the individualistic behavior Marx ascribed to the peasants has now become the hallmark of the colonized proletariat.

Furthermore, and this is essential for an understanding of Fanon on the peasantry, he appears to consider the lumpenproletariat as merely an extension of the peasantry, its urban arm, so to speak. He refers, for example, to "the landless peasants, who make up the lumpenproletariat." The significant role which he assigns to the lumpenproletariat is partly masked by the Marx-like rhetoric in which he appears to denounce this classless element. Compare Marx, in *The Communist Manifesto*,

> The "dangerous class," the social scum, that passively rotting mass thrown off by the lowest layers of old society, may, here and there, be swept into the movement by a proletarian revolution. Its conditions of life, however, prepare it far more for the part of a bribed tool of reactionary intrigue.

with Fanon,

> For the lumpenproletariat, that horde of starving men, uprooted from their tribe and from their clan, constitutes one of the most spontaneous and the most radically revolutionary forces of a colonized people (1967d, p. 103).

The rhetoric is similar but the difference is clear. For Fanon, the revolutionary possibilities inherent in the lumpenproletariat have become revolutionary potential of the greatest significance, *and the lumpenproletariat is but an urban extension of the peasantry*.[4] And it is for them, more than any other element, that the revolutionary violence will prove a magnificent rehabilitation:

> The prostitutes too, and the maids who are paid two pounds a month, all the hopeless dregs of humanity, all who turn in circles between suicide and madness will recover their balance . . . and march proudly in the great procession of the awakened nation.

However, the difference with Marx must not be overstressed, for Fanon recognizes that, if not mobilized, the lumpenproletariat will be used against the revolution.

In his analysis of the colonized bourgeoisie and the process of decolonization, Fanon is at his most brilliant. He ruthlessly exposed the essential difference between a true bourgeoisie of the classical Marxist variety and the caricature that masqueraded under that name in the colonies. For the colonized so-called bourgeoisie were, and still are, insignificant as accumulators of capital and are devoid of the capitalistic ethic which, in metropolitan countries, drives the bourgeoisie relentlessly forward in a ceaseless quest for invention and expansion—"the psychology of the national bourgeoisie is that of the businessman, not that of a captain of industry," and there must be scarcely an economic journal in the Third World which will not reveal copious lamentations over this fact. Indeed, even the bourgeois-nationalist type of reactionary leader that Fanon describes can sometimes be heard to cry out in exasperation at the effeteness of his bourgeois-parasitic cronies (see, e.g., Trinidad 1964–1968, p. 4). Whereas for a true bourgeoisie the capitalist system "exercises a psychological compulsion to boundless extension" (Sombart, "Capitalism," *Encyclopedia of Social Science*), for Fanon, the colonized bourgeoisie is, quite literally, good for nothing.

This bourgeoisie has a central role in Fanon's model of decolonization, a model, moreover, whose predictive aspects can be successfully demonstrated by reference to almost any random sample of countries which have become independent in the last decade or so. The model runs, in outline, as follows. Independence is achieved to the accompaniment of a wave of sterile nationalism. The national bourgeoisie soon finds its role as intermediaries for the exploitation of the economy by foreign capitalists and attempts to reinforce its position as looters of the public purse by calling for nationalization of some industries. The economy, nevertheless, continues to be characterized by the neocolonial assembly-plant type of base. Meanwhile, the country is rapidly transformed into a rest house and brothel for the foreign bourgeoisie. This process is known as tourism. The national bourgeoisie excels itself in ostentatious living. The workers and other less privileged elements get carried away by the nationalistic fervor. At their level, however, the only persons for them to turn against are foreign African traders and people like the Lebanese small-traders. Nationalism, therefore, is transformed into ultranationalism, from thence to chauvinism, and finally into tribalism. Meanwhile, protestations of African Unity fly thick and fast. Nor is the colonialist rear guard slow to exacerbate these differences. The Church takes its rightful place among the neocolonialist agents inciting division. The bourgeoisie seeks solace in a single party and takes cover behind a nationalist leader, who expects the people to live forever on the charisma he generated during the preindependence period. The leader exposes himself as "the general president of that company of profiteers." Slowly and painfully realization dawns on the people. National flags and radio appearances by the leader cannot feed empty bellies. The militants are excommunicated. Party organization disintegrates. The army and police loom as oppressive factors. A few honest intellectuals are disconcerted. They must be mobilized. The bourgeois phase in the Third World must be resolutely opposed and where possible prevented from appearing. To effect this, the middleman sector of the economy must be nationalized and given over to cooperatives of the people. "True liberation is not that pseudo-independence in which ministers having a limited responsibility hobnob with an economy dominated by the colonial pact" (Fanon 1967c, p. 105).

On the political level, a true neutralism must be achieved, aloof from the cold war, and most of all from "the United States [who has] plunged in everywhere, dollars in the vanguard, with Armstrong as herald and American Negro diplomats, scholarships, the emissaries of the Voice of America . . ." (1967c, p. 178).

There is one interesting theatre of the struggle against neocolonialism which Fanon identifies in several places but which seems to have escaped the attention of all the commentators. This is the more surprising since this subject has already emerged as the cause of much strident debate. This is the question of the role of Africanist scholars from the metropolis. In A *Dying Colonialism,* for example, he points out that "it is on the basis of the analyses of sociologists and ethnologists that the specialists in so-called native affairs and the heads of the Arab Bureaus co-ordinated their work" of systematically attacking Algerian cultural resistance. Psychologists and sociologists seem to be the Africanists he singles out for most abuse. His vehemence on this subject gives a clear indication that he harbors no illusions about the potency of academic weapons if enlisted in the struggle against the Third World (1976b, p. 37; 1967d, pp. 109, 111, 229).

It is inevitable that a model of decolonization as fiercely uncompromising as this should attract at least an occasional backlash. This "historic mission," as Fanon might have called it, was duly performed by the French author of a Christian Socialist review, who came to the defense of colonialism by affirming, in between strident denunciations of Fanon and Sartre, that colonialism, contrary to Fanon, had preserved native culture and made decolonization possible by refraining from exterminating the natives! Nor was there any trace of humor in this article, which was severely condemned in a later issue of the same magazine by, of all persons, an unnamed "French cleric working in black Africa" (Domenach 1962, pp. 454–463, 634–645; "A Propos . . ." 1962, p. 349).

TOWARDS A TRUE DECOLONIZATION

Just as the process of decolonization outlined above shows the course that will be taken by those who accept the constitutionalist version of independence based on compromise with the colonial overlord, Fanon also explicitly maps out the course that will need to be taken by those who desire true decolonization. There is only one way for this to be achieved—through violence. Colonialism itself is the incarnation of violence. It is imposed and sustained by fire and sword, and Fanon cannot bring himself to believe that such a situation can be changed fundamentally by inviting the Queen to preside over a flag-raising ceremony. The only road to real freedom is by making a clean break with colonialism. And a clean break necessitates violence.

Several of Fanon's interpreters suggest that he became aware of the necessity for violence as a result of his Algerian experience. This does not seem to be the case. For as early as his first book, written in 1950 but published in 1952, Fanon had unmistakably arrived at this conclusion by way of Hegel. In a section of that book devoted to "The Negro and Hegel," Fanon used the plight of the African to elaborate a theory of the conditions under which the African could liberate himself. Quoting Hegel's *The Phenomenology of Mind,* Fanon established that freedom of the human spirit can only be established by a dialectical progression in which the subjected individual imposes himself on the other in a violent demand for acceptance. In his own words, which at this point assume a Hegelian ponderosity,

> When it encounters resistance from the other, self-consciousness undergoes the experience of *desire*—the first milestone on the road that leads to the dignity of the spirit. Self-consciousness accepts the risk of its life, and consequently it threatens the other in his physical being. "It is solely by risking life that freedom is obtained; only thus is it tried and proved that the essential nature of self-consciousness is not *bare existence . . .*"
> (1967a, p. 218; quotation from Hegel 1949, p. 233).

Furthermore, the peculiar influence of *The Eighteenth Brumaire* on Fanon has already been mentioned, and here the message is the same, " . . . unheroic as bourgeois society is, it nevertheless took heroism, sacrifice, terror, civil war and battles of peoples to bring it into being." And Fanon's endearment to this work dates, as has been mentioned, from his first book.

As usual, here as elsewhere, Fanon is on the lookout for ways in which the peculiarities of the colonial situation must call for a modification of the traditional line. This time it is Engels whom he collides with. He explains, as against Engels' view that the poorly armed cannot defeat the mighty, that the new features of the cold war, support from socialist countries, and competition for spheres of influence among capitalist countries, not to mention the new techniques of peoples' war and guerilla warfare, all militate in favor of the weak and poorly armed in their struggle against the powerful. Further, he is fully aware of the deleterious influence of protracted struggle on the economic and political situation within the metropolitan countries themselves. And he can hardly be wrong when he says that no power can indefinitely occupy a subject country which has gone over to a peoples' war. But perhaps most important of all for him are the examples of Korea, Indochina, Cuba and his own Algerian struggle. He constantly reminds his African brothers that now is the time to strike—

now, while France is already weakened to the point of exhaustion by the Algerian conflagration. He points out that the proferring of the *Loi-Cadre* as a palliative to Africa is evidence of France's weakness and fear. His arguments here are at one with Che Guevara's "many Viet Nams" thesis. He even goes so far as to spearhead the formation, at the Accra Conference of 1958, of an African Legion to liberate the continent.[5]

But Fanon can never forget the price that the damned must pay for their freedom. The 45,000 innocent victims of French bombing at Sétif in 1945, the 90,000 slaughtered in Madagascar in 1947, the fact that no Frenchman has ever been disciplined for the torture of Algerians, the perpetration of frighteningly unethical practices on Algerians by French doctors—all these are considerations which return to trouble him again and again.

Yet the fight must go on. For without a violent break, only suffering and neocolonialism lie ahead. And the brotherhood of revolutionary violence cleanses, purifies, unifies, as Sartre remarked after viewing the new man produced by the Cuban revolution (de Beauvoir 1963, p. 619).

Here, as elsewhere, Fanon's critics have not been at a loss for wildly ridiculous arguments to oppose to his thesis. One critic, who should know better, concludes that

> He has not freed himself from the White Mask and still believes that the blacks *are* less than men. Terrorism and murder are necessary because unless European institutions are totally destroyed they will prevail and corrupt the new world (Zolberg 1966, p. 62).

This quotation contains almost as many misconceptions as words. It ignores the history of French brutality in Algeria and presents the violence of the damned as an action rather than a reaction. It fails to take cognisance of (or disbelieves) Fanon's own words:

> Having to react in rapid succession to the massacre of Algerian civilians in the mountains and in the cities, the revolutionary leadership found that if it wanted to prevent the people from being gripped by terror it had no choice but to adopt forms of terror which until then it had rejected. This phenomenon has not been sufficiently analyzed . . . (1967b, p. 54).

It presents the violence of the damned as a confirmation of the White Mask, whereas for the Hegelian basis of Fanon's thinking, revolutionary violence constitutes the very rending of the mask, the decisive action by which, to use Hegel's terminology, self-consciousness wrings acceptance from the other. It uses the term "European institutions," which can mean anything—the Church, Westminster-type government, racism, European-owned factories. It skillfully opposes the words "terrorism and murder" to "European institutions," thereby making a thinly-veiled allegation that Fanon was possessed of a blind undiscriminating hatred of Europe *per se*. This was not the case as I shall endeavor to show.

Though Fanon's violence is usually to be taken quite literally, there seems to be at least one situation in which a violent break may be made with the colonial past without any blood being shed. This conclusion is being deduced here by inference from his often-expressed admiration for Sékou Touré. It would appear that Sékou Touré, by mobilizing a revolutionary intellectual elite in communion with the masses, and by taking a step against French colonialism which at least exposed him to the very real *risk* of a violent retort, may have fulfilled the requirements for a violent break. Fanon seems to be saying here that if, once you have showed your determination for a fight, colonialism withdraws without a violent confrontation, then there is no necessity to pursue the retreating enemy and pick a fight simply for the sake of shedding blood (1967d, pp. 66, 161, 166).

NEGRITUDE, PAN-AFRICANISM AND RACE

Fanon's thought has often been presented in the form of an evolutionary process culminating in *The Wretched of the Earth*. While there is nothing inherently wrong in this approach, it occasionally leads to misconceptions. It has already been shown that Fanon's theory of violence was stated clearly as early as his first book. The same is true concerning his position on Negritude and Negro-ism, contrary to the view, sometimes expressed, that he started with an acceptance of the concept of Negritude and ended by rejecting it in his final work.

From the mass of material, especially in his first and last books, on this subject, the following picture emerges. Fanon appreciates the necessity to rehabilitate the past—"this tearing away [from European cultural domination] painful and difficult though it may be, is, however, necessary." He nevertheless moves on to an apparently contradictory position against Negritude. This is because he perceives the adherents of Negritude overreaching themselves and going to the other extreme of completely whitewashing the past, so that what emerges tends uncomfortably towards a blind mystification of the past and a "banal exoticism." Furthermore, the Negritude school is in danger of living in the past, which violates Fanon's *Eighteenth Brumaire* philosophy. For important as knowledge of the past is, progress for the present generation must be made in terms of contemporary realities. Culture should thus be subordinated to this goal. On a cultural level, the heterogeneity of Black cultures should be recognized. This does not rule out the possibility—in fact, the necessity—for cooperation on a political level. And as long as exponents of Negro-ism like Senghor and Rabemananjara can vote with France against the Algerian revolution, then something must clearly be wrong somewhere.

Thus unravelled (and the mass of scattered detail makes unravelling difficult), his apparently contradictory acceptance-rejection of Negritude is resolved. That Fanon's arguments were often expounded in a dialectical fashion (he uses the world itself continuously) often masks his meaning to the superficial reader.

His rejection of Negro-ism is influenced, further, by the fact that the generic term "Negro" is the creation of the white man. It is a term, nevertheless, which was created to designate the white man's conception of the "quintessence of evil" and bestiality. Therefore, he cannot see why Black people should revel in the fallacy of an undifferentiated Negro-ness created for them by their oppressors.

This analysis he backed up, characteristically, in action. Through the pages of *El Moudjahid* there poured a steady stream of exhortations to African Unity. And he frequently expressed pain at the obscurantism and chauvinism of people like Senghor, and, most of all, the "traitor Houphouët-Boigny," who was "objectively the most conscious curb on the evolution and liberation of Africa."

He was at pains to point out, in this regard, that his advocacy of national culture was not the same as nationalism. It was, on the contrary, the only real basis for a solid universalism which would include all humanity.

> The Negro is not. Any more than the white man. Both must turn their backs on the inhuman voices which were those of their respective ancestors in order that authentic communication be possible (1967a, p. 231).

This quotation is a succinct statement of the ideal to which all of Fanon's work pointed—the ideal of a new humanity.

This statement also throws considerable light on Fanon's attitudes towards race relations. His sensitivity, his inability to separate an overview of social relationships from relationships at the level of the individual, his dialectical approach to most problems—all of this made it logically necessary that his unrelenting hatred of racism, and his uncompromising struggle to lift the Black man out of the quagmire of psychological complexes into which racism had induced him, should be strictly divorced from a hatred of white people *per se*. For Fanon, there was no logical connection between the struggle against white racism and neo-colonialism and the undiscriminating hatred of white people. Any white person who proved his sincere desire for a true humanism was a friend for Fanon, just as a Black conservative like Houphouët-Boigny would remain an implacable object of detestation. This is why Fanon's books are replete with expressions of concern for the Frenchmen working undercover for the revolution, for the French soldiers who deserted to the Algerian side, for an end of the egocentric paternalism of the French left (see 1967a, p. 12; 1967b, 149). This is why, as Simone de Beauvior (1963) tells us, he could jokingly say that he would pay 20,000 francs a day to converse with Sartre for a fortnight (p. 619).

This is why, too, he sets out with such honesty in *Black Skin, White Masks* to analyze the pathetic complexes which exposure to white racism has induced in the Black people who come under his keen observation. All this is admirably borne out in the much misunderstood chapter "The Man of Color and the White Woman." Here, because he starts the chapter in the first person, superficial critics have been eager to associate him with the condition he describes.

The chapter revolves around the character Jean Veneuse, in René Maran's novel *Un Homme Pareil Aux Autres*, whose love affair with a white woman displays all the negative qualities that Fanon would like to eradicate. His conclusions concerning Jean Veneuse leave the careful reader in no doubt as to where Fanon's own position lies:

> . . . there would be a . . . lack of objectivity . . . in trying to extend the attitude of Veneuse to the man of colour as such. . . .
>
> This sexual myth—the quest for white flesh—perpetuated by alienated psyches, must no longer be allowed to impede active understanding.
>
> It is clear to me that Jean Veneuse, alias René Maran, is neither more nor less than a black abandonment-neurotic . . . who needs to be emancipated from his infantile fantasies . . . but let us remember that our purpose is to make possible a healthy encounter between black and white.

And the way to this healthy encounter, in characteristic Fanon fashion, is through "a restructuring of the world."

The impact of Fanon's ideas on Algeria (where, nevertheless, some critics suggest he may have been disappointed with the results of the revolution), on the student left in Europe, and on the Black liberation-struggle in the United States, has been documented in several places (Gordon 1966, Worsley 1969). But the greatest battles over the applicability of Fanon's ideas are still to be fought. They will be fought in Africa and the Caribbean, the areas in which Fanon was most interested and where disenchantment with the results of the Black versions of bourgeois nationalism is already plain to see.

References Cited

Ali, Bashir Hadj. "Some Lessons of the Liberation Struggle in Algeria." *World Marxist Review* (January 1965).

"A propos des damnés de la terre." *Esprit*, Vol. XXX, Pt. 2 (September 1962).

Armah, Ayi Kwei. "Fanon: The Awakener." *Negro Digest* (October 1969).

Barnard, Roger. "Frantz Fanon." *New Society* (January 4, 1968).

Brace, Richard and Joan. *Algerian Voices*. Princeton, N. J.: Van Nostrand, 1965.

Cherif, Mohammed. "Frantz Fanon and the African Revolution." *Présence Africaine*, Vol. LVIII (1966).

Davies, Ioan. *African Trade Unions*. Middlesex: Penguin Books, 1966.

de Beauvoir, Simone. *La force des choses*. Paris: Gallimard, 1963.

Denis, Manuel Maldonado. "Frantz Fanon (1924–1961) y el pensamiento anti-colonialista contemporáneo." *Revista de Ciencias Sociales*, Vol. XI, No. 1 (March 1967).

Dieng. "Les damnés de la terre et les problemes d'Afrique noire." *Présence Africaine*, Vol. LXII (1967).

Domenach, Jean-Marie. "Les damnés de la terre." *Esprit*, Vol. XXI, Pt. 1 (1962).

Fanon, Frantz. *Black Skin, White Masks*. New York: Grove Press, 1967a.

——— *A Dying Colonialism*. New York: Grove Press, 1967b.

——— *Toward the African Revolution*. New York: Grove Press, 1967c.

——— *The Wretched of the Earth*. Middlesex: Penguin Books, 1967d.

Geismar, Peter. "Frantz Fanon: Evolution of a Revolutionary." *Monthly Review* (May 1969).

Ghe, Nghuyen. "Frantz Fanon et les problemes de l'indépendence." *La Pensée*, Vol. CVII (February 1963).

Gordon, David C. *The Passing of French Algeria*. London: Oxford University Press, 1966.

Grohs, J. R. "Frantz Fanon and the African Revolution." *Journal of Modern African Studies* (December 1968).

Hegel, Georg Wilhelm Friedrich. *The Phenomenology of Mind*. Trans. by J. B. Baillie. 2nd rev. ed. London: Allen and Unwin, 1949.

"Homage to Frantz Fanon." *Présence Africaine*, Vol. XL (1962).

Isaacs, Harold I. "Portrait of a Revolutionary." *Commentary* (July 1965).

Seigel, J. E. "On Frantz Fanon." *American Scholar* (Winter 1968).

Trinidad and Tobago, National Planning Commission. *Draft Second Five Year Plan*, 1964–1968.

Worsley, Peter. "Revolutionary Theories." *Monthly Review* (May 1969).

Zolberg, Aristide R. "Frantz Fanon: A Gospel for the Damned." *Encounter*, Vol. XXVII, No. 5 (November 1966).

Notes

1. See, e.g., Geismar 1969; de Beauvoir 1963; "Homage to Frantz Fanon" 1962, especially the contribution of Dr. Bertene Juminer; Gordon 1966.
2. Karl Marx, *Theses on Feuerbach*. Fanon himself quotes part of this line approvingly, though he does not give its source. See Fanon 1967a, p. 17.
3. See Domenach 1962, pp. 634–45. Domenach also links Fanon, through Sorel, to Mussolini. For a similar view see Barnard 1968, p. 12.
4. This point has been overlooked by some critics, e.g. Cherif 1966. But for an interesting discussion of this point, see Worsley 1969, pp. 40ff.
5. 1967c, pp. 130, 145, 156; 1967d, pp. 50, 55–59, 62. For a sterile and inaccurate attack on Fanon for his position *vis-à-vis* Engels, see Dieng 1967.

PART II

Documents

13

Benito Sylvain of Haiti on the Pan-African Conference of 1900*

The Pan-African Conference of 1900, organized chiefly by Trinidad barrister Henry Sylvester Williams, is widely acclaimed for its pioneering effort in the field of international Black cooperation. Yet, apart from numerous fleeting references, very little has been written about it. What little has been written has usually been based almost entirely on the London *Times'* accounts of the proceedings and Bishop Alexander Walters' *My Life and Work* published in New York in 1917. Even W. E. B. Du Bois, perhaps the most famous participant, wrote very little about the conference in the remaining sixty-three years of his life.

What follows is a translation of a long forgotten account of the Pan-African Conference published in 1901 by Benito Sylvain, a participant. Sylvain had a distinguished career in the cause of Black people. He visited Ethiopia several times and described himself as aide-de-camp to that country's Emperor Menelik. He belonged to various race organizations and founded the Black Youth Association of Paris (1898) and later the Universal Association for the Moral Improvement of Mankind (1905). He was also a regular participant in conferences of all kinds on the racial question. Like many other Black activists of his type and time he probably would not qualify as very radical by today's standards. Yet the commitment to the protracted struggle for racial justice exhibited by many of the "talented tenth" of the race at this period cannot be gainsaid. Theirs was a real contribution.

In the context of this special issue on West Indian Struggles,* the achievements of people like Williams and Sylvain remind us that the Afro-West Indian, possibly because of his tendency to global wander-

*Originally published in *Pan-African Journal* in 1975

ings, has always distinguished himself in the wider Pan-African struggles waged by the Black race on an international scale.

There are some minor differences between Sylvain's account and
Bishop Walters'. Sylvain lists twenty-eight delegates, Walters thirty-
two. Two of Sylvain's twenty-eight do not appear in Walters' list and six
of Walters' are not in Sylvain's. There are also some differences in the
countries of origin (or domicile) assigned to delegates. For example,
C. E. French, a St. Lucian according to Sylvain, was from St. Kitts
according to Walters, and J. L. Love, an Antiguan according to Sylvain, was from Washington according to Walters. In some cases both
are probably correct, one listing the country of birth and the other the
country of current domicile.

THE PAN-AFRICAN ASSOCIATION*

On the 23rd of July, 1900, a new event, astonishing for many, dis-
turbing for some, and of overwhelming importance for us, took place in
the capital of Great Britain: educated Black people from the most
distant and diverse territories gathered at the Town Hall in ancient
Westminster Abbey not far from the House of Commons, in order to
examine the situation facing the African race in every corner of the
globe, to solemnly protest the unjust contempt and odious treatment
which are still heaped upon the race everywhere, and finally to create a
central organization which would in due course coordinate the common efforts and safeguard, by means of methodical and continuous
action, the economic interests as well as the political and social rights of
their exploited and oppressed brethren.

The English newspapers, with one or two exceptions, contented
themselves with impartial and detailed accounts of what transpired,
without adding any comment, favorable or otherwise. The rare French
newspapers which took any notice of the event described it as a
"strange occurrence" (manifestation bizarre).

As a general delegate to the Pan-African Conference, it is our special
responsibility to make known this work of which we were the principal
promoter.

On the 2nd of January 1895, long before an eminent member of the
French Academy had forcefully and authoritatively denounced the

*From Benito Sylvain, *Du Sort des Indigènes dans les Colonies d'Exploitation* (Paris: L.
Boyer, 1901), translated by Tony Martin.

"bankruptcy of Science," in that lofty arena where only scholars are subject to investigation, we addressed the following letter to our fellow countryman Anténor Firmin then visiting Paris:

Eminent and dear compatriot,

Since I am certain of obtaining from you both encouragement and support, as well as the judicious counsel which will assure success, I would like to communicate to you a project, the realization of which, I believe, will advance to a very great degree the work of rehabilitating the Black race, a work which you hold dear, and a work to which, as you well know, I am devoted body and soul.

The detractors of our race are of two sorts:

1. Those who, incapable of seeking out the whys and wherefores of phenomena which astound their narrow minds, receive and transmit, without even suspecting the gravity of what they are doing, unfortunate ideas which the apologists for slavery had such a great interest in propagating and which they were able to make the ignorant masses accept without too much trouble;

2. Those who, being in a position to deflate the a priori judgements commonly foisted upon people of color, are nevertheless restrained from so doing by a stubborn racial chauvinism. These latter, instead of trying to stop it, deliberately go along with a prejudice which is compounded by the fact that it originates in errors which are being passed off as science.

Now I am convinced, as you are, that the execrable theory of inferior and superior races is a moral monstrosity which is based, whatever one might say, solely on the idea of the exploitation of man by man. It has served, in centuries past, as a justification for the most revolting of social inequities; it still exercises in our time an even more evil influence.

What! In this century of enlightenment, in which no theory is accepted unless it has been supported by irrefutable proof, is the dogmatic opinion concerning the inferiority of Blacks to be maintained still, without any other basis than the self-interested belief of those who profess it? That cannot be.

No, the Black man was not created to be a footstool for white power. To all those who dare to support this position we reply fearlessly, whatever may be their high standing in scientific circles: "You insult the objectivity of science!"

The African race today contains too many outstanding men, both in terms of intelligence and moral uprightness, to continue to exist in the same state of prostration, under the burden of a scorn as outrageous as it is unjustified. Scholars, in order to calm the conscience of pro-slavery Europe, proclaimed in times past the dogma of the innate inferiority of Blacks; we appeal from this sentence to modern science, more impartial and better informed.

For the rehearing of this great case, which will certainly excite all good men, I intend to appeal to the honesty of the most illustrious scholars. Each country will delegate one or several representatives in order to constitute this imposing tribunal. These highly qualified individuals, who will of course be joined by the most authoritative spokesmen of the slandered race, would assemble in a Congress at the next universal exposition in Paris.

There all the arguments, old and new, which our detractors invoke for the support of their odious ethnological hierarchization, the perfect inanity of which, my eminent and dear compatriot, you have so definitively demonstrated, will be subjected to the close scrutiny of scientific discussion for the complete edification of the whole world.

You are better placed than any other person to extract from this idea, a fruitful one in my opinion, whatever usefulness it contains for the work which we are engaged in. In requesting your evaluation and practical advice, I am happy to avail myself of this opportunity of paying homage publicly to one of the men bringing most honor to my race—and I make bold to add: to humanity.

Please accept the sincere expression of my respectful admiration and great affection.

The author of *The Equality of Human Races* replied by way of this letter:

Paris, 3 January 1895

My dear compatriot,

I received your letter of yesterday's date, and I read it with great interest.

The idea that you put forward is assuredly an absolutely new and very beautiful one, namely that of convening a Congress of scholars from different nations to examine, during the Universal Exposition in Paris in 1900, the very controversial and emotional question of the equality or inequality of human races. Thus the twentieth century would open by shedding some light on a problem whose solution ought to influence powerfully the course of politics and philosophy.

In fact international relations between the civilized races and the backward races will take on a different character depending on whether one considers human races equal or not in their potential for moral and intellectual development.

First of all, as we approach the end of this century European governments are all so preoccupied with transcontinental colonization that one can predict, without being a prophet, that the politics of the first half of the twentieth century at least, will be dominated by colonial questions, that is to say by the study of the best means to follow in the assimilation of distant colonies to their respective metropoles. It does not require much effort to prove the universal desire to know how to treat the people of different degrees of civilization who inhabit the colonized territories and without whom nothing worthwhile will ever be extracted from these areas.

Furthermore, it is clear that the European mind will have broadened remarkably, enabling it to appreciate all the relevant historical, artistic and philosophical facts, if the day ever comes when scholars and thinkers desist from their stubborn adherence to the unenlightened doctrine of the natural inferiority of certain races as against certain others. From this broadening of the mind will come a thousand new aptitudes; but it is especially the sentiments of respect and solidarity which will have made significant progress, thereby opening up a larger, more profound moral horizon for twentieth century man, whose evolution will leave our own civilization very far behind.

So you see how fruitful the realization of your project might be. Some might perhaps find in it too ambitious an initiative for Haiti; as for me, I approve of your idea without any reservation. It can only show to the world that Haitians, light-skinned and Black, believe sincerely and seriously in the equality of races and in the consequences which flow from that fact. This would in turn increase respect for our race and provoke the admiration of all noble minds.

I wish I could add some practical suggestions to support my approval; but this would require more time and reflexion. You have, moreover, five years ahead of you: this point could be dealt with later, if need be.

In the meantime kindly believe, my dear compatriot, my sentiments of deep affection and my sincere regards.

Signed:
A. Firmin

Editor of a journal *(La Fraternité)* which we had founded at the end of 1890 to defend the interests of the Black race in Europe; president of the Oriental and African Committee of the Ethnographic Society of Paris; recently in charge of a special delegation to the Antilles from the managing committee of the *Alliance Francaise*, after having represented the Republic of Haiti at the first anti-slavery Congresses which took place in Paris and Brussels, we thought that we were duly qualified to bring to fruition the project which we have just described. However, because of a very unpleasant series of events for which our own fellow-countrymen are to blame, and which for four years dampened the initiative on all our enterprises, it became impossible for us to devote to the preparation of this great ethnological Congress either the time or the resources which it needed.[1]

In the month of December 1897, returning from Haiti after our first voyage to Abyssinia, we came in contact with Professor Booker T. Washington, the famous Black educator from the United States, and we decided to join an African Association which had just been formed in London through the zealous efforts of a clergyman, the Rev. Joseph Mason, and a young student, Henry Sylvester Williams, originally from Trinidad. Two months later (February 1898), after a banquet honoring the explorer Jean Hess for the publication of his moving work on *The Negro Soul,* we founded the Black Youth Association of Paris. The idea of a Congress was once more taken up, but the earlier plan had to be modified: instead of a meeting of Caucasian scholars, among whom some of the most eminent members of the Black race would be seated, we were now going to have a meeting of delegates of African origin, among whom there would be European scholars, philanthropists and politicians.

This meeting took place in London from the 23 to 26 [sic] July 1900. It is our duty to give the widest publicity possible to the proceedings and resolutions adopted during the course of this triduum.

Here first of all are the names of the various delegates:

United States: Bishop Alexander Walters of the Zion Church; Hon. Henry F. Downing, ex-consul at Luanda; Miss Anna Jones, educator from Kansas City; Mrs. Anna J. Cooper and Miss Barier from Washington; Professor Burghardt du Bois; Thomas Calloway; Augustus Straker, former judge in Michigan.

Liberia: Hon. F. R. Johnson, ex-attorney general.

Gold Coast: A. F. Ribero, lawyer.

Sierra Leone: G. W. Dove, lawyer.

Ivory Coast: Dr. R. K. Savage of Edinburgh University.

Jamaica: A. R. Hamilton

Antigua: Rev. Joseph Mason, pastor of a London parish; Prof. J. Love.

Trinidad: H. Sylvester Williams; R. E. Phipps, lawyer; A. Pierre.

St. Lucia: C. W. French; John E. Quinland, land surveyor.

Dominica: George Christian.

Canada: Rev. Henry Brown.

Scotland: Dr. Mayer.*

Ireland: Mr. and Mrs. J. F. Loudin; Miss Adams.

Cuba: Dr. John Alcindor.

Haiti and Ethiopia: Benito Sylvain.

These delegates, all of African origin, were joined by several English and American philanthropists and publicists among whom we must mention Mrs. Jane Cobden-Unwin, daughter of Richard Cobden, the famous free-trade economist; Dr. Colenso, son of the great abolitionist bishop; Dr. Clarke, the courageous Liberal member of parliament; Fox Bourne, secretary general of the English Aborigines Rights Protection Society; Sir Fowel Buxton, son of the illustrious companion of Wilberforce and Clarkson, president of the London Anti-slavery Society; Harford Battersby, member of the Committee Against the Alcoholization of Natives.[2]

His grace the Lord Bishop of London at the opening ceremony quite willingly called for the blessings of the Most High to descend upon the work of the Congress, the presidency of which was conferred upon Bishop Walters, who acquitted himself with remarkable distinction.

It was decided:

1. That a general association comprising the intellectual elite of civilized Blacks would be established under the name Pan-African Association, to centralize or control the activities of all organizations, whether in independent countries or colonies, which have as their objective the protection and education of peoples of African origin.

2. That a Pan-African Congress would be organized every two years, either in a major European or American city or in the capital of a Black independent State.

3. That the 1902 Congress would take place in the United States, and that of 1904 in Haiti, in order to add lustre to the celebration of Haiti's one hundredth anniversary as an independent nation.

*Delegate from the Afro-West Indian Literary Society of Edinburgh—(The *Times*, July 25, 1900, p. 15).

4. That a manifesto would be drawn up, appealing to the justice, political wisdom and humanity of Christian nations; and that a special address signed by Congress members who are British subjects would be sent to Her Britannic Majesty protesting the cruel treatment inflicted upon the indigenous people of the South African colonies.

5. That a memorial would be addressed to the Emperor Menelik and to the Presidents of the Republics of Haiti and Liberia, proclaiming them Grand Protectors of the Pan-African Association in order to direct their attention to the urgent necessity of consolidating and harmonizing their diplomatic efforts, with a view to reacting against the policy of extermination and degradation which prevails in Europe in regard to Black and colored people.

We reproduce here the address to the Christian nations:

TO THE NATIONS OF THE WORLD*

In the metropolis of the modern world, in this the closing year of the nineteenth century, there has been assembled a Congress of men and women of African blood, to deliberate solemnly upon the present situation and outlook of the darker races of mankind. The problem of the twentieth century is the problem of the color-line, the question as to how far differences of race—which show themselves chiefly in the color of the skin and the texture of the hair—will hereafter be made the basis of denying to over half the world the right of sharing to their utmost ability the opportunities and privileges of modern civilization.

To be sure, the darker races are today the least advanced in culture according to European standards. This has not, however, always been the case in the past, and certainly the world's history, both ancient and modern, has given many instances of no despicable ability and capacity among the blackest races of men.

In any case, the modern world must remember that in this age when the ends of the world are being brought so near together the millions of Black men in Africa, America, and the Islands of the Sea, not to speak of the brown and yellow myriads elsewhere, are bound to have a great influence upon the world in the future, by reason of sheer numbers

*Instead of making my own translation of Sylvain's text of the address, I am substituting the original English version as found in W. E. B. Du Bois, *An ABC of Color* (New York: International Publishers, 1969), pp. 20–23.

and physical contact. If now the world of culture bends itself towards giving Negroes and other dark men the largest and broadest opportunity for education and self-development, then this contact and influence is bound to have a beneficial effect upon the world and hasten human progress. But if, by reason of carelessness, prejudice, greed and injustice, the Black world is to be exploited and ravished and degraded, the results must be deplorable, if not fatal—not simply to them, but to the high ideals of justice, freedom and culture which a thousand years of Christian civilization have held before Europe.

And now, therefore, to these ideals of civilization, to the broader humanity of the followers of the Prince of Peace, we, the men and women of Africa in world Congress assembled, do now solemnly appeal:

Let the world take no backward step in that slow but sure progress which has successively refused to let the spirit of class, of caste, of privilege, or of birth, debar from life, liberty and the pursuit of happiness a striving human soul.

Let not color or race be a feature of distinction between white and Black men, regardless of worth or ability.

Let not the natives of Africa be sacrificed to the greed of gold, their liberties taken away, their family life debauched, their just aspirations repressed, and avenues of advancement and culture taken from them.

Let not the cloak of Christian missionary enterprise be allowed in the future, as so often in the past, to hide the ruthless economic exploitation and political downfall of less developed nations, whose chief fault has been reliance on the plighted faith of the Christian church.

Let the British nation, the first modern champion of Negro freedom, hasten to crown the work of Wilberforce, and Clarkson, and Buxton, and Sharpe, Bishop Colenso, and Livingstone, and give, as soon as practicable, the rights of responsible government to the Black colonies of Africa and the West Indies.

Let not the spirit of Garrison, Phillips, and Douglass wholly die out in America; may the conscience of a great nation rise and rebuke all dishonesty and unrighteous oppression toward the American Negro, and grant to him the right of franchise, security of person and property, and generous recognition of the great work he has accomplished in a generation toward raising nine millions of human beings from slavery to manhood.

Let the German Empire, the French Republic, true to their great past, remember that the true worth of colonies lies in their prosperity and progress, and that justice, impartial alike to Black and White, is the first element of prosperity.

Let the Congo Free State become a great central Negro State of the world, and let its prosperity be counted not simply in cash and commerce, but in the happiness and true advancement of its Black people.

Let the nations of the World respect the integrity and independence of the free Negro States of Abyssinia, Liberia, Haiti, and the rest, and let the inhabitants of these States, the independent tribes of Africa, the Negroes of the West Indies and America, and the Black subjects of all nations take courage, strive ceaselessly, and fight bravely, that they may prove to the world their incontestible right to be counted among the great brotherhood of mankind.

Thus we appeal with boldness and confidence to the Great Powers of the civilized world, trusting in the wide spirit of humanity, and the deep sense of justice of our age, for a generous recognition of the righteousness of our cause.

ALEXANDER WALTERS (BISHOP)
  President Pan-African Association
HENRY B. BROWN
  Vice-President
H. SYLVESTER-WILLIAMS
  General Secretary
W. E. BURGHARDT DU BOIS
  *Chairman Committee on Address**

At a time when the spirit of association is working such great wonders, when the least affinity of race, a mere connection, even in the absense of a complete community of interest, justifies the most unexpected political alliances and economic syndicates, was it not strange to see Africans and their most direct descendants continuing to live indifferent, if not hostile to one another, under the oppressive contempt of their tyrannical and scornful detractors?

God helps those who help themselves! goes the well-known saying. The Pan-African Association is a fundamentally and essentially peaceful body, but one which intends to pursue its objectives as much in a spirit of relentless firmness as in a spirit of calm and moderation. Adopting as its own the cause of all natives of the exploited colonies, it will organize

---

*The signatories are omitted from Sylvain's text.

in every important city a center of active propaganda, with the certainty that it will not appeal in vain to the generosity and spirit of justice of the young people, and especially the women of Europe. Thanks to this cooperation of young people and women, from which we expect a lot of good results, it will be possible to organize in the capital of each important colonial power, a group of people who can provide assistance and temporary accommodation for persons from the colonies who for one reason or another find themselves stranded in Europe.

The Pan-African Association will exert, to good advantage, direct control over the contracting of natives as free laborers; it will be an arbitrator for the settlement of disputes, so frequent among the pseudo-free workers and their unscrupulous employers.

The Association, finally, will acknowledge and encourage the efforts of all philanthropic organizations which, pursuing a parallel objective, are working to propagate the principle of peaceful, equitable and morally uplifting colonization.

Despite the short time of its existence, the Pan-African Association has already had to examine two rather important questions, relative to the role to be played by civilized Blacks from America in the politics of the colonial powers in Africa.

For several of our kinsmen from the United States did us the honor of asking our advice on their plan to enroll in the British army in order to fight the Boers at Transvaal. We dissuaded them, and they took our advice. There is no doubt that the Boers have been guilty of perpetrating the worst atrocities against the native Kaffirs and Hottentots; but the English have not shown themselves any more humane in their treatment of Black peoples. On the whole, the two belligerents deserve each other. We ought to abstain and wait and see what happens at the end of this War.

The growing influence of the Association has also been tapped, this time much more profitably, over the question of the Congolese in Cuba.

Representing a group of eighteen thousand Blacks from the Congo living in Cuba, whither they were brought as slaves some thirty years ago, Fr. Emanuel proceeded to Belgium in March 1901 to negotiate with King Leopold II over the repatriation of these Black people to, and their employment in their native land, which had since become a Belgian colony. An interview granted by Fr. Emanuel to a writer for the journal *Essor économique universel* published at Anvers, describes the progress of this interesting attempt:

———— Well then, will this association of eighteen thousand Negroes consent to return to the Congo in exchange for benefits accorded them by the king?

———— No, not all, a certain number who were born in the Congo, a thousand to fifteen hundred perhaps, men, women and children. Those who were born in Cuba, married there and have a job, will doubtless remain there. It is only the Congolese, therefore, with their families, who wish to return to their country.

———— Are they not satisfied with Cuba? Why do they wish to leave; aren't they able to earn a living?

———— It is not merely discontent which induces them to leave. Naturally the state of war which has obtained there for these last few years does not help but *the principal reason is a moral one and is dictated by their consciences. My Negroes are experiencing a very real desire to set themselves up in the Congo, where they can establish centers of civilization.* [Emphasis here, and throughout this interview, in the original]. The vast majority of them are workmen in the employ of local bosses who are not always particularly concerned with their welfare. Since their country, the Congo, contains immense undeveloped areas, it seems to them that the king should grant them, without any difficulty, concessions where they would cultivate tropical crops such as tobacco, in the cultivation of which they excel, rubber, cocoa, coffee, etc.

But I must say that as a first step, they wish to become *free citizens* of the Congo Free State. The exact area where they will settle matters little to them. These are quiet, peaceful people who will always suit their behaviour to the circumstances; many of them would not object to serving the king as soldiers; they place themselves entirely at the disposal of the Congo State.

Ideally, they will engage in agriculture and resell their produce to the commercial societies which have been established in the Congo; if the conditions are right, they will even willingly hire themselves out to the societies.

The immigration of these civilized workmen into the Congo would present the greatest advantages. First of all, everybody would gain by it, beginning with the State itself, the colonial societies and my proteges. Also, consider the great advance which would accrue to civilization in the Congo. And the Catholic religion in the bargain! Wouldn't we be valuable auxiliaries for the missionaries who go there to preach our faith? Truly, everything is in our favor and no serious obstacle stands in the way of our dreams.

And think of the growth in the import business which would take place. These civilized men have much greater needs than the inhabitants of the Congo. Many of their requirements would have to be imported; the Congolese native, who is a great imitator, would soon experience similar desires and the consumption of Belgian products will greatly increase as a result.

—— Is it a long time since you communicated with the government of the Free State concerning all this?

—— Yes, a very long time: more than four years. I am accompanied, by the way, by four Cuban Negroes who have just returned from three years in the Congo. They are so delighted by their stay in Africa that they are going back, this time for good, with their wives and children who were left behind in Cuba. A fifth Cuban Black is still in the Congo.

I was saying that I have been corresponding for a long while with Baron Van Eetvelde, and it is at the invitation of the secretary of the Free State himself that I decided to come to Belgium in the hope of settling once and for all this question of immigration.

—— You were accorded a meeting with M. de Cuvelier, who took over from Baron Van Eetvelde. Would it be indiscreet of me to ask you what was the result of that interview?

—— There was no immediate result. I thought that the negotiations would have been easy, but I was wrong. I encountered obstacles which I never even suspected. I am still hopeful. I have not completely lost confidence in the eventual outcome.

—— Some persons have attributed to you the intention of offering your services to some other country, in the event that you fail in your bid to obtain a concession in the Belgian Congo. England, France and Portugal have been mentioned.

—— No, no the Africans in Cuba want to return to the Congo, because it is their country, their motherland. *They want to return home* and not go to a strange country. The Americans* are in no way unpleasant to us; the American generals, to whom I have had occasion to speak, have assured me of the favorable intentions of their country in our regard, and the American authorities consider me, as the

*This was shortly after the Cuban-Spanish-American War.

Spaniards did before the war, as the legal representative of this association of 18,000 Black people.

I have no immediate plan in case of non-success. I will begin, of course, by reporting my lack of success to my constituents, and it is only then that we will examine the future.

I am entirely dedicated to the amelioration of the lot of Black people and it would be very painful to me to fail at the very moment when I thought I could see my most ardent wishes about to be realized.

"This interview," said the *Essor économique universel* in its preliminary remarks, "is all the more interesting in that it presents the question of the immigration of this colony of Cubans in a new light. It is not really a question of some sort of invasion of 18,000 Blacks to the Congo, but only the return of one or two thousand former Congolese to the land of their birth. . . . Emancipated many years ago, these Blacks actually possess in Cuba properties approaching a value of around one million dollars or 25 million francs.

"Given these conditions it seems, at least at first sight, that Mr. Emanuel's project would be perfectly realizable.

"Only a few practical difficulties would arise, and we believe that it would be easy to resolve them under careful examination. The project is surely worth the trouble. Perhaps the most serious objection which may arise concerning the establishment of these Cuban Blacks in the Congo, would be the increase in the price of labor; the newcomers, indeed, would probably not be content with the wages paid to the natives by the Free State and the various commercial societies. The demands of the natives would doubtless be raised significantly, and the cost of certain products, in particular rubber, would increase enough to reduce considerably the profits now made by certain colonial societies."

We reply that the objection concerning wages is invalid. It is indeed true that the commercial societies and others in the Congo Free State scandalously exploit the native workers, who, as is well known, receive a contemptible remuneration. The Congolese in Cuba would not accept that, and they would be a thousand times correct! The Belgian government has extracted enough super profits from goods produced by the unpaid or poorly paid for sweat of the Africans in order to consider with a little fairness today the question of colonial wages.

His Majesty King Leopold II who personally is a fine man, ought not to forget at this point the imperfect nature and transitory character of his *rights* of sovereignty over the Congo, rights which can still be challenged and which have never been recognized by the descendants of the legitimate rulers of this territory.

Be that as it may, Fr. Emanuel has consented to adjourn his decision until the next Pan-African Congress, which, as we have said, should convene in the United States in August or September of 1902. If in the intervening period the king of the Belgians has not benefited from wiser counsel and gotten rid of the purely artificial obstacles placed in the way of this just and promising enterprise, the Pan-African Association will advise on the most practical means to repatriate the Congolese in Cuba to the land of their ancestors which they would never have dreamed of leaving were it not for the criminally brutal force of the European slave traders.

The idea of transporting to various parts of Africa Blacks who are being so cruelly treated in the southern United States has been, since the Cuban War, the object of serious study by leaders of the developing Africano-American struggle. Professor Booker T. Washington does not favor a general exodus: "We are," he said recently in a Boston meeting, "the only Americans who came to this land without having either requested or desired it. They came to seek us where we were and brought us here at great cost, at the price of a thousand dangers and a thousand sacrifices. Well, we do not wish these sacrifices to have been in vain. We are here; we like it here, and we have every intention of remaining."

But in the absence of mass emigration, which is neither necessary nor practical, we must encourage the very laudable impulse which brings more or less compact groups of civilized Blacks from the United States or from other countries in America to want to contribute to the education and moral uplift of their brothers in Africa. The German colonial office already officially recognized the advantages of this participation when it had recourse last year to the Normal and Industrial Institute directed by Professor Booker Washington for good mechanical and agricultural supervisory personnel to work in the Cameroon colony.

The German authorities, for reasons which have not properly been explained, have recommended that silence be maintained concerning this negotiation. We believe that we should take no notice of this curious recommendation, for it is the most decisive reply which we can oppose, in concluding, to those who, forgetful of the teachings of history, are wont to assign narrow limits to the future of the African race, whose remarkable aptitude they fail to appreciate, while denying, contrary to all evidence, the very tangible development taking place at the present time.

Notes (Sylvain's)

1. The journal *La Fraternité* (the first every edited by a Black person in Paris) was honored by the collaboration of Jules Simon, Léon de Rosny, Mrs. Adam and Séverine (who allowed the reprinting of their articles), Anténor Firmin, Senator Isaac, deputy Gerville-Réache, Jean Hess, Edmond Thiaudière, Léon Audain, Wesner Menos, Emmanuel des Essarts, Derville Charles-Pierre, Marc Legraud and Paul Vibert. The journal was forced to cease publication in 1897, victim of a coalition of politicians and Haitian students who envied our independent opinions, our affairs for charitable purposes which were graced by the cooperation of the greatest performers in Paris, and above all the distinctions which were bestowed upon us in French literary and scientific circles. The Haitian government in 1895 encouraged those who were envious of our success by cutting off the subsidy which had been voted to the journal by parliament, under the title "rewards for service to the nation," a subsidy which, however, was paid very irregularly, according to the whims of the Ministry of Finance. . . . The production of this book will be our best vindication.
2. Mrs. Jane Cobden-Unwin had all the delegates to the Congress admitted free of charge to membership in the New Reform Club of London; Dr. Clarke and Mr. Fox Bourne held luncheons in their honor, the first in the restaurant at the House of Commons and the second at the Liberal Club; the Lord Bishop did the same on the grounds of his magnificent residence situated near London.
3. A large piece of ground around the spot where the heart of Livingstone lies buried (near Lake Nyasa) was offered in 1899 by the British South Africa Company to the Linvingstone Memorial Company. The company decided to have a forty foot high granite column erected on the site to perpetuate the memory in Southern Africa of the illustrious explorer who was so fond of Black people.
   There is a double monument to Cardinal Lavigerie: one in Tunis and the other in Bayonne. Our journal *La Fraternité*, "organ representing the interests of Haiti and the Black race," paid him homage by subscribing 500 francs.
   Victor Schoelcher also has his statue, in Guadeloupe, though there is still none in France.
   Our brothers in the British colonies ought to take the initiative in launching a subscription drive intended to glorify in marble or bronze the memory of Wilberforce, of Clarkson and of Buxton. Thus will everywhere be justified the words of Michelet: "Gratitude is a Black virtue."

14

The Yorubas of Carapichaima, Trinidad, Pre-1910

(Sam Manning)[1]

Introduction

African survivals in the Caribbean are stronger than many of the region's own inhabitants realize. In the years after slavery in Trinidad, communities of Yorubas, Congoes, Hausas, Mandingoes, Radas and other Africans developed. Some of these maintained their own distinct identities well into the twentieth century.

The author of the following article, Sam Manning, died in West Africa in the early 1960s. He seems to have grown up in or near the Yoruba community in Trinidad which he describes. He was for years a well-known Trinidad calypsonian. He was also one of the major popularizers of calypso music in North America.

* * * *

The Yorubas who lived unobtrusively in the settlement of Carapichaima were surrounded by a multiracial and aggressive group of fellow citizens. Nevertheless they held their ground as a distinct force in the progress of the people. They were the cocoa planters and owners of vast tracts of land acquired by thrift and foresight. They were agrarians, and by some deep ingrained characteristic which the rigors of slavery could not destroy, maintained a poise that was the envy of their rivals, the Congoes of Alexander Village.

Their independent attitude and industrious manner made them very unpopular with the Hindus and Chinamen not to mention their own kind from a different part of Africa. True they were all aliens in a foreign land brought there under the same conditions, chattel slaves, to till in the broiling Caribbean sun, but the Yorubas were different, as

1. Undated manuscript in the possession of Lionel Yard of Brooklyn, New York.

people are all over the world. The Yorubas were a proud, independent people. A people who through everything still clung to the beliefs and culture of their tribe. Their opposites the Congoes seem to have had less powers of resistance. The visitations of slavery left them thoroughly demoralized. The progress of the Yorubas and their evident pride in their achievements incurred the envy of the less prosperous Congoes, who settled in Alexander Village which in racial composition of its inhabitants was no different to the Carapichaima area of which the Yoruba settlement was a dominant part. The area Carapichaima was composed of sugar estates, and the cocoa plantations of the Yorubas. The village of Carapichaima which was the shopping center was virtually controlled by Portuguese, and Chinese merchants with one or two establishments run by Hindus who had served their term of indenture, and whose thrift matched that of the Yorubas. These were the human elements which formed the integral ingredients of the multi-racial group which inhabited these two settlements in the heart of the Island of La Trinity in the Caribbean in the years preceding the turn of the Twentieth Century, and almost as late as 1910. (Alexander Village where a colony of Congoes had settled, was of little importance beyond its residential area in the center of the sugar plantations. The bulk of its income came from the workers on the sugar plantations).

The Yorubas for several reasons did not look favorably on the intermarriage of any of their group with outsiders especially the Congoes or the mixed breeds of the many human strains from Alexander Village. Perhaps the protection of their hard won property rights and the fruit of their labor was one reason for this taboo. In any case the consorting of Yorubas with a Congo man or woman would invite certain maledictions on the head of the Yoruba man or woman who dared to violate this taboo, and this feeling was not lessened in the case of the mixed breeds—mulattoes, santones or douglas. The mulatto was a mixture of Blacks and whites, the santone a mixture of the Portuguese and Blacks, the "dougla" the East Indian and the Blacks.

[Author's note: an unfinished second draft of the same article by Sam Manning reads as follows—]

The Yorubas . . . were a distinct group of Africans who had survived the rigors of slavery. Their adversaries were the Congo people from the village of Alexander, not too far distant from the South. The Congoes expressed the view that the Yorubas were too proud and arrogant, and the Yorubas despised the Congoes for their easy mixing with their slave masters.

15

The Birth of the Universal Negro Improvement Association

(Amy Ashwood Garvey)

Introduction

The following is an engaging account of the birth of Marcus Garvey's Universal Negro Improvement Association. Amy Ashwood Garvey, the author, later became the first Mrs. Garvey. It may be that she exaggerated her own role in the formation of the organization. It cannot be denied, however, that hers was a very important role in the early days of the UNIA, both in Jamaica and in the United States of America.

Her account of Garvey's amorous advances provides a rare glimpse into Garvey's private life. Even his love life, it would seem, was closely intertwined with the question of African struggle.

Amy Ashwood Garvey was an accomplished political activist and Pan-Africanist in her own right. In later life she also fought for many feminist causes. She married Garvey in 1919 after a lengthy courtship. The marriage itself was disappointingly short lived. Its break-up, however, did not deter her from her life of Pan-African and feminist struggle. In Manchester, England in 1945, she chaired the opening session of the Fifth Pan-African Congress, organized by George Padmore of Trinidad and Kwame Nkrumah of Ghana.

Garvey's second wife, Amy Jacques Garvey, was every bit as much an activist in her own right as was the first. She too played a pivotal role within the organization. To Garvey, therefore, falls the unusual distinction of having had two wives with the same name, and both extraordinarily powerful personalities in their own right.

* * * *

A few months after his arrival from Britain it seemed to Garvey that for a time he might be chasing a will o' the wisp. Dreaming of greatness in itself alone failed to satisfy Garvey for long. His ardent spirit and passionate devotion to an ideal clamored for action. He wanted to see his race marching triumphantly in the human conclave ever onwards; he wanted officers and co-workers around him who had caught his spirit and would thus prove loyal bodyguards. Grandiose schemes would avail naught unless thay could be translated into reality. If as he considered, he was a Napoleon, he would need a Josephine. He had reached that moment in the life of all great men when the testing period between ideas and their execution became more challenging and acute. This is the period of well-nigh frustration through which all leaders must pass—the potter's fire of the refining gold and the elimination of the dross therefrom. It was a phase that was causing him to champ at the stirrup.

It was just at this period that our paths met. Marcus Garvey and I met for the first time as if by some design of fate and conspiracy of destiny. It was no casual meeting, for its timing was significant for both of us. It changed much in the life of each of us.

The occasion was a simple one. It was my custom at that time to attend the weekly literary debate at the Baptist Church Hall in Kingston, Jamaica. On that particular Tuesday evening in the late July of 1914, I had proposed the motion that "Morality does not increase with civilization". I had argued my case as strongly as I could, and then sat down to hear what my opponents had to say. As the debate progressed I had become so absorbed in the literary thrusts and parries that I paid little if any attention to the individual speakers themselves, not even among my own supporters, one of whom had been a pronouncedly outspoken young man.

When the meeting had dispersed, I went off to catch the usual tram home. But waiting at the stop was a stocky figure with slightly drooping shoulders. He seemed vaguely familiar, and then I realised that he was the gentleman who had argued so forcibly for my point of view. At closer quarters the stranger arrested my attention. Excitement over the debate had vanished, and I saw clearly that an intense light shone from the eyes of my unknown supporter. In that evening light they were such black twinkling eyes. A world shone from them.

Then followed the greatest surprise of my life. The bold stranger came forward impulsively, and without any invitation addressed me in the most amazing fashion.

"At last," he said in his rich deep voice, "I have found my star of destiny! I have found by Josephine!"

Not even the romantic spell of the Caribbean night could banish or conceal my astonishment on hearing so startling a declaration. Who was this strange Romeo who had appeared as if by magic out of the night? Yet I must admit that I was inwardly thrilled by such an amorous outburst of gallantry. Other admirers had paid me compliments, but none of them had equalled him in his sheer audacity, dash, and flattery of approach.

I was seventeen years old upon the occasion of this unusual tribute of affection, an age when I could have easily been swept off my feet. Yet somehow I managed to keep my balance and, I remember courteously declining his offer that evening to see me home. Such was my meeting with the imperious, young and daring Marcus Garvey in the springtime of our youth. True to his nature Marcus swept on regardlessly. Here was no timid suitor. The very next day, at eight in the morning to be precise, he was knocking on the door of my home. On that morning, I too felt a strange unaccountable sense of elation. It was a happy sunny morning. The birds were mingling merrily with the flowers and all nature seemed friendly; for me, there was an atmosphere of great expectations about the day.

Marcus spent no time talking of trivialities. Almost at once he plunged into relating his life to me, seemingly pressed by a sense of urgency. His manner of speaking fascinated me. Throughout the whole flow of his story there was never any suggestion nor visible consciousness that he was addressing one whom he had hardly known. He might have known me for years. The complete story of his heart, an outpouring of his most intimate self [sic]. At times he would stumble for the most fitting or appropriate words, but, nothing was hid and he was obviously sincere. How vividly he recalled the scenes of his unruly boyhood days, the nature and disposition of his parents, his father's prophecy, his first struggles to gain a livelihood, and how his heart went out to the Colored masses so oppressed by poverty and ignorance - his yearnings, hopes and aspirations for their betterment.

Continuing his story, Marcus went on to relate how he came to admire men who had fought their way to the top. Toussaint L'Ouverture, Napoleon, Antonio Maceo, Booker T. Washington - all serving their race in their own way and according to their own lights in the circumstances of their particular times. He glowed with pride when he spoke of the Jamaican Maroons and the many slaves who had fought all their years to keep alive the spirit of freedom and resistance to the shackles amongst their people. Listening to all this I instinctively felt that love for the African race was a powerful influence on his life.

The narration poured forth like some turbulent stream, gaining in power and depth and warmth of intensity as it flowed. The hidden-most recesses of his heart were revealed to me. Marcus spoke of the inner-compelling force driving him to the devotion of his mortal life to the awakening of his race and people. He earnestly desired to see them all obtain a higher social, political, cultural, and economic standard of living. One could sense his deep sorrow for the sad condition of so many West Indians; and what angered him to the core was the fact that they accepted their lot in life so fatalistically. Why did not a mighty roar of protest arise from their midst? Had Toussaint, the Maroons and other Afro-American leaders fought their battles for freedom merely that the descendants of the slaves might decay in frustration and apathy?

The "Napoleon" was now boiling over with indignation. He maintained forcibly that although the Afro-American people were legally "free" as a people, something of the slave mentality was still characteristic of them. Mentally they were still in chains on account of the crippling effect of an inferiority complex. Somehow the sunlight must be allowed to flood in the dark confines of their minds, so that they could be truly free and truly men, confident of holding their own with men of other races. The logic and simplicity of his contention needed no illumination.

It was obvious that Marcus had penetrated to the very core of the afflictions of the man of African origin. He divined accurately and precisely the cause and effect of the spirit of his people being broken and distraught, and he was intent on finding an elixir - a drastic remedy to heal the festered and chronic wound. He denounced all those who had placed obstacles in their path. By what sanction, human or divine, he asked, were his people prevented from taking their rightful place in the onward march of mankind? He cried out that all artificial and unjust hindrances should be swept away in one grand swoop. At the moment I discerned that a powerful inner flame was consuming the man, that a force of volcanic nature was gathering in the depths of his being.

This leader of small stature, but taller yet in vision and perspicacity, was no reed broken by the wind. In this respect he never hesitated, his convictions and beliefs were granite sure and firm. His master invocation was "Let my people go!" Already it was evident that Marcus considered himself the uncrowned emperor of a spiritual Africa of his own imagination; he believed that it was his destiny to lead all people of African descent towards a more glorious future.

When the glowing recital ended, I remained silent for a while. I wanted to be reassured that my feet were still on terra firma - solidly placed on the earth. I had heard so much in a short time that it had acted like heady wine. Such a deluge of dreams was overwhelming. I was disturbed, too, because Marcus was assuming that I, just as much as himself, was prepared to shoulder the herculean responsibilities of working for the uplifting of our race with all the implications of its formidable challenges.

As I sat in reverie, I saw the stern face of my mother uttering words of solemn maternal warnings. My mother was imbued with a strong sense of realism; the responsibilities of a family left her little time for flights of fancy, even had she been temperamentally so inclined. As for Marcus and his vision, they would have received scant sympathy from her. My doubts and hesitations did not deter the Black Moses. He must have read my mind, for he then addressed me in a much quieter voice and invited me to speak about my life and ambitions.

Before long I was relating how a sense of racial consciousness had been awakened in my own breast at the age of 12. It went back to an incident in my student days at Westwood. My school had been collecting money for a mission fund, the Dorcas Society. Later I had visited Mrs. Webb, the wife of the Rev. William Webb, the founder of our school. I told her the amount we had collected for the fund. Her reply somewhat nettled and startled me. She said that it was a pity it was not going "to your people". I explained to Marcus that I had thought Mrs. Webb meant my own parents. The good lady, however, had noticed my confusion and then added that by my "people" she meant the people of Africa. When I asked her to explain she replied that the people of far-away Africa were living in heathen darkness and needed help from Christian missionaries. No one before had told me that I was of African descent. Being so young I was very puzzled by this bit of news and naturally I asked the lady many more questions about Africa.

At first her story of Africa had intrigued me; but when I was told that my forebears had been brought from Africa as slaves and sold to white plantation owners in the West Indies, I was horrified and frightened. I heard about slave ships and slave markets and cruel practices. I asked Mrs. Webb who had brought my ancestors from their land. I remember how she replied in a low voice that English traders had done this many years before. She then explained more fully what a great and thriving business the slave trade had been. By that time I was unable to listen further. I recoiled in horror as if from the presence of a newly-discovered enemy, and rushed out of the room.

It was this incident, I explained to Garvey, that had caused the birth of racial consciousness within me. Marcus, of course, was eager to learn what happened after that. Immediately I told him that I had written a long letter to my father. In it I had asked him, "Who are you? What is your name?" In his answer to my anguished queries my father seemed very puzzled as to what was troubling me. I did not find the reply satisfactory, despite the fact that he related the story of how an African King had proposed to Queen Victoria after the death of Albert. In my youthful agitation I hurriedly sent off another letter beseeching my father, "I want to know something about myself immediately! I am told that my ancestors were slaves right here in Jamaica!"

This time my father really was worried; so much so that he hurried back from Panama to Jamaica. His remedy for me was to take me to see my very old Grandmother. This old matriarch told me a very strange story. She had been born many years before in Jaubin the land of Ashanti, then Gold Coast, now Ghana. When she had been still a girl of about sixteen, she had been kidnapped by a warring tribe along with her two sisters and sold into slavery. Along with many others she had been brought in a great ship across the ocean and sold again to a white master. In Ashanti her family name was Dabas, meaning iron or strong will; her first name was Boahimaa. The old lady was very proud of her lineage. She was very emphatic about the virility of her people and their prowess in war, producing the highest type of Ashanti. (In 1946 when the Asantehene, Sir Asi Agyeman Prempeh II, King of Ashanti, Custodian of Akan custom and culture, confirmed me an Ashanti and returned me to my family, I then learned that Amporte, one of Ashanti's greatest military generals, was my great, great-uncle).

Marcus still urged me to continue with my story. So I had to tell him that after the meeting with Grannie Dabas, I returned to school proud of my family and my people. I told him how this pride increased and how I often used to ask myself, "How shall I get back to Africa?" I explained how I felt impelled to be of use and service to my race in some positive way. I even told him that I had thought of becoming a missionary, but yet felt that this was not the right road for me: I had yet to discover by what means my ambition to help Africa, and all her sons and daughters could be realised. Thus deep in my own heart I was in full sympathy with what Marcus had said concerning the future welfare of the African race.

In a short space of time, Marcus had already revealed his heart's secret to me. In response I had made my own confession of faith to him. Throughout my outpouring, he listened intently. He only rose when I had finished speaking, once again to astonish me with a sweeping and completely self-confident statement.

"Together" he said, "we can conquer the world; together we can help to educate our people; together we can help to awaken the Negro to his sense of racial insecurity! When I met you last night our fate was sealed. We are neither of us able to resist the other in this hour of need . . ." I was all the more astonished and thrilled because of the sincerity and old-world courtesy with which he addressed me.

This meeting of ours on a July morning a few days before the outbreak of the Great War was a wonderful event. It was a memorable occasion, not only for the two of us, but also, as later events proved, for the whole or our race. Neither Marcus, nor I, fully realised what had taken place, nevertheless we sensed that events of far-reaching consequences had been set afoot. As far as we were personally concerned, both of us felt that our private dreams were beginning to take tangible form. Hitherto, we had been groping in the dark. Now there was light and a way ahead. Each had helped the other to understand how better to serve the cause of Africa and her peoples.

Our joint love for Africa and our concern for the welfare of our race urged us on to immediate action. Together we talked over the possibility of founding an organisation to serve the needs of the peoples of African origin. We spent many hours deliberating what exactly our aims should be and what means we should employ to achieve those aims. Out of this lengthy tete-a-tete we finally improvised a policy and formulated a programme for our infant "organisation." In fact the two member movement was christened the Universal Negro Improvement Association and African Communities Imperial League. (The imperial was dropped later.)

The birth of what was to grow into a world-wide mass movement could not have been simpler or less pretentious. It began with a membership of two, but grew eventually, like a grain of mustard seed, into an organic whole of several millions. Doubtless, anyone who might have witnessed the foundation of the U.N.I.A. would have hooted with scorn and derision, dismissing its two founders as vague starry-eyed idealists. Certainly the vast majority of Afro-Americans at that time would have laughed loudly at our seemingly crazy notions.

Before the lengthy conference finally broke up for that day, it ended upon a most solemn note. Marcus Garvey stood before me and said in a very earnest voice, "Amy Ashwood, I appoint you secretary of the Universal Negro Improvement Association". I replied with an equal earnestness, " And Marcus Garvey, I appoint you president."

16

My Advent, Work, Persecution, Indictment, Conviction, Appeal, Imprisonment and Liberation in the United States of America— The Land of My Friends and My Enemies

(Speech delivered by Marcus Garvey at the Ward Theatre, Kingston, Jamaica, on Sunday December 18, 1927)

Mr. Chairman, Lady [Henrietta Vinton] Davis, High Commissioner, President [C.D.] Johnson [of the Kingston UNIA], members and friends of the Kingston Division of the Universal Negro Improvement Association, fellow citizens, I am pleased to welcome you back to the Ward Theatre to hear me tonight. I am not going to deliver an oration; but will recite a narrative in which I will explain my activities in the country known as the United States of America. You have heard so much bearing on the work of the organization that I represent, and about myself, that a large number of you naturally are curious to see a man late from the penitentiary. You are curious because you do not understand. It is my duty to explain to you tonight, so that you may understand that the prison, the gallows and the guillotine have been the agencies through which human reforms have been brought about (hear, hear). I happened at this late hour of our civilization to represent a new reform movement; a reform movement that seeks the freedom of 400 million Black men, women and children. It is not an easy task. Those of you who are acquainted with history will readily realize that we have a tremendous task before us. Much has been said misrepresentative of the aims and objects of its leader, but I may point out to you the indestructible words of William Cullen Bryant:

> Truth crushed to earth shall rise again,
>   The eternal years of God are hers;
> But Error, wounded, writhes in pain
>   And dies among his worshippers.
> (Applause).

Arrival in the United States

My subject for tonight is: My Advent, Work, Persecution, Indictment, Conviction, Appeal, Imprisonment and Liberation in the United States of America. I went to the United States in 1916, landing in New York on the 23rd of March. My purpose was to carry out a program that was started in Jamaica in 1914 under the auspices of the organization known as the Universal Negro Improvement Association and African Communities League. After a lengthy correspondence with that great man of America, Booker T. Washington, who founded the Tuskegee Institute in Alabama, I was invited by him and others to visit the United States in furtherance of the work I had started in Jamaica. Just before the time I was ready to go I received news of the death of Dr. Washington. I therefore deferred my visit from November of 1915 to the spring of 1916. On arriving in the city of New York in the little district of Harlem where, then, about 100,000 Negroes lived, I met a few of my countrymen and a few West Indians who had been living there for some time. They thought that I had come specially to advocate the cause of West Indians. At the time the West Indians who were living in America made the American Negroes understand that they were not Negroes but Indians, and the American Negroes, who were very ignorant of the geography and history of their own race, believed that the West Indians were a branch of the Indian race, so that the West Indians were getting by as Indians.

Pulling Against Each Other

You all know how the different West Indians despise each other, how the Jamaican despises the Barbadian and the Barbadian despises the Jamaican and all the other islanders hate each other to the point where in America, they would not assimilate. They worked against each other and the American Negroes worked against them and they were all pulling against each other. The Universal Negro Improvement Association was founded in 1914 after my experience of travel in South America, in Central America, in all the West Indian islands and in Europe, seeing well the need for greater unity amongst the Black people of the world. It was because of that urge to unity that I came back from England to Jamaica and founded here in 1914 the Universal Negro Improvement Association. So when I arrived in Harlem in New York the Jamaicans thought that I had come to speak to them especially. But I disappointed them and I spoke to the Negro people, and I told the Negro people of Harlem, including Americans, West Indians—Negroes all—the truth of their history. I told them that we were one, the same branch of one human family; that it was only a question of accident what made some of us American Negroes and others West Indian Negroes. I told them that the slave trade as it was instituted, brought from Africa Negroes, millions of them, against their wish and distributed them in the British colonies of the Western world without any regard for geographical boundaries, from whence they came or to the places to which they were taken. If it suited the whim and caprice of the slave master in Virginia, I told them, or in any part of America, the African husband would be sold in Virginia, and if it suited the whim and caprice of the slave master in Jamaica, the African wife would be sold in Jamaica and the two who were one would go away separated against their wish or will. The American Negroes remained in bondage for 250 years and the West Indian Negroes for 230 years.

Duty to Reunite the Negroes

You who know your history know that you were liberated in the British islands through the good services of Victoria the Good; and the American Negroes were liberated in 1865 through that great man, Abraham Lincoln. Therefore the American Negroes and the West Indian Negroes are one, and they are relics of the great African race which was brought into the Western world and kept here for 300 years. I told them in Harlem that it was my duty to reunite the Negroes of the Western world with the Negroes of Africa, to make a great nation of Black men (applause). And I offered no apology then when I spoke in Harlem and I offer no apology now (hear, hear). If it is right for white men to divide themselves into national entities like the German nation, the French nation, the Italian nation, the English nation, the American nation, then it is right for the Negro peoples of the world to divide themselves into an African nationality (applause). And Marcus Garvey in America, in Jamaica, in England, in France or in Italy shall stand on the same platform and tell the world that the time has come for the Black man to be regarded as a man. (Applause).

Studied Conditions in U. S.

That was my work, that was the nature of my work in the United States of America for ten years. Before I started properly the propaganda as explained, I first travelled through thirty-eight states in the Union. I travelled through thirty-eight states, making a sociological study of the condition of Negroes in relationship with other groups. In America we have many different races. We have minority groups living there. America as a country has 115 million people, and 15 million are colored people; we call them Negroes, but when we say Negroes we mean all from the Black man right up to the border of the white man. We accept that and we work on that, but out here the classification is a little different. When we say Negro we mean the Black man or the Brown man, but not that other fellow that you can mistake for somebody else. He resents the idea of being called a Negro, poor fellow, because he doesn't know any better. One day he will be glad to be a Negro like anybody else, because the Negro is going to return to his own and he is returning at a rapid rate (hear, hear). He is proud of himself. (Applause). I tell you, bring into the Ward Theatre tonight two billion dollars, make the offer of being President of the United States, or king of any country in the world, and say: "Garvey, we will make you this if you become white, and you can be white, we can make you white," and I would say: "Go away, I am proud of being Black." (Applause).

To Be Black Is to Be Honest

To be Black in the twentieth century is to be honest, because for the last 3,000 years the Negro has to his credit all that God would desire from his creature. He has no murder, no theft, no wholesale robbery attached to his history, but on the contrary he has been robbed and murdered and abused all down the line. Who would not be proud, therefore, of such an honorable race? (Loud applause). A race that was so noble that when they sought out someone to be next to the Christ, someone next as perfect and as worthy as the Christ, to help Him in

His last agony and misery in the world, they looked to all. They looked to the Greek and turned away, they looked on the Roman and turned away, they looked on the Samaritan and turned away; and then God Almighty from heaven, through His direction to His angels, turned to Simon of Cyrene [in North Africa] and said: "Help the Christ with His cross." (Applause). The Black man has been the inspiration of the world ever since God Almighty said "Let there be light;" and not only the Black man, but his country, has been the solace of the world. When in the infant stage, they ran the Christ out of Judea, where did God advise that they take him for protection? Not to Asia, not to Europe; but to the land of our fathers—Africa. (Applause). Therefore I am proud to be a Black man (applause); it is an honor to be a Black man. They try to make it a disgrace, but God Almighty knows it is an honor and it is because of that honor why I am proud to be one like you.

UNIA Brought Into Being

It took me, after I had travelled through thirty-eight states, one year on my return to New York to organize the New York division of the Universal Negro Improvement Association. I appealed to the hearts and to the souls and to the minds of the Negroes in Harlem and they responded. I cannot go into minute details because the subject is very lengthy, taking in so many branches, and I desire to give you the satisfaction for coming to hear me, so I can't go into minute details of my early organizing work in Harlem. Suffice it to say that in the first year I organized and brought into the Universal Negro Improvement Association one million Negroes. (Applause). That was between 1918 and 1919 after travelling through thirty-eight states—you know there are forty-eight states.

The Black Star Line, Inc.

In the latter part of 1919, after having organized so many into the Universal Negro Improvement Association, I was directed by them to launch the Black Star Line as a steamship commercial auxiliary to the Universal Negro Improvement Association. In doing that I only carried out the orders of the members of the organization. When we started, the doubtful Negroes—you will always find them everywhere—and the discouraging of other races said it could not be done—Black men couldn't run ships. Some Negroes were as ignorant as to say that the sea was belonging to the white man, so how could we run ships? (Laughter). They tried to discourage us, but we went forward and we proved that the Negroes could run ships. They asked. "Where are you going to get a crew, where are you going to get a Negro captain?" You in Jamaica saw the first ship of the Black Star Line, the steamship "Frederick Douglass"—proof to the world. We worked on in 1919 and by August 1920, we had two million Negroes as members of the Universal Negro Improvement Association.

The First Great Convention

Then it was that we called the first great convention of the Negro peoples of the world, and then my troubles started in the United States of America. Without any immodesty in that I am explaining my work, I would tell you that I happened to be the first and only Negro to address at one time, in one place, one building, 25,000 people. That was at the opening of the International Convention of the Negro Peoples of the World at Madison Square Garden in August 1920. For the first time in the history of the world a Black man was able to bring Black men from all parts of the world, in their thousands, to attend an international conference of the race. Men came from all parts of Africa, from Central and South America, delegates came from all parts of the world—I believe you sent a man named Stewart—and we had a parade in Harlem that was ten miles long (applause), a procession which made an entire circuit of Harlem. That is to say, we had a starting point and we ended the parade at the same point where we started, and when the first line marched around and came back to the starting point after travelling ten miles they came in time to see the last line march off—and they were marching ten abreast. (Loud applause).

Something New in Negrodom

That opened the eyes of the world that something was about to happen in Negrodom, and something did happen when I appeared at Madison Square Garden that night and mounted the rostrum to speak to the 25,000 assembled delegates and members. It was a wonderful scene, and it was written down in the history of Madison Square Garden. Madison Square Garden is over 100 years old and that gathering was recorded as the third greatest celebration held there. Many great celebrations have been held there; the great Roosevelt has been there, the great presidents have been there; political conventions were held there to arouse the people from certain fears, and the 1920 convention of the Universal Negro Improvement Association held third place among them all. That night as I spoke I looked down upon an ocean of reporters from the rostrum, reporters representing every press in Europe, every press in South America, the German press, the Italian, French, Japanese, the Chinese, Hungarian press were all there. The British Reuters, the Associated Press, the United Press, the Illustrated Press, every branch of the newspaper profession was represented there, reporting what I had to say. I spoke until about 11 o'clock that night, and the wires were kept busy. They were all eager to hear news of the new Negro who gave expression to himself at Madison Square Garden that night. The wires of Europe became busy about this little Negro, the Black man from Jamaica, and they started to hound me down from one part of the country to the next. The great United States government got men to investigate me; all manner of Secret Service people were set after me, and 20 per cent of my employees were the United States Secret Service. I believe I must have cost the United States government about five million dollars in ten years.

A Costly Single Proposition

I happened to be a costly single proposition, but nevertheless I was not disloyal to anything American, to anything British, or to any constituted government in the world. All I was interested in was the liberation of the people who look like me. I stood on that platform at Madison Square Garden as I stand uncompromisingly on this platform now. I have not retreated one inch, have not changed my ideas one bit, for I am as firm tonight as when I made my advent into the United States, and with the blessing of Almighty God I shall be as firm the day that I am laid in my grave as I am tonight. (Applause). Nothing in the world shall change me but God Almighty; because of my experience I am determined. No man can convince be contrary to my belief, because my belief is founded upon a hard and horrible experience, not a personal experience, but a racial experience. The world has made being Black a crime, and I have felt it in common with men who suffer like me, and instead of making it a crime I hope to make it a virtue. (Applause). That was all I had in mind when I travelled from one part of America to the next.

Government in America

For ten years the American government was unable to get anything on me by way of sedition or disloyalty. When I say the American government I want you to understand that government is only executive control exercised in the interest of those governed. Government exists only by the will of those governed, and when government fails to express the wish or desire of those governed, those who are governed change the government to suit themselves (hear, hear). Sometimes in America we have a Republican government by the choice of the people. Then sometimes the president is elected by a small and meagre majority of his party followers. In a country with 115 million people the people may do a very small amount of voting. Seven million votes was all the last president elected got, leaving 108 million who had not expressed their will. Even so, when the government goes into power it goes into power by the mandate of but seven million out of 115 million people. So it does not mean always that the president expresses the entire will of all the people, because he was elected by a majority of his party, but naturally he officiates as head of the government and during the time he and his party are in control of the government all the people have to abide by what they do and say. They are supposed to be in power for four years and if in that four years they do things not satisfactory to the people who put them there, at the next election they put them out of power, but while they are in power they can do anything. They can make war, they can steal, they can lie, they can put anybody in prison, they can do anything to any individual person. There is really no appeal, because each judge is generally in line with the government in power, and an appeal is only appealing to the same party.

From Caesar to Caesar

If the president is against you for personal reasons, then it is a foregone conclusion that the chief justice is against you, so that if you complain against the attitude of the president it will simply be appealing from Caesar to Caesar. You can understand the position in America; it is a question of party politics and men. Now it happened that I was never in politics. I was just a Negro and that was not a very nice thing to be in America. When I went to America all the Negroes were Republicans, so to speak, because they believed in the party of Lincoln, who freed them. It happened that I had a lot of power in Harlem, where we had 35,000 members and I represented a tremendous power amongst the Negroes in the country, and you know a man will make mistakes sometimes. Well it happened that John F. Hylan was running for the position of mayor of New York City and a man by the name of Alfred Smith was running for governor of New York State on the Democratic ticket. New York was somewhat Democratic before and they were determined to carry the state because it was a hot year in politics.

Some of my friends inveigled me to give Liberty Hall to Governor Smith and John F. Hylan. I never thought much of the thing and so I did it. They asked me to speak. I did so and every Negro who used to vote Republican, voted Democratic because I told them to do it. Then the great Republican party turned on me. I kept New York Democratic among Negroes with the influence I had there, until I went for two and a half years to Atlanta. They broke my power there only after they had kept me locked up for two and a half years. The Negroes went back Republican only two months ago. In America certain states are Democratic, even though they have the federal government of Republicans. The whole country is never Republican or Democratic at the same time. Sometimes twenty of the states may be Republican, and the rest Democratic or 25 Democratic and the rest Republican, yet the federal government would be Republican. Up to 1920 they were Democratic and because my friends were in power, they did not do me anything. They knew that nothing could be done in New York, and the only way of forcing me out would be by the federal government at Washington, which was Republican.

A Bogus Charge

It was with this idea that they set up a bogus charge against me of using the mails to defraud, which was a federal violation and could only be tried in a federal court, and not a Democratic state court, where the Democrats would be in power. Now, to be able to get that indictment what did they do? They couldn't get the indictment against me through the Universal Negro Improvement Association because the UNIA was and is a fraternal organization. We had a constitution and book of rules, the officers were properly elected and they acted by direction given in the book of rules, the constitution, so it was almost impossible for them to indict me through the Universal Negro Improvement Association. Now it happened that I, by virtue of my position as president general of the Universal Negro Improvement Association, became president of all the auxiliary movements and so, automatically, I was president of the Black Star Line.

Trying to Silence the Leader

The Black Star Line was a business organization, chartered to do business in a certain way, and the laws in America are strict on business corporations. Well, we started the Black Star Line, and they tried to handicap us as much as they could. I am not saying this of the government themselves, but I am saying this of the individuals who were interested in having me torn away from the leadership of the Negro people so as to break up the organization. Negroes were involved in that, white men were involved in that and many governments were involved in that, because of the speech I made on the 1st of August, 1920. They were then scared and believed that Garvey represented too much. Black people, white people, governments all turned and wanted to silence me so that I could not advocate the cause of Negroes. They decided to get me through the Black Star Line. I, in common with the other directors, conducted the business of the company. We had made a bold statement to the world that we were going to prove Black men could run ships. My reputation was at stake, the honor of the race was at stake, because we made that statement and other people said we could not do it. We got the ships and we got Black men and placed them on the ships—you saw them when they came here. That was all we as directors could do. When we placed them on the ships, we, as directors, had done our duty, and it was for them to so conduct themselves as to uphold our honor. They did not.

Cockburn

That man Cockburn! May God damn him in eternal oblivion. That man had in his hands the commercial destiny on the seas of the Black man. He sold it, every bit of it, for a mess of pottage. He took our ship, and on the first voyage out, if it were not for a faithful engineer and a faithful oiler, the S. S. *Frederick Douglass* would not have reached here; it would have been stranded on some sand bank near Cuba. They did everything to make it impossible for the Black Star Line to succeed. We bought The S. S. *Kanawha* and renamed it the S. S. *Antonio Maceo*, after the name of the Cuban patriot, and after we spent $120,000 reconditioning that yacht, which was a first class boat, we sent it off the docks at New York, and it was not out at sea 12 hours before they dismantled it and had over eight hundred of the tubes blown out, and we had to send a tug to bring her back, and spend another $25,000 again. It was not 24 hours after she was put in condition again that we heard the boat was stranded in Cuba, and we had to send her on to Jamaica to be reconditioned there. She was not out of Kingston six hours before they broke up her engine again, and I had to mend and refit her again. It was not long after that they wrecked it again and that boat is now lying at Antilla, Cuba, a total loss of $200,000. Well, in that way they handicapped the company. You remember when I was out here, I got permission to leave the United States for thirty days, but no sooner was I gone than they tried to keep me out altogether. They said now we will keep him away and break up the organization. They kept me out for five months. I had to use certain powers to get my passport signed. I had to get Mr. Hughes, who was a friend of mine, and President Harding, to sanction my return to the United States, and by the time I got back they had robbed half of the assets of the Black Star Line.

The Business of Indicting

The whole lot of them were surprised to know that I had landed in New Orleans, even the employees, and I was not there two months before the government indicted me for using the mails to defraud in the failure of the Black Star Line. Well, they were out to get nobody else but Garvey. It was a big corporation, having a regular board of directors and all the regular officers according to law, yet the only person they indicted was Garvey. Then they thought it over and said: Well, we will change the indictment; but they indicted me first only to get into their hands the books of the corporation. They could not get the books into their hands except they had a legal warrant by indicting one of the officers.

They indicted me and they seized the books of the corporation, and, after they seized the books, this is what they did. They sent out a questionnaire to every member who had stock in the Black Star Line, asking questions like these: "Do you know Marcus Garvey? Were you promised any dividends? Are you satisfied with your investment? Have you any complaints to make?" That was sent to 35,000 people and out of the 35,000 they got 18 people to say that they were not satisfied, and they had got no dividends. When they got the statement from these people, they again went back to the Grand Jury—that first indictment did not mean anything, but to allow them to get the books. But when they got those statements, they went and indicted Garvey and three other officers of the Black Star Line—you see they couldn't do otherwise but bring in the other men for a sham. They returned an indictment with 26 counts. They thought then that I would have packed my baggage and run out of the United States, but I paid them no attention whatever, because I knew my conscience was my guide (hear, hear).

Organization Grew, Notwithstanding

I paid no attention to the indictment; I went about my business just as I did before, and the organization drew in more Negroes than ever. (Applause). When they saw I wouldn't leave, they said they would call the case. I said: "Go ahead, I want you to try it now." And so Marcus Garvey, George Tobias, Elie Garcia and Orlando Thompson were called. And just by way of explanation, I might tell you that these three colleagues were in with the government to let them out and get Garvey. I knew of it, but I paid no attention whatever to them. We went into court; we had several lawyers representing us on the case. The leading counsel was supposed to be my counsel, and the other six were taking care of the case generally and looking after the other three men. That was on our side, but the government had a room full of men. There were Secret Service men, Department of Justice men, in fact, every second man in that room was a Department of Justice man or from the Secret Service. Lawyers and judges and ex-judges were there and we had a jury, a white jury, a white judge, a white district attorney prosecuting—prosecuting a Black man. The lawyers we had were Black men, but the first day of the trial I discovered that the Black men were in league with the white men to get Garvey, and so I kicked them out and took charge of my case (hear, hear).

Saw Through the Scheme

And that is why I am here tonight. If I had not kicked that man out, I would have been sent to Atlanta for 100 years and I would have become decrepit in Atlanta. That was the scheme they had, but they would have to come cleaner than that to fool Marcus Garvey. I found there was a scheme to get me in prison among the other men and get out themselves, but I said, boys, I will go through alone. If I go to prison I will go alone, but I will not allow anyone to send me. I found out the first day that there was some kind of arrangement by which I was to be compromised and railroaded. The first thing that happened which struck me was this: years before, I had two employees, fellows who I had to dismiss for dishonesty, and for three years I never saw those boys, never knew they still existed. When I went into court that morning, the first two men on the witness box were those two boys. I was surprised and curious to know what they could have to say. They went to the witness box and reeled off the vilest lies possible, and I whispered to my attorney and said, "I have the dope on them." In

America we use slang. I told my attorney that I had facts as to why they were dismissed from my service and I could bring proof from the office which would nullify their story. I asked him to keep them on the stand until the next morning so that during the night we could get the proofs. He said to me: "Oh, it isn't necessary to keep them on the stand until tomorrow for we can always get them back." I said: "Are you sure?" He said: "Oh, sure, you can get them back."

Dismisses Counsel

I was a little hazy about the matter, but I doubted what he said from certain things which went on before. He did not impress me that the witnesses could be called back tomorrow morning. I asked him again and he said: "Yes, they can be called back." So the boys went through their testimony and some sort of cross-examination. The next morning when I came into court I said to my attorney: "Now, I have the proofs and we will recall those witnesses." He said to me: "Well, you know, you can't bring them back except you bring them back as your witnesses and you will be bound by what they say." A different aspect entirely. My idea was to bring them back as government witnesses because they were hostile to me. When I found the man was double-crossing I just simply said to him: "Look here, I want you out of my case, and I will take it myself." He got hostile, but I said: "Please retire." Then he started shuffling around, but I was determined and I told him to leave the case. He reluctantly went up to the judge and whispered something to him. After that he came back and said: "I want to make a statement to the court. My client has expressed a desire that I retire from the case." I took charge of my case that morning and the afternoon papers, the big metropolitan evening dailies came out with headlines announcing: "Marcus Garvey dismisses counsel and conducts case himself with marked ability."

Now they have about 200,000 lawyers living off six million people in New York and they do it well. When a big man gets into trouble, it means half a million for some lawyer. Sometimes if he is a man with several million dollars they leave him to mourn over his lost millions. These lawyers are all members of the Bar Association. The judges are all members of the Bar Association, and when the papers announced that day that Garvey was conducting his case, the Bar Association immediately sent out to say that Garvey must not win his case, he must not be allowed to win. They said that if Garvey was allowed to win his case, it would be a slap to the entire bar of New York. You see, they thought, well, I was a big man, and that every millionaire, if I won, would try to do the same thing, and that would lessen their chances of big fees. That was the position and you can realize what I had on my shoulders then.

Hostile Courtroom Atmosphere

I was pleading my case before a white jury, a white judge, and with a courtroom crowded with white Secret Service men. All influences were at work against me. They kept those white people and all enemies in, and all my friends who wanted to come in they kept out. They had everything against me, with the hope, you know, that the jury would get the spirit of the mob. Now my lawyer seemed to have made some arrangement with the district attorney to dispose of my case in three weeks. He was to put in the defence in one week so that the judge, who was a Jew, should attend some Zionist movement abroad. So that when I dismissed my attorney, they said to me: "You know there is an arrangement that this case be disposed of in three weeks." "Yes?" I said, "well, this case is not going to be heard until all the evidence is in. I do not care what arrangements you have to go to Europe; you are not going to Europe at my expense." Then I knew that the judge had been picked to railroad me; he was a member of the hostile organization to me. I realized that when I petitioned him to retire from the trial and give me a change of venue. He denied the application, and he lessened my respect for him as a man—not as a judge of the court, because I respect the court. And I made him know I did not think much of what he said, even though he was laughing in my face and saying he would give me a fair trial. Instead of dismissing the case in three weeks, I kept him there for six weeks. When my case was closed this man who was trying to get away to Europe, who had been impressing the jury that I was keeping them there longer than was necessary and pointing out that they were business men, who, no doubt, wanted to go on vacation, after I closed my case on Friday at 11 o'clock and when he found out that even though it was a jury of white men, and even though the court was bent on convicting me now, what did he do?

After I had spoken to the jury for three hours he saw that the jury was disposed to acquit me, and do you know what he did? At that 11 o'clock he said: "Gentlemen, court is adjourned until 10 a.m. on Monday." That gave the district attorney and others Friday evening, Saturday and Monday morning to fill the papers with the vilest of attacks against me. They published in the papers articles saying that Garvey had an army of a million men to kill all the white people in America and that he had all the ammunition stored up in his Liberty Hall in Harlem, and they had this sensational viciousness scattered on the front page of all the New York papers so that the jury came back with a biased heart. Then there was a judge, one of the ablest men on the bench, a man who could wiggle in and wiggle out of the law, a man who when they have a technical case where the law has to be interpreted in a certain sense, he is called in and can do it in a way to baffle and bother the supreme court; such was the man who tried me. He started by trying to pay me a compliment. "With all due deference to the lawyers in the case," he said, he thought that Garvey had conducted his case with marked ability. The case came to a close, and the jury was out in the jury room for twelve and a half hours. Even though they had that biasing propaganda from Friday until Monday the jury remained out for twelve and a half hours to midnight Monday night.

Find One Guilty

Then the judge got nervous; he began to think that they wanted to let me go, and so, without any request from the jury—it is customary to allow a jury to come to their conclusion, but after the judge found they were out until 12 o'clock, he said: "Come in gentlemen. The government has spent a lot of money over the case, and the defendant, too"—as if he cared anything for the poor defendant—"if you can't find all guilty, then why not find one guilty," as if to emphasize the idea: get Garvey, who is the man we want. Now I was indicted on 26 counts. In ten minutes after the judge said that, the jury returned with a verdict of guilty; guilty on one count, one count out of 26, against me. The judge discharged them. We took the records, and looking over the records, and looking over the count on which I was convicted, ladies and gentlemen of Jamaica and ladies and gentlemen of the world—because my explanation is not so much for Jamaica but for my friends throughout the civilized world to which I intend to lay my case for justification. (Applause). My case is not tried yet. My case shall be tried before the bar of public opinion in Europe, and my case shall be tried before the bar of public opinion in America, and I shall not fail through my friends and myself to expose the chicanery and the trickery by which I was railroaded in the United States of America.

The Famous Count

Now this count. When we turned it was this. A man named Benny Dancy, who I never saw in all my life, never knew a Negro like that existed anywhere—he was brought to testify against me. He said he was a railroad employee of the government. The prosecutor handed him an envelope and said: "Benny Dancy, do you recognize that envelope? It bears your name, typewritten, and in the corner there it has a rubber stamp of the Black Star Line." The answer was: "Yes, sir."

Do you know what was in it? A. No.

Can you identify anything that was in it? No.

Benny Dancy, can you tell what was in it? No.

I show you some circulars. Can you identify any of them? (Benny Dancy looks at them). No, sir. All right, Benny Dancy. I present this, your honor, in evidence as a fair assumption that it contained printed matter from the Black Star Line, because it bears on it the imprint of a stamp from the Black Star Line. He tendered into evidence the rubber stamp envelope, which was not identified, as a rubber stamp of the Black Star Line!

Any of my enemies could have stamped a rubber stamp on the envelope, but the imprint was never identified as having been made by the stamp of the Black Star Line. He presented the envelope as a "fair assumption" that it contained matter from the Black Star Line. That was the case, and on that I was convicted of using the mails to defraud and was given the maximum penalty of five years in Atlanta prison. When we appealed to the higher court for a discharge of the verdict of the lower court, my secret service men reported to me that two of the judges who were to hear the appeal laughed and said the thing was a farce and a joke, and that there was no evidence on which I could be convicted. Well, we put in our application and the thing remained before the circuit court of appeal and nobody heard anything about it for months.

Nothing was heard until we bought the steamship *General Goethals*. When they found out that we had bought the steamship *General Goethals* to trade with the West Indies in bananas and citrus fruit, the quiet and silent influences that were operating against me said: "Now we must stop this thing because they have another big ship." And our ship sailed out from New York for Havana and for Kingston.

Rushed to Prison

Just then the circuit court came in with a decision refusing the appeal. Ordinarily it takes ten or fifteen days after the opinion of the circuit court of appeal is given for the prisoner to be surrendered. The district attorney told my attorney that I would have all the time necessary to fix my business, and do you know that in spite of that inside of

24 hours after the refusal was announced they had me on my way to Atlanta prison (Voices: "What a disgrace!") with the ship out at sea without directions. They purposely did that so that the ship would arrive here, without any cargo, would get none, and we would lose a lot of money and break up the thing. They would not even give me time to appeal to the supreme court. Ordinarily they would have given me time on bond, but they rushed me off to prison and they said: "You can appeal from prison."

And this is what happened: the supreme court refused to review my case because they could not do it. You know under the rules there are certain opinions that become laws. Now, the opinion of the supreme court becomes a kind of unwritten law, and that was why they couldn't review my case. They did not want it to be made an unwritten law, they did not want to make it binding that any citizen could be convicted on an unidentified envelope with a stamp unidentified and a person's name in typewriting, and the supreme court could refuse to review the case. They sent me to Atlanta prison, thinking I would have died, but the God whom, as I say, took care of Daniel in the lion's den, took care of me. And the two good judges, whom I had hoped to meet later on, and to present to them legal opinion of other men who saw how wrong they were—what have become of them? They have passed to the Great Beyond, but I am still here. I hope to meet them somewhere some day. Well, I don't know about that, for I don't see how I could go to the same place as they. But you know of the old Bible story where they told of Lazarus and Dives, the man who was flourishing in wealth.

Politics in the Courts

You remember how Lazarus was asked to dip his fingertips in water to quench Dives' thirst? Lazarus was in the bosom of Abraham, and when Dives asked to send Lazarus to his brothers they said his brothers had Moses and the prophets. Well, I don't want to be disobedient and I will do anything my God tells me to do, but if I should get to heaven and see those two judges down in hell I don't even think that if Gabriel tells me to dip my fingers in the pail of water and touch those fellows' tongues I would do it. (Laughter). Because men who could so disrespect the rights of other men are not worthy of the respect of God or man. But I am not blaming the great American people. It was all politics. You know in the jurisprudence of America I have had this experience. Judges would get upon the bench, and if the prosecutor was a college mate of a chum he would have the advantage in the case, he would get the preference. They would meet in chambers and he would say: "Oh, it's all right." It was all a question of knowing you or belonging to the same party or being a friend. It is not a question of the right, and when the man is sent to prison it is nothing.

Inmates of Atlanta Prison

Why, do you know that a prison like where I was, they had 3,000 people there—2,300 white men and 700 colored men. We had a white governor of a state there. You know what a governor is? Well, we had one. We had white federal judges, and we had state judges; we had municipal judges and mayors; we had members of congress; we had doctors by the hundreds, lawyers by the hundreds, bankers by the hundreds, big businessmen by the hundreds, presidents of corporations, and all kinds of people. We had some men serving 100 years, some serving 90, some 50, some 20 years, and some life, and others two years and ten years. There was a governor who came in just ahead of me; he was doing ten years. (Laughter).

He was a strapping well-built white man from the great Republican state of Indiana, a state about ten times the size of Jamaica. While governor he signed some notes and got money from a bank. He was a rich man, and had cattle farms, but he signed notes for more than he had, and his political enemies got behind him and impeached him, and they indicted him for fraud. A similar charge to mine, using the mails to defraud, but the difference was that he was charged with 50 counts, and he was found guilty of all 50. He got ten years. I was indicted on 26 counts and found guilty of one, and was given the maximum of five years. He was a good Christian, but the only trouble he was crying all the tir   (Laughter).

Resort for Friendless Politicians

Then there was a white mayor, also from Indiana, named Johnson. When I went to Indiana in 1921 he was then mayor and presided at the meeting and introduced me. The next place I met him was in Atlanta prison. He served a year and a day and then he made parole and went home. Then the next person I met from Indiana was a judge who, curiously enough, was at the same meeting where the mayor presided. Then we had Eugene Victor Debs. He was sent for ten years in the prison; a man who ran for the presidency. He was nominated in prison and ran against Harding, and I believe got two million votes. So that just shows the make-up of the penitentiary there. It is just a health resort for politicians whose friends are not in power, and for crooks. Now don't you doubt that there are crooks there, and a large number of them, villains who would pick your pocket with your eyes open and with your eyes closed. You have there villains who have held up trains with two guns and got everybody off, and then they take away two million dollars worth of mail. Most of the villains down there are Jews; all races are to be found there.

So I spent two years and ten months out of five years, and I was never disturbed one minute of the day, for my conscience was clear. I was so busy for the seven years preceding my conviction that I was not able to open a book. I had a library of 18,000 books, and I had not even time to open one of them for about seven and a half years. In Atlanta I had a library of 2,000 books; and I had all the time to read and reflect; therefore I feel good now and well. I feel ready for another ten years. I will not worry you much more tonight with these details, because a narrative is not pleasant, it is always monotonous. But I want to thank you for listening to all that I have explained relative to my indictment and imprisonment, and I want to talk for five minutes about my liberation. You out here were good enough to stage a Release Week or something of the kind. It was not necessary. I felt extremely glad and happy when I heard of it, and I wish to tell you that I appreciated it very much.

But I can tell you that inside of two weeks three million petitions were in Washington asking for my release. Two weeks after my imprisonment, three million people, citizens of America, sent asking for my release, and two weeks later petitions came from Africa and Europe and all over the world. They thought in America it was a good policy to keep me in prison. They thought that they would be able to break up the Universal Negro Improvement Association; you see the organization had become a power in the world. They wanted to keep us off the seas because that would mean commercial rivalry. That was one group of men working against us. Another group of men who saw we wanted to enter into certain commercial enterprises desired to get us out of business. Then in America where I had to lead people the American leaders became jealous of me. There is no man now and there was no man then who could have gotten 200 Negroes to follow him in America, and because I was able to get up four million Negroes in America to unite and seven million abroad they were against me. They went around and said it was a dangerous thing for one man to have all those votes and not with the party. Then another branch of the group of enemies was in the great enterprise of rubber.

Rubber you know has caused a lot of trouble in the world these last five years. The rubber shortage in 1922-24 got America scared, and the great American corporations like Firestone and Goodrich started searching the world for new rubber fields. During that time the Universal Negro Improvement Association had already entered into an agreement with the Liberian government to place at the disposal of the organization several million acres of land by which the people of America and the West Indies—the Negroes—would be able to colonize a part of the country and start an African state.

After we got the people ready, and we had 33,000 families ready to start, the thing was blocked. At that time we had experts sent down to Liberia to do certain work and prepare for the people—I think you had a man from Jamaica named Nicholas. After all that was done Firestone discovered that rubber could be grown in Liberia and on the lands which we had got as a concession. President King was immediately influenced by the United States government and with the propaganda of Dr. W.E.B. DuBois that I was going down to Liberia to start a war against the white man. They fixed it so that King was forced to recall the concessions he had granted to me and to the Universal Negro Improvement Association in Liberia. The result was that when the people arrived there they were seized and the materials which had gone on before had to be left in Liberia. They had therefore to keep me in prison until King was returned as president of Liberia, because if they had turned me out King would not have been re-elected. It is interesting to know that Firestone is a close friend of President Coolidge.

I have nothing more to say.

Paid the Usual Penalty

I could only be pardoned by President Coolidge after I was locked up so you can just understand whether it would be good policy to let out a man who would interfere with the business of your friend. The prison means nothing to the Negro who is thinking. It is only to the foolish, ignorant Negro that the prison means so much. The greatest creatures who ever graced God Almighty's universe were men who slept and died in prison. The great philosphers, the great reformers, teachers from the time of Socrates to Jesus Christ, and from the time of Jesus Christ to the modern martyrs, all have paid the price. What did the Greeks do to the greatest of their philosophers,Socrates? They gave him the hemlock. Voltaire, Karl Marx and the great apostles, they ridiculed them and imprisoned them. What did the world do to the Christ of Judea? What did the world do to the greatest of all reformers, the man Jesus? They buffetted Him, they spat upon Him, they kicked Him all around and finally they crucified Him between two thieves. They crucified Him in preference to crucifying Barabbas, the murderer, and simply because He was a reformer and a teacher seeking the salvation of human souls.

What did they do to Buddha, the great Indian teacher? They hounded him from one place to another; but that did not kill Buddhism. What did they do to Mohammed? They drove him out of Mecca; but that did not kill Mohammedism. Mohammed returned triumphant to Mecca. Through all the misery, the anger and everything else, I am willing to pay the price, every bit of it. I accept the Christ of Galilee as my teacher and my leader and I shall follow Him anywhere He leads. I want to reassure you, my people in Jamaica, my people in Jamaica and the Negro peoples all over the world, that my mission is not to create disturbance among mankind. My mission is to plead the cause of Negroes, and I shall do it anywhere—at morningtime, at noontime, and afternoontime and at evening. I shall always be doing it in the cause of righteousness. My creed is:

> I would be true, for there are those who trust me.
> I would be pure, for there are those who care.
> I would be strong, for there is much to suffer;
> I would be brave, for there is much to dare;
> I would be friend of all—the foe, the friendless;
> I would be giving and forget the gift.
> I would be humble, for I know my weakness.
> I would look up and laugh and love and lift. (Applause).

Index